With best wishes from

[signature]

Tübingen, 18 April 1986

ISSN 0340-6687

VERÖFFENTLICHUNGEN DES OSTASIEN-INSTITUTS DER RUHR-UNIVERSITÄT BOCHUM

Band 25

Documents From Changjwa-ri

A Further Approach to the Analysis
of Korean Villages

by

DIETER EIKEMEIER

1980

OTTO HARRASSOWITZ · WIESBADEN

A part of the village, as seen from the sea (1973)

A village lane (1973)

Documents From Changjwa-ri

A Further Approach to the Analysis
of Korean Villages

by

DIETER EIKEMEIER

1980

OTTO HARRASSOWITZ · WIESBADEN

Herausgegeben von der Abteilung für Ostasienwissenschaften der Ruhr-Universität Bochum
Schriftleitung z. Z. Klaus Kracht

CIP-Kurztitelaufnahme der Deutschen Bibliothek

Eikemeier, Dieter:
Documents from Changjwa-ri: a further approach to the analysis
of Korean villages / by Dieter Eikemeier. — Wiesbaden: Harrassowitz, 1980.
 (Veröffentlichungen des Ostasien-Instituts der Ruhr-Universität Bochum; Bd. 25)
 ISBN 3-447-02044-X

© Otto Harrassowitz, Wiesbaden 1980
Alle Rechte vorbehalten
Photographische und photomechanische Wiedergabe nur mit
ausdrücklicher Genehmigung des Verlages
Gedruckt mit Unterstützung der Deutschen Forschungsgemeinschaft
Satz: H. E. Henniger, Wiesbaden-Dotzheim
Reproduktion, Druck und buchbinderische Verarbeitung:
fotokop wilhelm weihert KG, Darmstadt
Printed in Germany

ACKNOWLEDGEMENTS

It is my sincere hope that the publication of this book will bring some degree of satisfaction to those who have helped me during the past several years when it was under preparation.

I am convinced that nothing would have resulted from this and other efforts of mine in the field of Korean studies if I could not have relied on, and enjoyed, the friendliness and helpfulness which so many Koreans, both within and without scholarly circles, showed to me. I hope that the many who must remain anonymous here will forgive me for mentioning the names of two of their compatriots who have contributed to this book in a particular way. The one is Professor Dr. Duhyun Lee (Yi Tuhyŏn 李　杜　鉉) from Seoul National University. It is he who turned my attention towards Changjwa-ri 長　佐　里 and Wan Island (Wan-do 莞　島), and in the subsequent years, when there were repeated opportunities to enjoy his scholarship and friendship in either Korea or Europe, taught me more and more to appreciate Korean "folklife". I can hardly remember anything in that field which I did not learn through him. The other person is Mr. Hwang Chongu 黃　鍾　宇, a native of Changjwa-ri who now lives as a businessman in the township of Wan-do. Mr. Hwang and his family, together with the villagers from Changjwa-ri, have several times been my generous hosts as well as my kind and patient guides into everything concerning their island and their village. I am most grateful to Mr. Hwang for having responded to my manifold requests and for having supplied ample additional information on the village and the documents. He has thus helped to mend as many of the deficiencies ensuing from the shortness of my stays on Wan Island as was possible under the prevailing circumstances.

I am grateful to Dr. Tilemann Grimm, professor of Chinese History at Bochum University during most of the years I was working on this book and now at Tübingen University, for having allowed me to spend most of my time as research and teaching fellow in Chinese History on studying things Korean. To many a Sinologist, something like the documents from Changjwa-ri may appear to be a mere oddity from a far-off corner of what may be ranked as a middle-size Chinese province, in other words: something hardly worth being given any more serious consideration. This was certainly not Dr. Grimm's point of view. I am equally grateful to Professor Dr. Bruno Lewin of Bochum University. He, although being a linguist and a literary historian, took upon himself the task of defending this manuscript as a *Habilitationsschrift* with the Faculty of the

Department of Far Eastern Studies at Bochum University. He thus bore witness to a concept of broad scholarship which deserves to be highlighted at a time when even people in an infant academic field like Korean studies are in danger of falling victim to the idiosyncrasies of "disciplines". I am much indebted to Professor Dr. Karl Siegfried Bader (Zürich) who once spent a whole day on explaining to me the essence of his writing on Central European villages of the Middle Ages and thus contributed prominently to the formation of the set of terms and concepts used in this study. I also want to thank those scholars who, by means of their expertises on the original manuscript, offered constructive criticism. Most of it found its way into the final draft presented here.

Various grants extended by the Deutsche Forschungsgemeinschaft considerably facilitated the research underlying this book and altogether helped to smooth my way into Korean studies. Again it is by a generous grant from that institution that the publication of this book was made possible. My grateful acknowledgement of the support received from the Deutsche Forschungsgemeinschaft as well as that received from the persons mentioned above should, however, not be taken as to mean that any of the sponsors necessarily endorses the opinions expressed in this book.

I am grateful to the assistance rendered by my wife and by Mr. Terrence Toney (Bournemouth), who have made significant contributions to improving the style of my writing. Besides, my wife took upon herself the task of producing the typescript of the text. Last, but not least, I want to thank the printing office of Seoul National University which in a few days time succeeded in preparing the materials needed for the reproduction of the documents and the insertion of the parts in Chinese, Korean, and Japanese script into the text.

Witten-Annen, West-Germany   D. E.
February 25th, 1979

TABLE OF CONTENTS

ABBREVIATIONS

CS   *Chōsen no shuraku* 朝鮮の聚落

CWS   *Chosŏn wangjo sillok* 朝鮮王朝實錄

HMY   *Honam munhwa yŏn'gu* 湖南文化研究 , ed. Chŏllam taehakkyo Honam munhwa yŏn'guso 研究所 , [Kwangju 光州 :]
Chŏllam taehakkyo ch'ulp'anbu 出版部 , 1963—

MIH   *Munhwaillyuhak* 文化人類學 ed. Han'guk munhwaillyuhak
hoe 韓國文化人類學會 [Seoul:] 1968—

TKB   *Transactions of the Korea Branch of the Royal Asiatic Society,* Seoul:
1900—

CHAPTER 1: AN OLD SOCIETY

The Nature of the Material

When for the first time in February 1970, the author of this study went to the village of Changjwa-ri[1] 長 佐 里 to attend the yearly shrine festival there, he found a set of village documents which immediately stirred his curiosity. They were to require a good deal of his study time in the subsequent years, but this could not be foreseen at the time of that first encounter. For the first and somewhat casual reading of the documents suggested the idea of a simple, harmonious, and prosperous village society living a life of its own and remaining undisturbed by the demands and turmoil of the world around. It all seemed to fit so well into the picture of the farm-steads flocking at the edge of the sea, of the dignity and demureness of the peasants, the warm hospitality with which the present author was welcomed at the village, and the spell the magnificent natural surroundings exercised on him. It appeared to be a task both easy and rewarding to convey something of the charm of that happy small world to an outsider by simply translating the documents into a Western language. They would speak for themselves, it was thought, and analysis appeared to be superfluous.

A second look at the texts as well as growing insight into the realities of that and other villages revealed that Changjwa-ri could neither be a simple society nor an isolated one. It is the outcome of a long history of agrarian settlement and political action, the traces of which are all visible in the present village conditions. Changjwa-ri, like most other places on the Korean peninsula, has long since ceased to be virgin land, and likewise, it has time and again been exposed to influences from outside. The village today preserves as much of those former stages of agrarian history as it absorbs more recent stimuli; and agrarian techniques, behaviour patterns, and values have as much developed from the

[1] The transcription of Korean, Japanese, and Chinese words and names as well as the manner of quoting sources and literature follow the systems and principles outlined by this author in a former study. In order to facilitate reference to sources, the indication of *kwŏn* (Chin. *chüan* 卷), folio, and lines is followed by the reference to volumes and pages, when an edition has been used which is bound and paginated according to Western binding fashions. These references appear in parantheses and will be preceded by an equation mark. Where equation marks are lacking, the reference is not to Western pagination, but to the pages of a translation of the work quoted into a modern language.

Vid. Dieter Eikemeier, *Elemente im politischen Denken des Yŏn'am Pak Chiwŏn (1737-1805). Ein Beitrag zur Geschichte der kulturellen Beziehungen zwischen China und Korea,* Monographies du T'oung Pao, vol. VIII, Leiden: 1970, p. 11.

immediate concerns of the peasants themselves as they were imposed on the village from outside.

The final concept of village life which proceeded from the more thorough reading of the village documents owed much to Dr. Eric R. Wolf's view of a particular kind of social relationship which he thinks to be fundamental to peasant life as such and which at the same time explains why a village cannot be viewed as an insolated world of its own. In his booklet on peasants, outwardly unpretending but very rich in ideas, Dr. Wolf said that in more complex societies social relations are based upon a kind of exercise of power which coerces the tillers of the soil into rendering part of the produce of their labour to an overlord and which does not allow them to keep more than a portion of their produce for their own food consumption. The presence of overlords, who themselves are not engaged in agriculture, but maintain jurisdiction over some land and defend its peace in exchange for agricultural goods, means a permanent charge on the cultivator's production, who is thus forced to set aside a part of his produce to meet the superior's claims to his labour and land. Such charges to be paid out as the result of some superior's claim, Dr. Wolf calls rents, regardless of whether they are paid in labour, produce, or money. It is the necessity to reserve part of the agrarian produce to form rent funds which critically distinguishes the peasant from the primitive cultivator, from the farmer of more modern times, and, of course, from the industrial worker. The obligation to pay rent to an overlord is a determinant force behind all other ties a peasant may maintain with the world beyond his homestead, his village, and his valley. To a considerable degree, the necessity of forming funds of rent shapes power relations within a society and generates the different kinds of market organization.[2] Since in the relationship between peasant and overlord the dice are loaded against the former, the relationship is tinted, at least potentially, by frustration on the side of the peasants, and it tends to be a hotbed of conflict and struggle.

Korean society has been a complex one in Dr. Wolf's sense throughout all of its known history up to the present day. Therefore, it was no surprise to come across that old formative pattern in peasant-overlord relations again in the documents from Changjwa-ri. Only the actors who play the role of "overlord" and that of "peasant" have changed. Given the conditions of present-day Korea, it appeared to be most appropriate to view the central government as the party which has assumed the role of overlord, and since in the case of Changjwa-ri the village pretends to act as a whole, it was convenient to regard the relationship between peasant and overlord as having assumed the shape of a relationship between village and central government and to view much of what could be found in the documents as having been determined by the tension

---

[2] Vid. Eric R. Wolf, *Peasants*, Foundations of Modern Anthropology Series, ed. Marshall D. Sahlins, Englewood Cliffs/N. J.: 1969, pp. 9 s.

inherent in that relationship. This view of things greatly helped to co-ordinate the outwardly incoherent bits of information on peasant desires and government policies, on old customs and innovative inspirations.

The emphasis on the peasant-overlord pattern has not only been dictated by the object of this study, *viz.* peasantry, but by the wording of the documents themselves. Much of the material clearly bears the stamp of government planning and action, and this again caused the author to view the village and the villagers within the frame of their dealings with superior authorities. Government impact has been efficient to such a degree, it seems, that conflict and struggle between peasantry and government have virtually disappeared. It appears that the conflicts inherent in the peasant-overlord relationship, with an overlord demanding ever more and a peasantry unwilling to yield to the demands and to abandon vested interests, have been settled to the almost total advantage of the superiors. It is not only the documents from Changjwa-ri which intimate such an impression, but other material as well. In modern South Korean legislation villages have not been ranked among the local self-government corporations (*chibang chach'i tanch'e* 地 方 自 治 團 體) and have not been granted any kind of local autonomy.[3] That means that virtually none of the rights and interests of villages have been recognized as being worthy of protection from superior demands.

The impression that Korean villages have more or less completely resigned themselves to government demands gains support from quite another angle. At about the same time as the present author started working on the documents of Changjwa-ri, Mr. Gregory Henderson published his challenging book on Korean politics, in which he compares them to a vortex which irresistibly pulls all political energy towards the centre, *i. e.* the capital, thus divesting the countryside of both the necessity and the possibility of regional autonomy.

More characteristics of the material have to be discussed here. Most of the material is law. It is meant to be law by its authors, and it agrees with more general concepts of law. Consequently, this study, in many parts, had to be a legal one. As a legal one, it was subject to decisive limitations, which are all described and commented upon in chapters 3 and 4 of this study. Suffice it to say here that the village code entitled *Regulations of Changjwa-ri* (*Changjwa-ri kyuyak* 規 約), which is at the centre of the present investigation, and most of the other provisions as law belong to the category of abstract rules. Other kinds of law, such as abstractions from actual decisions or statements of older observances, are always intimately linked to reality and provide immediate insights at least into the legal practices of a society, if not into the economic and social ones. Contrary to abstractions from actual decisions and

---

[3] The details of South Korean legislation concerning local self-government have been provided in Appendix 1 of this study.

statements, abstract rules are not so strongly rooted in reality as the other kinds of law are; instead they have their origins in the imagination of a legislator. Alienation from reality and, as a consequence, limited value as a source of information seem to be characteristic of any written material concerning rural conditions, not only of abstract rules of law, which in most cases are written law. Abstract rules will contain imperatives to be observed in future times, and as such they will tell hardly anything about reality, not even the legal one. If they are considered as revealing phenomena beyond themselves at all, they will at best provide insights into the concepts of the legislator, into his wishes of how things should be.

A further limitation imposed on this study is that of time. Except for some pieces of minor importance, all the documents pertain to the period between September 1952, when the *Regulations of Changjwa-ri* were enacted, and May 1964, when the *Regulations* were changed. The latter document, a protocol of a village meeting, is almost the latest document of all available to the author of this study. Documents of any kind posterior to the year 1964 do not seem to exist, with the exception of Document IV, dating from 1966. It is a fortunate coincidence that the period of time covered by the documents is identical with one of the most interesting periods in the recent history of Korean society. In 1952, village life is imagined to have returned to normal after the Korean War, and in the early sixties, drastic changes in the over-all political scene in Korea ushered in a new period of village history. Thus, the years between 1952 and 1964 bring to full light the diffusion and diversity in village life talked about above.

The Prospects of the Study

In the preceding section of this chapter the author has tried to explain why the necessity for the peasants to form rent funds and the character of the subsequent relationship between peasant and overlord should be assigned an important place in writings on rural affairs. Such a view of things is in accordance with a basic feature of peasant life and, in the particular case of Changjwa-ri, it is provoked by the character of the research material itself.

However, a dissertation on peasant-overlord relations and how they affect village life is not what a reader primarily expects from a village study. Peasants devote most of their time and energy to producing the food which is basic to their lives and that of their families, they have to find and work the material to be used for tools and clothes, they build and repair their homesteads, and they join their fellow peasants in social ceremonies by means of which they demonstrate the values underlying their lives and teach the younger generation to pursue them, thus insuring the stability of their social surroundings. Most of the peasant energy is thus devoted to what in the terminology of Dr. Wolf is called the provision of the "caloric minima" and the formation of replacement funds and ceremonial funds.[4]

A genuine village study should therefore concentrate on the phenomena of crops, field system, agricultural tools, co-operative and individual ways of farming, housing, family system and family life, religious and other ceremonies, oral traditions, etc. Indeed, these and others have been the foci in that paragon of community studies by Dr. Edit Fél and Dr. Tamás Hofer which has justly been called *Proper Peasants*.[5] The present author feels that it is in this respect that his study will be found most wanting. This again is largely due to the nature of the material available. As abstract rules of law the various regulations and decisions contained in the documents from Changjwa-ri will tell us about actual economic, social, and cultural conditions in an indirect manner only, if at all. Such deficiencies should have been outweighed by data obtained by means of field research. However, proper field research would have required an extended and continuous stay in the village for at least one agrarian cycle. The academic routine the present author is subject to did not allow him to stay that long. The more grateful this author is to his main informant, Mr. Hwang Chongu 黃鍾宇. His interest in the author's endeavours, his ample command of information concerning the village and its surroundings, and his patience enabled the author to mend as many deficiencies inherent in his study as was possible under the prevailing circumstances.

What then can be well expected from this study? Much could be said to have been achieved if the reader is left with a knowledge of the basic constituents of Korean village life — institutions, procedures, values — and the terms associated with them. Such a knowledge naturally transcends the experiences of Changjwa-ri, and it may better enable researchers to put the right questions when trying to grasp in detail the actual events and constellations of other Korean rural communities in future research. If a considerable number of researchers could agree upon a set of constituents which they considered to be both typical of, and all-pervasive in, Korean village life and which they would accept as a common guideline in future studies, a certain uniformity of community research in and about Korea would be in sight. Such uniformity can hardly said to have been achieved, and the lack of uniformity of procedure is the main reason why the community case-studies concerning Korea are so poorly comparable with each other.

[4] Vid. Wolf, *Peasants*, pp. 4-9.
[5] This famous study has been followed by another volume pertaining to the same village as *Proper Peasants*. The more recent volume is entitled *Bäuerliche Denkweise in Wirtschaft und Haushalt*. These two studies by Dr. E. Fél and Dr. T. Hofer have been reviewed in *Current Anthropology*, vol. XIII, nos. 3/4, 1972, pp. 479-497 and in *The Journal of Peasant Studies*, ed. T.J. Byres/C.A. Curwen/Teodor Shanin, vol. 2, no. 2, London: 1975, pp. 243-245, respectively.

Secondly, it is hoped that the reader may get an idea as to why the village of Changjwa-ri, and most other Korean villages as well, did not really claim any vested interests of its own and did not develop into a nucleus of local autonomy in the economic and political spheres. The tentative answers to that question can be found in the passages dealing with the forces which erode corporate village unity and thus prevent it from establishing rights and interests which belong to the village as such and are to be defended from the inroads of an "overlord".

Thirdly, the author has tried to make due allowance to cultural elements in village life. In doing so, he has emphasized an approach which in most other village studies concerning Korea has only been assigned a rank of secondary importance, if it was followed at all. However, since cultural phenomena do not figure prominently in most of the documents, which are of a legal nature, they had to be left out of the body of the main analysis and were assigned to an appendix instead. Yet, this is by no means meant to depreciate their importance.

Fourthly, this study, largely being based on written material most of which is law, may help to give an idea of the advantages and disadvantages inherent in that kind of material with regard to village studies, and it may better help to determine the limitations of future studies of the kind presented here.

The present study can in many ways be said to be a novelty in the field of Korean studies. Until now, the writing on rural Korea has mostly been done by sociologists, anthropologists, or local residents and travellers not pretending any scholarly ambitions. Their works differ greatly in size and quality, but almost all of them provide larger or smaller bits of information useful to the author of the present study. They will be quoted in their proper places, but the frequency — or infrequency — of quotation should not be taken as a judgment on the qualities of those works. The choice of quotations is exclusively due to the usefulness of single portions of the works, and not to that of the whole books or articles, which the authors wrote with quite different aims in mind. The only real precedent, though not model, of writing on village law is a long-forgotten article by Mr. Philip L. Gillet. The present author could not find out anything about Mr. Gillet except that he served as Treasurer and Recording Secretary of the Royal Asiatic Society, Korea Branch, in 1911/12. Occasional remarks in his article reveal that by travelling in the countryside he brought together a whole collection of village codes.[6] Of course, such a collection would be of immense

---

[6] G.St.G.M. Gompertz has mentioned a few items which may be of value in considerations of former Korean rural life and of its legal aspects in particular. Unfortunately, the present author was unable to obtain the articles and the monograph in question.

Vid. P[hilip] L. Gillet, "The Village Gilds of Old Korea", *TKB*, vol. IV, part II, 1913, pp. 13-44; G.St.G. M Gompertz, "(The First Sections of a Revised and Annotated) Bibliography of Western Literature on Korea from the Earliest Times until 1950. Based on Horace G. Underwood's *Partial Bibliography of Occidental Literature on Korea*", *loc. cit.*, vol. XL, 1963, nos. 777, 913, 932, 970, 980, 1080.

value in further inquiries into the topic, but hitherto, the present author has
been unable to find out the whereabouts of that collection.

Community and Commune

Trying to combine the thought stimulated by the peasant-overlord pattern
with the investigations of the proper village affairs the author has found it
helpful to make use of a distinction between community and commune. The
circumstances affecting village life as differential factors were regarded as
belonging to one of the two spheres of orientation and rules, each of the two
terms summarizing either the incitements, demands, and habits of the villagers
or those of the government. The division of the material along the lines of
community and commune helped to account for the diffusion and diversity in
village society as well as for the sources of the diffusion and thus appeard to be
the only concept doing full justice to the complexity of the village society and to
its age. The distinction has been adopted from the writings of Professor Dr. Karl
Siegfried Bader (Zürich). It occurs as a *Leitmotiv* in his studies on the legal
history of medieval villages, published in three volumes. The present author has
tried to follow the directions indicated by Dr. Bader as closely as possible. His
concept has indeed turned out to be widely applicable, and everybody familiar
with Dr. Bader's writings will notice that the present author owes much more
inspiration and guidance to him than the few explicit references to his work
could demonstrate.

One may question the feasability of a transfer of concepts and terms to
circumstances which are as far removed both in space and time from the ones
they were derived from as medieval Central Europe is removed from the Korea
of the fifties of this century. However, there are some fundamental similarities
between the villages of the two spheres. During the greater part of the period
under investigation by Dr. Bader, the villages were basically self-sufficient units,
the effects of a market-economy becoming palpable only towards the end of the
period. By and large, the same can be said about Changjwa-ri and other Korean
villages of the last two decades, if one takes into consideration that in modern
times the pace of development is generally faster than it was several centuries
ago. Secondly, the political overlords in both spheres were not in a position to
sway village life completely; they had to leave the decision on, and realization of,
many affairs to the villagers. In Korea, this peculiar instability of power turned
to the favour of the government only later in the period under discussion here.
Thus, emphasizing the aspects of instability and transition, we may well take the
case of Changjwa-ri as a miniature of the more extended developments which
took place in many parts of medieval Central Europe, and if cautiously applied,
the duality of community and commune will also prove helpful in the analysis of
Korean villages.

To an English-speaking person the close juxtaposition of the terms community and commune in the discussion of small human societies may appear to be somewhat artificial both in thought and language. Indeed, the division does not fully correspond to experiences of the Anglo-Saxon world. The terminology employed here is closely associated with investigations and theories concerning the rural past of the Germanic countries. Within that framework, viewing things in the light of the community-commune contrast marks a big step away from an older approach, largely considered outdated today. Many scholars of an earlier period tended to view almost every phenomenon in the social and legal life of the countryside, and even more than that, as being shaped by community (*Genossenschaft*) values and practices, somewhat unilaterally emphasizing the effects of equality and autonomy among the peasants.[7] It seems to the present author that a great many Korean scholars' thought on rural affairs is, directly or indirectly, determined by such older concepts.[8] Since Korean scholarly thought in the field of rural studies has for some time been associated with a particular academic "school" and the phenomena of a certain area, it can hardly avoid following the more recent developments — coming from that school and referring to the same area — which either supplement or replace the older ones. In doing so, rural studies in Korea remain attached to both the theories and terminology of research concerning the Germanic countries. This is another reason why the present author has to introduce a nomenclature which admittedly sounds awkward to Anglo-Saxon ears.

Whereever families live together as neighbours, tasks will arise which call for joint action. This is particularly true under rural conditions, where simple and occasional co-operation tends to grow into a whole of behavioural rules aiming at accomodation and restraint of individual ambition. The number of goods is limited, and if somebody takes an overdue portion for himself, he will by this

---

[7] The best documentation of those views and the main source of inspiration for subsequent authors has been the important work by Otto von Gierke (1841–1921) on *Genossenschaftsrecht.*

Vid. Otto von Gierke, *Das deutsche Genossenschaftsrecht,* 4 Bd., Berlin: 1868–1913.

[8] When writing about villages and other rural associations these authors make *kongdongch'e* 共同體 the key term in their discussions, without succeeding in giving it any technical meaning and making it a useful tool in analysis. Their failure is largely due to the fact that they indiscriminately equate *kongdongch'e* with a series of terms taken from older German sociology and jurisprudence, such as *Gemeinschaft, Gesellschaft, Genossenschaft,* without realizing that these terms have been subject in scholarship to a continous process of differentiation and limitation. The two authors quoted below are only the more prominent ones of a much larger group.

Vid. *Han'guk sahoe kyŏngje sa yŏn'gu. Kyeui yŏn'gu,* comp. Kim Samsu, rev. ed., Seoul: Pagyŏngsa, 1966³, pp. 19-25, 41-60 *et passim; Han'guk nongch'onui ch'ollak kujo,* comp. Yang Hoesu, Asea munje yŏn'guso, Han'guk sahoegwahak yŏn'gu ch'ongsŏ, no. 9, Seoul: Asea munje yŏn'guso, 1967, pp. 127, 129, 377-390 *et passim.*

encroachment inevitably divest his neighbour of his due, which in turn means a serious threat to the others' welfare and thus potentially to the equilibrium of the small society.[9] Such conditions entail a certain kind of equality among the members of such a society. Rural people are equal among each other in the sense that they are all equally subject to the conditions dictated by the limitations in goods. This, in turn, often creates a sense of equity in economic matters, a desire to give everybody his due and, in spite of actual differences in wealth and power, not to let him drift towards the verge of ruin. Where such equality and equity prevail, and where initial agreements and co-operation have grown into a more formal and stable set of rules, we talk of a community. In this sense, and only in this one, does community come close to, or is it identical to, the *Dorfgenossenschaft* known from pre-modern rural conditions in Central Europe. In scholarly investigation, the concept of community is meant to be susceptible to legal considerations, and, therefore, the term should not be applied to less formalized societies, even if they, too, are based on modes of co-operation. Here already, a warning is in place. The equality is not an equality necessarily embracing all of the inhabitants of a rural locality. For equality as the power to participate as equals in decisions about the distribution and use of goods can be meaningfully applied only to those who own some property. Therefore, people such as farm labourers, petty farmers, and artisans are generally excluded from the community. In other words, the community as a society of equals is for all practical matters a community of the wealthier peasants only.

When juxtaposing village community to village commune (*Dorfgemeinde*), we are not talking about entirely different entities in terms of territory and people. The object under investigation is the village, where both modes of

[9] The quantity of goods cannot be increased by any working techniques which may be applied and by any amount of labour which may be invested. This "image of the limited good" has been made the key by Professor Dr. George Foster in analyzing peasant economy and life and the peasants' view of them. Dr. Foster generalizes on his basic assumption by outlining two kinds of possible reactions to this fundamental condition, *viz.* maximum co-operation and even communism, or extreme individualism. He takes the second alternative to be the normal one. This assumption, however, can in no way be substantiated. If nothing else, the experience of basically pre-modern rural societies like the one under discussion here will confine his generalization.

Dr. Wolf, too, associates the virtues of restraint and accomodation with peasant life. However, he tends to view their appearance as being limited to rural societies where we find what he calls "network markets" and/or where food production and distribution are co-ordinated by extended families. The Korean experience contradicts his statements. For, at least during the last few centuries, the basic co-ordinating unit in Korean rural life has not been the extended family, but the smaller household consisting of 5 to 6 persons on average, and yet those virtues have always been there.

Vid. George M. Foster, "Peasant Society and the Image of the Limited Good", *American Anthropologist,* ed. American Anthropological Association, vol. 67, Menasha/Wn.: 1965, pp. 293-315; Wolf, *Peasants,* pp. 41-48, 65-67, 69 s, 80.

organization are closely interlocked with each other in one place and within one group of people. Viewing the village or parts thereof as a community, we emphasize the neighbourly union of a considerable number or of all of the villagers, as they join hands to care for, and exploit jointly, certain tracts of soil, woodlands, and waters. Following Dr. Bader's line of distinction, we talk of a village commune, when we want to portray the village as a body corporate that lays claim to, and actually exercises, rights which are both more comprehensive and exacting than those concerning a common usufruct of land and waters.[10] In Korea, a village as a commune will deal, for instance, with the construction and maintenance of roads, schools, water reservoirs, with police matters, and with the local organization and realization of government-inspired modernization campaigns. The rules of a commune are not only more comprehensive than those of the community, they are less subject to changes and individual discretion. In the eyes of the villagers, the village as a commune thus tends to live a life of its own and to become a "personality", as it were, that, in terms of time and influence, goes beyond the lives of any of its members.

The distinction between community and commune is not a very sharp one. Both modes of organization influence each other intensely, and either of them may gain the upper hand over the other at some time in the course of history, again becoming the weaker one afterwards. As far as our present knowledge of Changjwa-ri and that of Korean agrarian and legal history in general goes, we are unable to decide whether either of them marks a certain period in history as the prevalent mode of rural society, to the exclusion of the other. Thus, the community mode of organization may not safely be said to have flourished at an earlier period of agrarian history and to have subsequently been displaced by the commune. We can only say that a certain combination of community and commune modes as observed in the period under investigation here has since then been seriously distorted to the advantage of the commune. We may further say that this distortion is due to the various pressures and needs of an increasingly more powerful and rational government, which tends to command everything from beginning to end. The dominance of the commune is very likely to destroy the community, because the former unilaterally favours the educated people and because it introduces and emphasizes values which are utterly alien to community thought, such as individuality, competition, and strife for material recompense for effort. We therefore expect the community to die out or at least to be even more deeply penetrated by commune objectives and necessities than we witness in the years under discussion here.

Such considerations closely link the community-commune contrast to the peasant-overlord pattern introduced before. The community-commune con-

---

[10] Vid. Karl Siegfried Bader, *Dorfgenossenschaft und Dorfgemeinde,* Studien zur Rechtsgeschichte des mittelalterlichen Dorfes, Zweiter Teil, Köln/Graz: 1962, erg. Neuauflage Wien/Köln/Graz: 1974², p. 29.

trast is just a way of describing the peasant-overlord pattern in terms better suited to "juridical" evaluation. The "juridical" way of describing the mixed nature of village organization appears to be more recommendable than the anthropological one. For the former does not only help to recognize the overlord's impact on villages as such, but also to determine the degree of his preponderance. In Changjwa-ri, none of the past and present village activities which are not of a strict community order emanated from among the local people themselves, but were initiated by the authorities. (This is not to say that, once introduced, they did not eventually win the favour of the local populace or that they may not occasionally do so in the future.) What the present author wants to say is that the village commune does not simply "flow from" the village community in such a way that community values and practices "automatically" extend to the realization of non-community aims or that they even "create" those aims. The village community, or communities within the village, are no real bases for the village communes. Rather, they are given some space within the commune, in the confines of which they can play economically, socially, and legally relevant parts. Whether this state of things can equally well be taken as implying a sequence of historical steps which followed each other in the genesis of the village[11], the present author is unable to tell. It can only be said that this state appears to be a constant one at any given time in the known past and present of Korean villages.

The community-commune contrast displays an even more important aspect. The very fact that the two modes of aims and organization are brought into some kind of equilibrium, unstable and different at various places as it may be, reveals the real preponderance of the government and its role in shaping villages. Village codes, which are the records of the order of things in a place, regularly seem to require the sanction of the authorities to become valid, and the authorities tend to reserve the right to future interference with current village affairs by inserting corresponding provisions into the texts of village codes. Not all Korean villages have their constitution written down in codes, but even where such codes are lacking, we are probably correct in assuming that not much can happen in such a place without at least the tacit consent of the authorities. Thus, a village as an ordered whole owes at least part of its existence to the government's participation in, or approval of, its current dealings. If there

---

[11] Writing about a somewhat different, though "structurally" related set of problems, *viz.* that of the relationship between guilds and towns in pre-modern Europe, Karl von Hegel (1813—1901) did make the superior order, *i. e.* that of the towns, precede that of the guilds both in time and substance. For this reason, the towns were put in front of the guilds in the title of his work. However, in the main text of his work, he presented enough material to somewhat mitigate his basic assumption.
Vid. Karl von Hegel, *Städte und Gilden der germanischen Völker im Mittelalter,* Bd. 1, Leipzig: 1891, Nachdr. Aalen: 1962, p. VII.

were no government, there would be no village in the sense the term is employed
in this study, *i.e.* as an ordered whole determined by both community and
commune modes.

In the documents from Changjwa-ri, there is comparatively little evidence of
direct government interference with either the wording of the *Regulations* or
with current village affairs. The authors of the documents seem to have been
eager to conceal any traces of such involvement. Yet, we cannot deny
government involvement and government domination. The mixed nature of
villages and an unstable equilibrium between peasant and government powers
are characteristic of rural conditions not only in Korea, but in other parts of the
world and in other periods of history as well.[12] Looking at Changjwa-ri in a
different way from the one suggested here would mean making Changjwa-ri an
exception to an obviously world-wide phenomenon both in space and time. The
differences between developments in different areas and different periods seem
to be differences in degree only, not in principle.

The Concept of Village

The term village has been used above in an "untechnical" manner, as far as
territory and people are concerned. Since much of the confusion in scholarly
disputes on villages is often due to nothing but the fact that people are not
talking about the same kind of society in terms of territory and people, the term
requires some explanation. In this study, village is the equivalent of *i* 里 , which
is the same as the *-ri, -ni,* or *-li* of the final syllables of the Sino-Korean
renderings of place-names. Both in matter and name, these *i* go back to the end
of the Koryŏ 高麗 (918—1392) and the beginning of the Yi 李 (1392—1910)
periods. They were created by the government for purely administrative
purposes. *I* appeared first as subdivisions of the capitals of the two dynasties and
were later mentioned as existing in the countryside as well. These villages and
capital quarters were meant to serve as one kind of instrument among others to
control the population of the kingdom, mainly people's changes of residence.
The inhabitants of an *i* were held responsible for each others' doings and
movings. Punishments were to be meted out to all office holders of an *i* and to
the families immediately concerned, if one of the members of such an *i* moved
away without authorization. It was hoped that by such a system of collective
responsibility and punishment the people could be deterred from changing their
residence and thus from fleeing from the services and contributions they were
expected to render to the government.

The implementation of *i* as instruments of control was part of a government
effort to model the administration of the Korean kingdom upon Chinese

----

[12] Cf. Bader, *op. cit.,* pp. 29, 335 *et passim.*

precedents. As a device imported from China, the establishment of *i* should have followed strict and uniform principles as to the number of households to be included in one *i*. But the Yi government, apparently deviating from the Chinese precedents, was less keen on following the model in this respect. The numbers of households which together constituted one *i* were far from uniform. The whole effort leaves us with the impression that Korean *i* were created either by lumping together several natural settlements, the existence of which preceded the creation of *i*, or by dividing natural settlements into smaller parts.[13]

The *i* of the Yi period could thus hardly have been anything but agglomerations or divisions of natural settlements, and as such, they cannot have been very different from the *i* of today. Today, most *i* are made up of one larger conglomeration of houses as their centres and several houses or groups of houses located at some distance from those central agglomerations. These agglomerations will be called hamlets here. Mostly, they are neighbourhoods inhabited by kin. Besides, we find *i* which are composed of several of such rather dense agglomerations, or in which no hamlets at all are discernable as subdivisions.[14]

The colloquial usage of the Koreans themselves does everything to obliterate the distinctions between hamlets and *i*. When talking about rural settlements, the Korean peasants will use the word *maŭl* 마을 . This term mostly means the hamlet, and it is to be taken as a generic term.[15] However, *maŭl* is also used to

[13] The duties of *i* as administrative divisions as well as the question of their extension have been dealt with in greater detail in an article by the author of this study. The sources, too, are listed there.
Vid. Dieter Eikemeier, "Villages and Quarters as Instruments of Local Control in Yi Dynasty Korea", *T'oung Pao,* vol. LXII, Leiden: 1976, pp. 73-78, 80-98.

[14] The distinction between these three types of *i* has been made by Professor Dr. Man-gap Lee (Yi Man'gap 李萬甲) of Seoul National University. He has based his generalizations on a very limited number of specimens, but experience justifies the generalizations presented here, at least with regard to areas where rice cultivation is the preponderant kind of agriculture. Practically the same distinction has been made by Professor Dr. Ch'oe Chaesŏk 崔 在 錫 . Its validity is confirmed by the drawings and short histories of the villages studied by Professor Dr. Pak Ki-Hyuk and Dr. Sidney D. Gamble.
Vid. *Han'guk nongch'onŭi sahoe kujo. Kyŏnggi-do yukkae ch'ollagŭi sahoehakchŏk yŏn'gu,* comp. Yi Man'gap, Han'guk yŏn'gu ch'ongsŏ, ed. Han'guk yŏn'gu tosŏgwan, vol. 5, Seoul: 1960, pp. 24-29; *Han'guk nong'chon sahoe yŏn'gu,* comp. Ch'oe Chaesŏk, Seoul: Ilchisa, 1975, pp. 66 s, 74-76; Pak Ki-Hyuk/Sidney D. Gamble, *The Changing Korean Village,* publ. for the Royal Asiatic Society, Korea Branch, by Shin-Hung Press, Seoul: 1975, pp. 76-79, 115-118, 142-146.

[15] Professor Dr. Yi Pyŏngdo 李丙燾 explains *maŭl* as having originally meant the meeting-place of the villagers. Since the middle of the last millenium, Dr. Yi says, the term has constantly reocurred as meaning the hamlets themselves, and in later times the local authorities and their office buildings. The later meaning is still alive at least among the rural populace of southern Korea, where we can hear the expression *maŭre kada,* meaning "to go to the magistrate's office".

mean the whole *i* unit, and it is sometimes difficult to decide in which sense the word is employed on a given occasion. The meaning apparently depends on the degree of integration the speaker is willing to attribute to either kind of unit, the better integrated one being called *maŭl*. This selective use of *maŭl* for the *i* unit proves that not all *i* are considered to be well-integrated societies. The colloquial usage thus reflects a condition which is of the utmost importance for considerations of Korean villages. There does not seem to have developed a truly native term for *i* after the inception of the administrative pattern described above. This could mean that the orientation towards the *i* seems to have always remained somewhat alien to the minds of the Koreans. *Nongch'on* 農村 or *purak* 部落 are both Sino-Korean words, which again are not only applied to *i* units, but to hamlets as well. This usage is the reverse of the use of *maŭl*. Today, *maŭl, nongch'on,* and *purak* seem to be indiscriminately used to mean that settlement which by its outward cohesion suggests social and economic integration, whether this be an *i*, a hamlet, or parts of an *i*. It is obvious that such indiscriminate usage does not promote scholarly distinction.[16] *I*, in turn, is no generic term at all; it only appears as the final element in Sino-Korean renderings of village names.

The matter is made even more complicated, at least to a foreign observer, by the occurrence of the term *tong* 洞 . In the first place, *tong* as the final element in place-names is an equivalent to *i*. Today, this usage is restricted to only a few village names and to the names of quarters in cities and towns. Secondly, it appears as the final element in the Sino-Korean renderings of hamlet names. Here, the Chinese character meaning "cave", "hole", which, in turn, is the Chinese equivalent of Korean *kol* 굴 , seems to be used to render an ancient Korean word *kol* meaning "settlement". This latter *kol* is preserved in many hamlet names up to the present day. *Tong* can thus be viewed as a translation into Chinese of a Korean word *kol* "cave" which because of homophony was mistaken for *kol* "settlement".[17]

Vid. *Han'guk kodae sahoewa kŭ munhwa,* comp. Yi Pyŏngdo, Sŏmun mun'go, no. 071, Seoul: Sŏmundang, 1973, pp. 21-23.

[16] This confusion in terminology is also attested by Dr. Ch'oe Chaesŏk. Like many other Korean scholars, he uses the term "natural village" (*chayŏn purak* 自然部落). This is to denote an agglomeration of smaller settlements. Dr. Ch'oe is aware of the fact that the "natural villages" are not always co-extensive with administrative units, and therefore he reserves the term "administrative village"(*haengjŏng* 行政 *purak*) for the latter. The distinction is of no importance here, because what would be considered the "natural village" of Changjwa-ri is co-extensive with the administrative unit. The term "village" will do here, because it covers both aspects.

Vid. *Han'guk nongch'on sahoe yŏn'gu,* comp. Ch'oe Chaesŏk, pp. 67, 75s.

[17] According to Professor Yi Tonju 李敦柱 , a relationship between *kol* "settlement" and the "cave" character has first explicitly been testified to by lexicographers of the early Yi period. Furthermore, many present-day Korean place-names carry the *tong* character in their

Lacking sufficient knowledge of the geography and history of settlement in Korea, we are not able to tell which have been the forces generating hamlets and those more or less dense agglomerations which were later grouped as *i*. But we may say that since the rules and behavioural patterns that govern life in the hamlets have been more closely adapted to the needs and concerns of the peasants, they are different from those grafted upon the settlements when they were turned into administrative units. We may also say that they are not only different in character, but also older than those ensuing from administrative purposes. Assuming that a certain degree of integration and solidarity prevailed in those supposedly earlier hamlets and hamlet agglomerations, the author has decided to translate *i* by "village". This translation emphasizes more its character as a socially integrated unit than as an administrative instrument.

For the large part, the diffuse state of village society is a result of the transformation of hamlet groupings into administrative units. The transformation being of rather an early date, the competition between commune and community modes is an old one. It is mainly for this reason that the village society of Korea has been called an old one. As an object of study, the village almost automatically offers itself to anybody intent on investigating the basic issues of the relationship between government and peasantry, which cannot be accounted for without taking into consideration those older constituents.

Sinicized renderings, when a *kol* appears in the popular native versions. Such observations support the interpretation offered here.

In a very few cases, this *kol* is not rendered by the *tong* character, but by the character *kok* 谷 "valley". This is probably due to the near-homophony between *kol* and *kok*. In the names of places which belonged to the ancient kingdom of Koguryŏ 高句麗 (trad. dates 37 B.C.-668), the *kok* character is used to render a *tun* morpheme, which in all probability meant "valley" and thus denoted places situated in valleys. Note the modern Japanese *kun* 訓 reading of 谷, viz. *tani*. In these instances, the *kok* character is a translation into Chinese, and not a phonographic rendering, of a Korean word. Because of the possibility of homonymic conflict between *kol* and *kok*, the *kok* character seems to have been restricted in its use to renderings of place-names where a "valley" morpheme appears in the native form. Its use in renderings of the "settlement" morpheme seems to have already been the exception since early times.

Vid. "Wan-do chibangŭi chimyŏng ko", comp. Yi Tonju, *HMY*, vol. 4, 1966, pp. 248-250; "Chŏnbuk chibang chŏllae chimyŏngŭi yŏn'gu", comp. Yu Chaeyŏng, [*Wŏn'gwang taehak-kyo*] *Nonmun chip*, ed. Pak Kilchin, vol. VI, [Iri:] Wŏn'gwang taehakkyo ch'ulp'anbu, 1972, p. 244.

CHAPTER 2: THE VILLAGE OF CHANGJWA-RI

Some Facts About the History and the Socio-Economic Background of the Village

The village of Changjwa-ri is situated on the eastern coast of Wan Island (Wan-do 莞 島). Wan Island is one of the two bigger islands which lie off the southernmost tip of the Korean peninsula, ranking fifth in size among the islands of all of Korea.[1] It measures about 20 km in length and about 15 km in width.[2] A road runs along the coast, and by this road Changjwa-ri is linked to the township of Wan-do (Wando-ŭp 邑), which is the centre of commercial and industrial activity on the island as well as seat of the county (*kun* 郡) administration. The distance by road from Changjwa-ri to Wan-do town is 8 km. Since there are no buses which run directly from Changjwa-ri to places on the mainland, the village is connected with the mainland only by the buses commuting between Wando-ŭp and Kangjin 康 津 or Haenam 海 南 , the nearest towns on the peninsula, or the provincial capital of Kwangju 光 州. Haenam is 56 km away from Wando-ŭp, and the distance from Wando-ŭp to Kwangju is 150 km. By express bus it takes about one hour to go to Haenam and about four hours to Kwangju. In terms of time, Kwangju is the closest train station as well as the nearest airport and thus the most convenient starting-point for travels from Wan Island to other parts of the Korean peninsula. Although bus services have improved considerably during the last few years, there being at least one bus per hour leaving for, or arriving from, one of the places mentioned above, Wan Island must still be considered a rather remote place. It was even more so during the period under consideration in this study, when there was not more than one bus a day during most of those years. Travel conditions will improve further in the near future, for there are plans to exploit the superb natural surroundings of the island for tourist purposes.

In historic times, Wan Island was a place of the utmost strategic importance. The adventurer and trader Chang Pogo 張 保 皐 (d.841?) was the first known person to have realized this. In the years 828/29 he established the

---

[1] Vid. *Tae Han min'guk chido* (*The Standard Atlas of Korea*), comp., ed. Im P'yo, Seoul: Sasŏ ch'ulp'anbu, 1960, map no. 12; [*Tae Han min'guk chido*], ed. Kungnip kŏnsŏl yŏn'guso, scale 1:50.000, Seoul: Han kongjido kongŏpsa, 1963-1969, leaves nos. 6516 (I, IV,), 6517 (IV).

In 1969, Wan-do ceased to be an island in the proper sense of the word, because in that year a bridge was completed which links it with the Korean mainland.

[2] Statistical data concerning Wan-do county can be obtained from the statistical yearbooks issued by the county administration. The latest issue available to the present author is the twelfth, which was published in 1972.

garrison of Ch'ŏnghae (Ch'ŏnghae-jin 清 海 鎮) on Wan Island. He was appointed Grand Envoyee (*taesa* 大 使) of Ch'ŏnghae-jin by the king of Silla 新 羅 (trad. dates 57 B.C.-935), whom he had summoned to protect the island and the rest of the coast from the raids of Chinese slave traders, who at that time used to harass the coastal waters of southern Korea and abduct Koreans into slavery. His extraordinary career as a merchant and politician was due to his success in controlling the sea routes used for trade between China, Japan, and Korea, for which purpose Wan Island served as his main base. Chuch'ŏng-ni 竹 青 里 , a village between Changjwa-ri and Wando-ŭp, is said to have been the site of the garrison.[3] In later centuries, too, Wan Island served as a stronghold in naval warfare and was fortified many times.[4] It was thus at the focus of attention for the government, but people now and then seem to have enjoyed a considerable degree of independence in their economic dealings, which probably did not differ too much from the ways in which Chang Pogo must have handled matters in his day. In accordance with a more moralistic nomenclature of the times, those people were called thieves by the court archivists. In one instance, the apprehensions of the court went so far as to order all agricultural activity to be stopped, *i. e.* all living and settling on the island to be forbidden.[5]

[3] Chang Pogo is also known by the name Kungbok 弓 福 . Before he was sent to the garrison of Ch'ŏnghae, Chang Pogo had spent several years in China. He seems to have risen there to a position of power and wealth among the Korean residents, whose head he seems to have been for some time. From 837 onwards Chang Pogo was involved in struggles for succession to the throne of Silla. He supported Ujing 祐徵 , whose father had been the rightful successor to the throne, but had been murdered before he could become king. With the help of Chang Pogo Ujing succeeded in ascending the throne of Silla in 839 as King Sinmu 神 武 . After the death of his protector, King Sinmu, which occured only three months after his accession to the throne, Chang Pogo tried to continue his attempts at winning influence at the court by marrying one of his daughters to the new king. This caused misgivings among the court officials, who, probably in 841, succeeded in having him assassinated.

The life and career of Chang Pogo have meticuously been reconstructed from Chinese, Japanese, and Korean sources by Professor Dr. Edwin O. Reischauer. This study was preceded by an article written by Professor Kim Sanggi 金 庠 基 . A short history of the area has been written by Professor Song Chŏnghyŏn 宋 正 炫 , who also wrote an article concerning the importance Wan Island had for the Japanese pirates of the Yi period.

Vid. "Kodaeŭi muyŏk hyŏnggt'aewa Ramarŭi haesang palchŏne ch'wihaya. Ch'ŏng-hae-jin taesa Chang Pogorŭl churo haya", comp. Kim Sanggi, *Chindan hakpo,* ed. Chindan hakhoe, vol. 1, Seoul: 1934, pp. 86-112; vol. 2, 1935, pp. 115-133, photolithogr. repr. Seoul: Kyŏngin munhwasa, 1973; Edwin O. Reischauer, *Ennin's Travels in T'ang China,* New York: 1955, pp. 287-294 *et passim*; "Wan-dowa waegu. Yijo sidaerŭl chungsimŭro", comp. Song Chŏnghyŏn, *HMY,* vol. 4, 1966, pp. 203-211; *Han'guk minsok chonghap chosa pogosŏ,* comp. Han'guk munhwaillyuhakhoe, publ. Munhwa kongbo pu, Munhwajae kwalliguk, vol. 1: Chŏlla namdo, Seoul: 1969, pp. 22-35.

[4] Such a case of fortifying the island is reported from the 16th year of the reign of king Chungjong 中宗 (February 2nd, 1521-January 27th, 1522).

Vid. *Chŭngbo munhŏn pigo,* k. 27.5a.5s (= vol. 1, p. 392).

[5] Vid.' *CWS: Sejong sillok,* k. 126.5b.16-6a.2 (= vol. 5, p. 151 — December 8th, 1449).

Memories of Chang Pogo are still quite alive among the people of Changjwa-ri. They use Ch'ŏnghae as the name of their primary school, and older people in the village would say that the correct name of the place is Changjae-ri, which should be written as 張 在 里, meaning "the village where the Chang family resided". Although, at present, there are no people who bear the family name Chang and claim descent from Chang Pogo, graves are shown in the vicinity of the village which carry that name. Besides, pieces of partly petrified wood are preserved at Ch'ŏnghae School, which are explained as being remnants of poles used in constructing stockades in the shallow waters around Wan Island. Larger stones with striations on them are said to have been used for grinding gunpowder. All these things and other artefacts emphasize the importance of the island as an ancient centre of civilization as well as its strategic role, but it is by no means sure that they all date from times as far back as those of Chang Pogo.

In terms of administration, the village of Changjwa-ri, at present, is part of the township of Wan-do, which in turn, belongs to the county of the same name, South Chŏlla Province (Chŏlla namdo 全 羅 南 道). There were 182 households (*ho* 戶) in the village, comprising, in 1966, a total of 1101 individuals.[6] Out of those 182 households, 166 were classified as basing their livelihood on agriculture. Therefore, Changjwa-ri can doubtlessly be called an agricultural village. However, in recent years, the breeding of domestic animals and, above all, the cultivation of seaweed (*haet'ae* 海 苔) have gained momentum. The two most widely spread kinds of seaweed are the *ch'angp'ojo* 菖 蒲 藻 [7], also

---

[6] These and the other data mentioned later in the text have been taken from an article written by Professor Dr. Duhyun Lee (Yi Tuhyŏn 李 杜 鉉). They were all collected in 1966.

The counting of a population by households is a traditional device in census-taking, which stems from the beginnings of the Yi period. At that time, the household was a unit established for strictly fiscal reasons, and it comprised the persons liable to taxation, labour services, and other contributions. However, as used throughout the *Regulations of Changjwa-ri,* "household" means all those kin, in-laws, and farm labourers living under one roof.

Vid. "Wando-ŭp Changjwa-ri tangje", comp. Yi Tuhyŏn, *Yi Sungnyŏng paksa songsu kinyŏm nonch'ong,* Seoul: 1968, pp. 432s; "Chosŏn ch'ogi hogu yŏn'gu", comp. Yi Sugŏn, [*Yŏngnam taehakkyo*] *Nonmun chip* (Inmun kwahak p'yŏn), ed. Yŏngnam taehakkyo nonmun chip p'yŏnch'an wiwŏnhoe, vol. 5, [Taegu:] Yŏngnam taehakkyo ch'ulp'anbu, 1972, pp. 107-162.

[7] The *ch'angp'ojo* should not be confused with a plant called *ch'angp'o* 菖蒲 (*acorus asiaticus*), a kind of iris. In former times, around the fifth day of the fifth month of the lunar calendar (*tano* 端午), women and children would pluck the stalks and adorn their hair by sticking the roots into it and thus using them as hairpins. In some regions, this custom is observed even today. Besides, they would soak the leaves of the plant in water and use it for bathing. In a work dating from the early 19th century, it is said that iris stalks were used as medical herbs to strengthen the eyesight. Moreover, its alleged power to drive away bad spells seems to have been, a welcome excuse for brewing liquor from it.

Vid. *Chuyŏng p'yŏn,* k.1 (= vol. 1, p. 219; vol. 1, p. 54), *Kugŏ tae sajŏn,* comp. Yi Hŭisŭng, Seoul: Minjung sŏgwan, 1972[19], p. 2773b.

called *kamt'ae* 甘苔 *(porphyra tenera)*, and *miŏk* 미역 or *myŏk* 멱 *(undaria pinnatifida)*. The *ch'angp'ojo* is more popularly known as *kim* 김 or *kiŭm* 기 음, but this term should correctly refer to dried seaweed only. The seaweed grown in the waters around Wan-do and other islands of the region is rated as the best of all Korean seaweed and thus figures prominently as an export item to Japan.[8] Due to the export of seaweed, the villagers of Changjwa-ri and other places have succeeded in acquiring some wealth, and they can be said to be rich, at least, if one compares their standard of living with that of the majority of Korean villagers.[9] Since seaweed is a source of wealth, the suspension of the assignment of lots to grow seaweed is one of the most serious punishments inflicted upon violators of the *Regulations*.[10] Likewise, in the attempt to increase their income as well as to gain additional eatables, the villagers have agreed upon the promotion of coastal fishery and rearing oysters as well as upon the encouragement of cattle rearing and swine feeding to the detriment of sheep and rabbit breeding.[11]

Among the villagers of Changjwa-ri, those between 20 and 39 years of age constituted, in 1966, by far the largest age group. This is a noteworthy fact, because migration from countryside to town is a prominent feature in present day Korean society as well as in the societies of other developing countries, and it tends to affect just this age group, leaving only the young and the old in the villages. There are two big lineages in the village, *viz.* that of the Hwang 黄 and that of the Kim 金. Each of them comprises an almost equal number of individuals, and each of them makes up about a quarter of the total population of the village. They outdo by far the other lineages, of which should be mentioned the Kwak 郭 (162 individuals), the Mun 文 (112 individuals), and the Kang 姜 (87 individuals) as the largest in number next to the Hwang and Kim. None of the clans claims descent from former *yangban* 兩班 [12].

---

[8] In former centuries, timber was another local product for which the island was known. The destructive lumbering of former times must be seen as the main cause for the rather desolate state of the woodlands on Wan Island today.

[9] At present, the government is encouraging the farmers to use slate and other materials instead of straw in roofing their houses. Farmers usually respond positively to such encouragement, considering a slate roof a sign of wealth and prestige. In 1973 slate roofs were still a rare sight in South Chŏlla Province, but at Changjwa-ri, about one fifth of the houses were already covered with slate. It is another sign of wealth and progress that in 1973 one farm house showed a television aerial, which was not there in 1970.

[10] Vid. *Regulations of Changjwa-ri*, Art. 31. Henceforth, all references will be to the *Regulations*, unless otherwise indicated.

[11] Vid. Arts. 7(13-15), 27(5).

[12] In writings about Korea, the reader will frequently encounter expressions such as "*yangban* lineage" or "*yangban* clan". However, the term *yangban* should only be applied to individuals and not to whole clans or lineages. Since the end of the Koryŏ period and throughout the Yi dynasty, the term *yangban* ("two classes") signified those people who had passed the civil and military examinations and thereby gained access to that class of persons

The Documents of Changjwa-ri

According to Document XII, which contains the latest and most comprehensive of all the listings of the documents preserved at Changjwa-ri, there existed twelve different items in the year 1957. If one adds a volume of household registers, which is mentioned in Document XI only, the total amount of separate documents which exist or have existed in Changjwa-ri would be 13.[13]

The documents which served as a basis for the present study are bound in three volumes. The first of these volumes does not bear any specific title; instead, the text of its first leaf is identical with what appears as Document I in Appendix 3 of this study. This volume contains all the material arranged as Documents I to XII inclusive. The second of the volumes is called *Collection of Decisions (Kyŏrŭi soch'ŏl* 決 議 書 綴), the larges part of which is a collection of the records of the village assemblies between the years 1952 and 1964 and contains amendments to the village regulations. Besides, it comprises a non-dated list showing the amounts of money the households had to pay into the funds for the village festival. The third volume bears the title *Collection of Papers Concerning Affairs on the Coast (Kaigan jiken shoruitoji* 海 岸 事 件 書 類 綴). By far the largest part of this volume consists of statements issued by the Japanese authorities concerning the rights of the villagers of Changjwa-ri to gather seaweed in the waters around Wan Island and other islands in the

---

from which government officials were recruited. In practice, such elevation and subsequent appointment to office entailed various privileges for a *yangban's* closer kin. It provided the opportunity to acquire wealth in landed property, which people often managed to bestow on their descendents, and exemption from military service. Since large areas of land meant the freedom to pursue educational ends and to seek official posts, an individual's elevation to *yangban* status usually ensured privileged positions for his living kin and for succeeding generations as well. It is in this sense that the term "*yangban* lineage" and the like have a meaning.

Even after the abolition of the traditional examination system and the old system of land tenure, the terms could be used to mean families which by their erudite tradition were well versed in literature written in the Chinese literary language and thereby maintained certain Chinese-inspired standards in social life and adhered to the old elaborate ancestor ritual. It is in this sense that the terms "*yangban* lineage" or "*yangban* clan" are used by present-day sociologists and ethnologists. The terms mainly serve as operational tools in classifying Korean villages with a view to their readiness in accepting innovations and the dominance of either an old hierarchical value system or an egalitarian community ethic. However, unless *yangban* lineages, by their "natural" lead in education, did acquire wealth again under the new economic modes, the term today does not necessarily imply richness and economic power.

Vid. William E. Henthorn, *Korea. The Mongol Invasions,* Leiden: 1963, p. 119 (note 21); Vincent S. R. Brandt, *A Korean Village. Between Farm and Sea,* Harvard East Asian Monograph Series, no. 65. Cambridge/Ms.: 1971, pp. 8-11.

[13] The leaves of land registers and the book of land registers mentioned in Document X are said to be identical with the three sets of land registers appearing in Documents XI and XII. Therefore, this material cannot be regarded as separate items.

vicinity. Since all these papers concern conditions in the period of Japanese occupation (1910—1945), and not those in the period at the focus of the present study, they are altogether left out of consideration here.

The volume called *Collection of Papers. . .* measures 29 cm x 17 cm, the one called *Collection of Decisions* measures 27 cm x 19 cm, and the third volume measures 28,5 cm x 26 cm. Most of the texts are written on cheap brown paper, but some of them are recorded on either simple letter paper or copy paper (*wŏn'goji* 原 稿 紙), intersected by horizontal and vertical lines so as to form squares into which the characters are inserted. Almost all of the documents are written by means of the traditional tools, *i.e.* brush and ink; only about half of the material contained in the *Collection of Papers. . .* is in printed form. When in 1970, the present author visited Changjwa-ri for the first time, the three volumes were kept at the office of the village rural co-operative (Inonghyŏp samuso 里 農 協 事 務 所). They are the only copies of the texts which ever existed until 1970, there are no others either in the village itself, or at a government office, or in any archive. In 1970, the author of this study had some handwritten copies made, which he checked during his second visit in 1973.

The *Collection of Papers . . .* is written or printed in the so-called Chinese-Japanese mixed style (*kanamajiribun* 假 名 交 り 文), in which the flexions of written Japanese are added to the Chinese characters, the word-order becoming that of the Japanese language. The documents contained in the other two volumes are written in a Chinese-Korean mixed style, *i.e.* the flexions of the Korean language are employed and Korean word-order is produced.

Both the *Collection of Decisions* and the *Collection of Papers . . .* appear as separate items in Documents XI and XII. With regard to the other pieces enumerated there, the present author's informant said that part of them is what makes up the third volume, *i.e.* the one which bears no title. This part comprises the "volume of important documents", the "set of other documents", and the "volume of agreements concerning musical instruments". In other words, out of the 13 items only five could be used for the purpose of this study. When asked where the documents concerning land, forests, village finances, and households were kept, the people would either answer that they simply did not know or that the persons in charge of those papers were away from the village. As these papers were inaccessible, certain serious limitations of the analysis had to be taken into consideration from the very beginning. There was no way out of it, because for various reasons the stays of the present author in Changjwa-ri had to be limited in time. In view of the readiness with which questions were answered and documents put at his disposal, the author of this study is inclined to regard those answers as truthful ones and not to consider them as sub-terfuges, by means of which the villagers tried to keep information from him. The ignorance of the location of certain documents rather seems to be indicative of something else, *viz.* that they are not all too important to the villagers or else that they contain information which is known to them anyway. The same kind of negligence towards written material is attested by the fact that several of the papers or volumes appear under slightly different names in different documents, although the items are doubtlessly the same in substance. Likewise, it is surprising to note that the volume of household registers mentioned in Document XI, a paper possibly considered to be of the utmost importance by an outsider, does not appear in Document XII, which was written only one year later, although, in 1973, it was said to be still extant. Such observations are apt to serve as further proof of what has already been said above, *viz.* that written material only opens a narrow alley towards information and thus cannot be considered the ideal tool in the investigation of the realities of village life.

CHAPTER 3: THE *REGULATIONS OF CHANGJWA-RI* AS LAW AMONG LAWS

Definitions of Law and the Position of a Historian of Law

The introductory chapter of this study has already provided an opportunity to point out that the authors of the *Regulations of Changjwa-ri* definitely wanted the provisions to be taken as law. In this chapter, the author will show that the *Regulations* do indeed correspond to a certain concept of law. Yet, his aim is not simply to confirm the nature of the *Regulations* as law, but to outline those prospects of the present study that can reasonably be hoped for, when one takes into consideration the fact that it is based on law.

The *Regulations of Changjwa-ri* were enacted on September 18th, 1952, by 134 household heads, six of them acting as village deputies, and one as village head. The formal act was that of taking an oath to put the provisions into effect and of sealing the text.[1] Although it is nowhere stated, we are probably correct if we assume that the people who as covenanters enacted the *Regulations* were identical with those who drafted the text, or at least that those who drafted the text were part of that larger group of household heads who enacted the *Regulations*. The whole process of drafting and enacting the rules suggests that the *Regulations of Changjwa-ri* were the result of an agreement reached and sworn to by villagers who were acting upon their own free will. Thus, the *Regulations* have the air of being a specimen of really autonomous legislation at the grassroots level. The impression of the *Regulations* having been an agreement between free villagers is further enhanced by the element of *kyuyak* in the name of the rules, literally meaning a "binding agreement on rules".

The pretensions to autonomy and liberty which the enactment, the taking of an oath in particular, suggests will turn out to be rather hollow. It is a matter of later discussion to show that the *Regulations* are anything but a free agreement between free villagers. The taking of an oath is no argument to the contrary. Readers familiar with the writings of Dr. Bader will be reminded of what he said about oaths of medieval peasants in the south-west of Germany and adjacent areas.[2] There, villages never manifested themselves as unitary corporations to

---

[1] Vid. Art. 35.

[2] It is a pity that the preconditions and effects of oaths in Korea cannot be discussed within the framework of Korean law. For as far as the present author knows, the question has altogether escaped the attention of Korean jurists, and there is no literature he could refer to.

The present author refers to Dr. Bader's writings not because he wants to enforce undue analogies between villages of medieval Europe and those of modern Korea, but because Dr.

the outside world by means of village codes and collective oaths. Taking oaths, even collective ones, was quite a common habit associated with many dealings in medieval peasant life, but whereever it occurred, such oaths either meant affirmations of agreements between peasantry and overlord or else they marked the entrance into a larger oath community (*Schwurverband*). These acts often initiated the growth of *Eidgenossenschaften*, which in turn were larger territorial units above the village level. Oaths never marked the "creation" or affirmation of village communities.[3] Therefore, on the surface, the oath of Changjwa-ri cannot be compared to any of the medieval oaths described by Dr. Bader. Other kinds of collective oaths marked seditious conjurations (*coniuratio*).[4] The oath of Changjwa-ri cannot be compard to such a conspiracy either, for it would be difficult to find people less seditious in mentiality than those of Changjwa-ri. Refuting critism of his view of oaths, Dr. Bader comments upon an instance of a collective oath which was once taken in some village. In his opinion, that procedure could not mean that the villages were imposing on themselves the obligation to follow autonomous regulations; instead it meant an act of homage (*Huldigungsvorgang*).[5] The present author wonders whether the taking of an oath and much else in the *Regulations of Changjwa-ri* should not be seen in the same light.

What has to be done here first is to determine the legal nature of such village codes as the *Regulations of Changjwa-ri*. The fact that matters most is that the village should be ruled by a code of its own. The existence of such a village code is a strange fact in itself, which calls for a word of comment. For the laws of the Republic of Korea neither provide for bodies of villagers to draft and enact village rules nor do they envisage village codes of any kind at all. This, in turn, is due to the fact that neither villages nor parts thereof are recognized as local self-government corporations, which, according to the laws valid since 1952, were the only bodies outside the central government agencies that were given the power to legislate.[6] Hence, people clinging to the view that the term "law"

Bader's remarks succinctly illustrate a dominant feature of peasant life all over the world and in all ages, *viz.* the almost total inability of peasants to form coalitions for the long-term pursuit of common aims on a basis of autonomy and freedom.

Dr. Eric Wolf comments on the same topic. His chapter on peasant coalitions is an illustration of, as well as a probing into, the reasons underlying that inability, which is neglected by many scholars often clinging to "romantic" views, but well realized by politicians and revolutionaries.

Vid. Wolf, *Peasants,* pp. 81-95, esp. pp. 91-93.

[3] Vid. Bader, *Dorfgenossenschaft und Dorfgemeinde,* pp. 252ss, 271-273, 464.

[4] Vid. *ibid.,* pp. 464,274.

[5] Vid. Karl Siegfried Bader, *Rechtsformen und Schichten der Liegenschaftsnutzung im mittelalterlichen Dorf,* Studien zur Rechtsgeschichte des mittelalterlichen Dorfes, Dritter Teil, mit Ergänzungen und Nachträgen zu den Teilen I und II der . . ., Wien/Köln/Graz: 1973, p. 303.

[6] Vid. Appendix 1 of this study.

should only be accorded to rules issued by a national government or by bodies given legislative powers by a national government, would certainly not classify the *Regulations of Changjwa-ri* as law. Yet, for reasons of a more general order, such a view should be discarded here, because it precludes the study of laws of organized communities which do not correspond to the definition of a nation.

Other scholars accord the status of law only to those rules which are adjudicated by courts of an organized community.[7] They would not find it difficult to regard the *Regulations* as law, for, indeed, they are adjudicated by a court, *viz.* the village committee.[8] Yet, making the adjudication by courts the only criterion, these scholars focus on the formal aspects of law only, and fail to grasp its very substance.

In search of a concept of law which will give due credit to both its substantial and formal aspects, the author of this study has found it useful to rely on the writings of legal anthropologists and other social scientists who are interested in legal matters. He welcomes a side-effect of such reference, *viz.* that Korean village codes such as the *Regulations of Changjwa-ri* are made comparable to legal phenomena in other parts of the world. Dr. Leopold Pospíšil has elaborated four attributes which together will suffice to classify an observance as law. These attributes are: statement by an authority, universal application, *obligatio,* and sanctions applied in cases of transgression and neglect.[9]

Dr. Pospíšil's criterion concerning authority refers to individual cases of dispute, where an authoritative individual or group have the litigants comply with a decision, either by persuasion or by force. This criterion can be applied in the case of the *Regulations* as well, if by decision is meant not only the adjudication in a single case but also the drafting and enacting of rules. Dr. Pospíšil himself has implicitly suggested this extension of the criterion by viewing judgements in single cases primarily as acts of creating or restating law.

[7] Such views are not only upheld by jurists. Two of the more recent statements of that view within the literature written in English were made by an anthropologist and a sociologist.

Vid. Alfred R. Radcliffe-Brown, "Primitive Law", *Structure and Function in Primitive Society. Essays and Addresses,* with a foreword by E. E. Evans-Pritchard/Fred Eggan, London: 1952, repr. 1956, p. 212; F. James Davis/Henry H. Foster/C. Ray Jeffery/E. Eugene Davis, *Society and the Law. New Meanings for an Old Profession,* New York: 1962, pp. 41, 45.

[8] Vid. Art. 17(9); chapter 10 of this study.

[9] Vid. Leopold Pospíšil, *Anthropology of Law. A Comparative Theory,* New York/Evanston/San Francisco/London: 1971, pp. 39-96.

The author of this study, although not being a specialist fully able to judge upon the value of the various writings in legal anthropology, has the impression that a concept of law such as that developed by Dr. Pospíšil will be a useful tool in comparative cross-cultural studies in the field of law, for it seems to be largely free from any bias conditioned by the author's ties to his own culture. The book by Dr. Pospíšil seems to be the most recent work of its kind and to summarize the relevant writings, which have hitherto appeared, in a fair way. Anybody who prefers to diverge from Dr. Pospíšil's views will find enough stimulation and support in the works discussed by him. Therefore, reference to earlier writings as well as further discussion will be avoided here.

As far as the second criterion is concerned, the very formulation of the *Regulations* suffices to show that they are not meant to judge single cases only, but to be applied to all those future circumstances which fall into the province of one article or the other.

It is only the term *obligatio* which requires some comment. Dr. Pospíšil takes it in the sense it had in Roman law and wants it to be distinguished from one-sided obligation. *Obligatio* in the case of Changjwa-ri is the implicit statement of the rights of individual villagers, households, or associations and corporations within the village on the one side, and the duties of the village as a corporation, represented by its various agents, on the other side of the relationship. A villager has a right to obtain compensation in cases of damage inflicted upon his property, and the village has the duty to bring about that indemnification.[10] Likewise, a villager as a member of a mutual benefit association (*kye* 契) or a corporation within the village has a right to have his financial or material contributions employed in a responsible way, and the village has to see to such adequate use by controlling the finances and the regulations of associations.[11] In more general terms, *obligatio* means the right of villagers and corporations to be protected from damage, and the duty of the village to bring about balance and order. *Vice versa,* the village has a right to have its property left intact, and the villagers have a duty to restore it to its former state in cases of damage.[12] Finally, there are sanctions, which will be applied in cases of neglect of the provisions, and thus the *Regulations* even correspond to the fourth of Dr. Pospíšil's attributes of law.[13]

Distinction of law from mere custom always causes much trouble, whenever one has to deal with rules which were not issued by a national government. Indeed, two of the attributes of law are shared by custom as well, *viz.* intended universal application and *obligatio*. But the difference between law and custom is equally well marked. In the first place, the criterion concerning authority is alien to custom, because custom is neither authoritatively created nor restated. Besides, law and custom are distinguished by the criterion of sanction. Dr. Pospíšil, in accordance with Professors Llewellyn and Hoebel, says that if a statement of an authority is not ensued by anything, if not even gossip or ridicule are to follow the transgression of it, an observance has to be regarded as mere neutral custom, although it may possess other attributes of law.[14]

Hitherto the quality of the *Regulations* as law has in such a way intruded upon the observer as to even make the analytical tools of Dr. Pospíšil appear as too subtle a device. The real problem, however, arises from quite a different

---

[10] Vid. Art. 31.
[11] Vid. Arts. 17(6), 22-24.
[12] Vid. Documents II, IX, X; Arts. 8(2), 10, 28(3, 5), 29, 30.
[13] Vid. Arts. 27-34.
[14] Vid. Pospíšil, *Anthropology of Law*, pp. 79, 95.

area. All of the scholars who have so far tried to determine the nature of law have made one and the same basic assumption, whether they have explicitly said so or not, *viz.* that law is a form of institutionalized social control. We cannot be sure whether the *Regulations of Changjwa-ri* do really excercise much control over the life in the village, because in terms of origin they are abstract rules. As a whole, they are neither a record of decisions taken nor a set of principles abstracted from actual behaviour which would thus be "legalized". Most of them have rather been elaborated without any explicit reference to already observed habits of any kind, and they pretend to mould village reality according to general principles rather than in accordance with traditional observances peculiar to the place. It is in this sense that the *Regulations* have to be called abstract rules and that they are somewhat removed from village reality and hardly have a chance to exercise much control over it. However, making either the realization of a scheme of social control a requirement of law or else viewing law as a set of rules abstracted from actual behaviour, both present several difficulties, because equating law with actually enforced behaviour would make the concept of law both meaningless and superfluous. Hardly any behavior conforms with the ideal attribute, and yet, nobody would deny the value of the ideal attribute and would cease to call it law. For this and other reasons succinctly stated by Dr. Pospíšil, we could hardly limit the term of law to actually exercised social control.[15]

In this respect the case of Changjwa-ri does not differ from cases in other parts of the world. The present study, it is hoped, will show how little of village life, if anything at all, is regulated by the rules laid down in the *Regulations*, and how little the provisions in the village code can be said to be abstractions of actual village life. This largely invalidates the *Regulations of Changjwa-ri* as a source of information on economic and social realities of the village, but it does not invalidate them as law, unless we insist on the criterion of social control, not only as an ideal, but as actual reality.

The limited material available does not only bar the present author from studying the economy and the social life of the village, but its legal life as well. Realizing the fact that law often maintains much of an ideal and thus presents more of a pretension in value and procedure than a reflection of real legal life, it almost goes without saying that deeper insight into the legal life of a community can be obtained by relying mainly or even exclusively on principles upheld by legal decisions than by referring to written abstract rules.[16] However, in most

---

[15] Vid. *ibid.*, pp. 24, 30s.

[16] The present author's interest in the nature and value of legal decisions as sources of information is different from that of Dr. Pospíšil's. Whereas the latter sets about to estimate the value of legal decisions, because he works with them in his study, the legal historian does so, because he is not in a position to use them. By comparing his abstract rules with legal decisions, the legal historian will learn in what respect his inquiries fall behind the studies which are based on legal decisions: other than legal decisions do, abstract rules almost entirely

cases it would be difficult to adduce past legal decisions from which to abstract legal principles. The difficulties the present author experiences with regard to the *Regulations of Changjwa-ri* are those of any historian of law. For, as a rule, the more the investigator is removed in time from the period under investigation, the more difficult it is to obtain records of decisions and the more hopeless it must appear to interrogate people who have memories of by-gone days. This is the more so in the rural areas of most of East Asia, because peasants there are not in the habit of recording things themselves, and government authorities on the other hand have never cared much for the internal life of villages and other rural corporations. In the light of such considerations Dr. Pospíšil's endeavours to make actual legal decisions the main sources of information about legal conditions must appear to be somewhat over-ambitious when applied to historical circumstances, however useful his concept of law may otherwise be.

Thus, village codes like the one from Changjwa-ri will hardly introduce us to any aspect of inner village life, and we shall not learn much from them about the social structure, the economy, and not even about the realities of the legal life of the village. Any investigator who, by means of such regulations, tries to gain deeper insight into the life of a Korean village, will quickly find himself pursuing a chimera. Yet, there is no reason to refrain from the study of such codes altogether. Despite the many shortcomings inherent in such laws as sources of information on legal aspects as well as on economic and social ones, they are useful when it comes to legal and political ideals. Written laws have a unique value as documents of the concepts of the powerful ones, which they reflect in a very succinct manner and better than any other kind of document. They can, therefore, be regarded as an appropriate means of access to the ideals of the power group in a society. Although the *Regulations of Changjwa-ri* pretend to be the work of the villagers themselves, we cannot *a priori* be sure that this is really the case. The problem concerning the nature of the *Regulations* not as law but as a piece of legislation is very complicated, and it must be further elucidated in the course of this study. Suffice it here to say that the *Regulations* are a strange result of interaction between villagers and government officials, and it is by no means evident that they exclusively reflect the ideals of either of them. The *Regulations of Changjwa-ri* lead us right into the middle of the conflict between government claims and village autonomy. Since this is likely to be true of any other village codes, the *Regulations* may be taken as an appropriate means to study the nature of that conflict as well as its history and its future prospects. In the light of such considerations, part of the aims pursued in this study can be re-formulated as follows. In the first place, the author has to bring to light

---

lack the behavioural aspect. This is not to mean that abstract rules are not law; as law they are just not a very convenient instrument in research, if by them one endeavours to gain insight into the real legal life of a society.

Vid. *ibid.*, pp. 31-37.

the discrepancy between real village life and the provisions in the *Regulations* pertaining to its economic, social, and legal aspects. This will be achieved by making as much of the village economy and social life known as is necessary and possible. Secondly, he will present the material in terms of community and commune activities, thus illustrating the complex nature of village life. Finally, he has to comment on the character of the *Regulations* as a specimen of legislation, which also reflects this complexity.

Multiplicity of Legal Systems

In order to illustrate further the relative insignificance of the *Regulations* both as law and as a source of information on social and economic matters, the present author will refer to a concept which has also been elaborated by Dr. Pospíšil, *viz.* that of the multiplicity of laws and legal systems.[17]

Underlying the whole of the *Regulations* is the assumption that the village is a well-integrated corporation, the well-being of which is at the focus of every individual's and every group's attention and aspiration. As might have already appeared from the above discussion of *obligatio*, the provisions of the *Regulations* do not so much deal with the relations of individuals to individuals or of corporations within the village to other corporations. Instead, they basically try to handle the relationships between individual villagers, households, and corporations within the village on the one hand and "the village" on the other. This implies that the village is thought of as an integrated corporation, which at the same time is opposed to, and associated with, less inclusive units, such as the individual villagers, households, etc.

However, as far as our present knowledge of Korean villages goes, we cannot but consider as largely fictitious the concept of the village as being the main rallying point of interest and aspiration within it. Likewise, we are reluctant to accept the idea of its being a corporation, a body of people acting in unison for a common reason.[18] The supposed weakness of Korean villages

---

[17] Vid. *ibid.*, pp. 97-126.

[18] The question of village solidarity and village coherence has hardly caught the attention of the authors who have hitherto written about Korean villages. They rather seem to have taken them for granted. This silence on the matter may in part be due to the fact that most of these authors have dealt with units other than the *i*. The question deserves our full attention here, because the validity of the assumption of village solidarity is quickly minimized when we look at the conditions of the Yi period. Having studied various entries in the *Veritable Records of the Royal Court of Chosŏn* (*Chosŏn wangjo sillok* 朝 鮮 王 朝 實 錄), the present author can safely state that by the government the villages were not considered to be efficient instruments in local control. This may have been conditioned by the very lack of village solidarity. Likewise, not many villages seem to have developed a penal jurisdiction of their own which could be taken as another manifestation of village coherence. Most of the few extant codes of that kind date from the latter part of the last or the beginning of the present

seems to have its roots in equally strong — or even stronger — allegiances of the individual villager to social units other than the village. He is part of a household, and he is very likely to belong to one or more of the mutual benefit associations and corporations within the village. Moreover, he may have close ties with a religious denomination or be a member of supra-village corporations such as the rural co-operatives. Each of these units is governed by a set of rules of its own, and thus the individual villager, by being associated with one or several of such units, is subject to several systems of rules at the same time, the village rules not necessarily being the strongest ones.

As far as these various systems of rules meet the requirements of law, the multiplicity of social units and of rules can adequately be portrayed as a multiplicity of laws. Although, according to Dr. Pospíšil's reasoning, the most inclusive unit is not the village, but a confederacy of villages or the modern state, there is nothing in that concept which would prohibit its application to such units as Korean villages and the legal systems within them. The multiplicity of legal systems usually occurs in two ways. Either each of the systems controls a specific area in the individual's life. It may be that inheritance is subject to the rules of lineage, whereas the kind and order of agricultural labour are subject to village rules, and the financing of innovations is regulated by the provisions of some kind of co-operative. Or the systems may all cover the same fields and thus tend to contradict each other. In either way, one system will have to get the better of another one at any given moment. A villager will spend more of his means, in terms of time or money, on the efforts of one group than on those of another, and he will thus obey the rules of the one and not those of the other system of rules. Although being the most inclusive one, the legal system at the village level can by no means be considered to be *a priori* the strongest one. Villagers may obey the commandments of their lineages more willingly than those of some village agency, and they may spend more money on enterprises of some mutual benefit association than any decision of a village assembly could ever raise. It is a matter of purely empirical

century. It seems as if village coherence, where it ever developed at all, was the result of a slow process which started comparatively late in history and has not attained its climax yet.

Even a cautious scholar as Dr. Ch'oe Chaesŏk still seems to cling to the traditional view. When comparing the constituents of Korean villages with those of Japanese ones, he portrays the Korean village as the primary group from which all sub-units within the village emanate. This alleged process he juxtaposes to Japanese conditions, with regard to which he emphasizes the idea that Japanese villages do not generate, but are made up of, smaller units, such as neighbourhoods, households, and associations.

Vid. Dieter Eikemeier, "Villages and Quarters as Instruments of Local Control in Yi Dynasty Korea", pp. 85, 89s, 92, 98-100; "Rechtswirkungen von heiligen Stangen, Pfeiler-gottheiten und Steinhaufengottheiten in Korea", *Oriens Extremus*, 21. Jg., Heft 2, Wiesbaden: 1974, pp. 175, 183-185; *Han'guk nongch'on sahoe yŏn'gu,* comp. Ch'oe Chaesŏk, pp. 56-58, 60s; pp. 45-47 of this study.

observation to decide which legal system is the strongest and why. In legal studies on Korean villages, particularly in those concerned with conditions of the past, one can at best provide a complete survey of all the legal systems in a village, including that of the village itself, without deciding on the individual power of any of them.

The immediate value of the concept of multiplicity consists firstly in urging the investigator to think of the village code as being merely one system among others, coexisting and competing with others. It will, secondly, prevent him from overestimating the impact of one legal level to the neglect of others. Likewise, it prevents the student from focusing his interest on the individual villager in such a way as to make him appear to be participating immediately in the life of the village as the one and all-inclusive society. The concept of the multiplicity of laws teaches him to think of the village as of a complex society of sub-groups rather than as of a jumble of interacting individuals oriented towards the village as the single focus of interest.

The validity of the concept of the multiplicity of legal systems is corroborated by an analogous distinction made in anthropology. Writing about peasant coalitions Dr. Wolf mentions a type of coalition which he characterizes as single-stranded, polyadic, and horizontal, which means that a number of people in equivalent relationships are organized around a single interest. His reference to associations or "sodalities", mutual aid clubs and parent-burial associations in particular, as the best examples of that kind of coalition, points to the category the mutual benefit associations of Korean villages should be assigned to. The kind of grouping from which part of the power is removed by the single-stranded polyadic horizontal associations also appears among Dr. Wolf's categories. It is the many-stranded polyadic horizontal coalition, to which he has on some other occasion given the name "closed corporate community". The latter communities restrict membership to people born and raised within their confines, they have the ultimate right to land, they develop equalizing and levelling arrangements, and they act as unitary groups with regard to outside claims for rent, taxes, and the like. They maintain their internal order by both formal and informal sanctions, and other than the rather short-lived associations they create enduring rights and duties upheld by a stable membership.[19] It is obvious that these characteristics pertain to the village community we have in mind here and that this village community should be regarded as the peculiar Korean manifestation of the many-stranded polyadic horizontal kind of peasant coalition. Although Dr. Wolf nowhere writes about competition among these various kinds of peasant coalitions, he admits that in practice they all interpenetrate and complement each other.[20]

[19] Vid. Wolf, *Peasants,* pp. 83s, 85s.
[20] Vid. *ibid.*, p. 89.

Hence, his distinctions can indeed be said to be parallel to what has elsewhere been described as a multiplicity of legal systems.

In the course of a conversation with the author of this study Professor Dr. Yi Kwanggyu 李光奎 of Seoul National University suggested a distinction between two levels of village life. One of the levels is formal and "official" in character. All social organizations belonging to it have been established or revitalized in more recent times in the course of campaigns of community development, such as the 4-H-Clubs, the Youth Society, the Women's Society, a local Red Cross Section, etc.[21] Village assemblies and village committees would also belong to this level. The other level, being a more or less "unofficial" one, comprises the mutual benefit associations and societies responsible for the organization of village ceremonies. Moreover, it comprises groups of co-operative farming called *p'umasi* 품앗이 and such informal groupings as the *maltanigi* 말 다 니 기, groups of villagers who would visit each others' houses in cases of sickness, provide medicine, and share other grievances or pleasures with each other.[22]

Here, Dr. Yi lumps together into one category what has been distinguished by Dr. Wolf as single-stranded polyadic horizontal coalitions and many-stranded ones of the same order. Nevertheless, Dr. Yi's distinctions further help us to get a feeling of what multiplicity of sub-groups and of smaller systems of rules means in a Korean village. Besides, they support Dr. Wolf's statement that single-interest peasant coalitions also serve to link those groups to the supra-village structure of power and interest.[23] Those distinctions are thus intimately related to the one between community and commune affairs which is to play an important part in this study.

---

[21] Vid. pp. 76s of this study.

[22] *P'umasi* is an informal kind of co-operation in farming and other kinds of work among neighbours. They join hands in working in the fields of each of the members of the group, lend oxen to each other, or help in building and roofing houses.

Vid. *Han'guk nongch'on sahoe tapsagi,* comp. Suzuki Eitarō, transl. Idae sahoehakkwa, Seoul: Idae ch'ulp'anbu, 1961, pp. 66-69; *Han'guk nongch'onŭi ch'ollak kujo,* comp. Yang Hoesu, p. 388; Brandt, *A Korean Village,* pp. 70-73.

[23] Vid. Wolf, *Peasants,* p. 84.

CHAPTER 4: THE *REGULATIONS OF CHANGJWA-RI* AS CUSTOMARY LAW

The Attributes of Customary Law and Their Application to the Regulations of Changjwa-ri

Whoever deals with rural law inevitably has to face the question of whether it is customary law or not. Most people will quickly equate rural law with customary law. Since changes are usually fewer and are brought about at a much slower pace in rural areas than in other parts of a country, many people tend to think that the law in the countryside tends to cling much more to the past than the law prevalent in towns and cities. However much this assumption may be true, it would mean jumping to conclusions, if we all too easily regarded any law of the countryside to be customary law. It is therefore necessary to elaborate certain criteria, by means of which we can decide whether the *Regulations of Changjwa-ri* can really be called customary law or not.

Following Dr. Pospíšil's reasoning and having disentangled law from custom and usage, the reader may not be inclined to give the term "customary law" any further consideration. He may rather discard it on the grounds of its being a *contradictio in adjecto*. Still, the term is used in juridical writing, even by Dr. Pospíšil himself, and in less "technical" language as well. It thus carries some meaning, and therefore it is open to definition, because definition anyway does not do anything but express tacitly acknowledged attributes of some phenomenon or concept. Although we can thus be certain of the possibility of definition, we have to consider a great many aspects of the concept, because most of the definitions we can adduce so far suffer from a remarkable degree of vagueness and are often quite meaningless.[1] Like the considerations pertaining to the concept of law, the following ones will help to determine further the province and the prospects of investigations of legal conditions in the countryside, particularly with regard to past times.

---

[1] As far as the present author's knowledge goes, the most recent writing on the topic is contained in the introduction to *Ideas and Procedures in African Customary Law*. This is a most thorough exposé of problems pertaining to the concept of customary law, but it does not contain any explicit definition of the term which might serve as an analytical tool here.

Vid. Max Gluckman, *Ideas and Procedures in African Customary Law. Studies Presented and Discussed at the Eighth International Seminar at the Haile Sellassie I University, Addis Ababa, January 1966*, ed. . . ., with an introduction by A. N. Allott/A. L. Epstein/M. Gluckman, publ. for the International African Institute by Oxford University Press, London: 1969, pp. 9-15.

In order to forestall a common, though not truly "professional" opinion, it must be said that the *Regulations of Changjwa-ri* should not be denied the status of customary law simply on the grounds that the rules have been written down. No contemporary writer, irrespective of the particular area he is concerned with, would *a priori* exclude legal rules from the province of customary law for that reason. At least, he would not do so, if his main concern was with a legal past, however remote it may be. As far as the area of pre-modern central European law is concerned, it may suffice to quote the most recent publications of Dr. Karl Heinz Burmeister and Dr. Theodor Bühler. They are, it is true, only two scholars among many who have dealt with the subject, but they do not adduce a single instance from the bulk of earlier literature which could support a view contrary to the one held here, nor was that ever their intention.[2] In a work like *Ideas and Procedures in African Customary Law*, the authors express misgivings as to whether and in what sense the recording of customary law could distort its meaning or hamper its meaningful application, but none of them ceases to call it customary law because it is written down.[3] As another example we may quote *La rédaction des coutumes dans le passé et dans le présent*, which by its title excludes any other view than the one sustained here.[4] Reviewing the many considerations which could be adduced in support of this view, the investigator orientated towards the past might emphasize that by regarding contracts, *Weistümer*, police regulations, *franchises, rôles*, and "restatements" as not containing customary law, he would finally cease to avail of the most important and sometimes only sources of law other than those promulgated by modern government institutions.

Occasionally, it is simply said that age is an essential attribute of customary law. This is a view often held even by recorders and specialists of customary

---

[2] Vid. Karl Heinz Burmeister, *Die Vorarlberger Landsbräuche und ihr Standort in der Weistumsforschung*, Rechtshistorische Arbeiten namens der Forschungsstelle für Rechtsgeschichte beim Rechtswissenschaftlichen Seminar der Universität Zürich, hrsg. Karl Siegfried Bader, Bd. 5, Zürich: 1970, pp. 12, 24, quoted as Burmeister, *Vorarlberger Landsbräuche*; Theodor Bühler, *Gewohnheitsrecht und Landesherrschaft im ehemaligen Fürstbistum Basel*, Rechtshistorische Arbeiten namens der Forschungsstelle für Rechtssprache, Rechtsarchäologie und Rechtliche Volkskunde beim Rechtswissenschaftlichen Seminar der Universität Zürich, hrsg. Karl Siegfried Bader, Bd. 8, Zürich: 1972, pp. 16s.

[3] Vid. Gluckman, *op. cit.*, pp. 15-21 *et passim*.

[4] Strangely enough, Professor Dr. Gilissen, as the editor of the work, insists on customary law as being non-written law. But neither he himself nor any of the other contributors would cease to continue talking of customary law after its having been written down.

Vid. John Gilissen, "La rédaction des coutumes dans le passé et dans le présent. Essai de synthèse", *La rédaction des coutumes dans le passé et dans le présent. Colloque organisé les 16 et 17 mai 1960 par le Centre d'Histoire et d'Ethnologie juridiques sous la direction de . . .*, Etudes d'histoire et d'ethnologie juridiques, publ. par le Centre d'Histoire et d'Ethnologie juridiques, no. 3, Bruxelles: 1962, p. 26.

law.[5] Yet, it is quite an unsuitable criterion, because nobody can tell how much time must elapse before a law can be regarded as an old and hence a customary law.

It would be equally unsatisfactory if we made a judgement dependent on the kind of language used in recording the law. Records of customary law are sometimes believed to be written in the language of the simple folk, conveying human warmth and faithfully portraying rustic imagination and the common man's soul (*Volksseele*).[6] Yet, if we look at some specimens which in other respects would well qualify as records of customary law, we would deem the language anything but pleasing and popular, because the texts are heavily loaden with loan words, which make the style extremely formal and clumsy.[7] Therefore, insistence on popular and imaginative language would require the exclusion, from the bulk of customary law, of a great many texts, which could easily be classified as containing customary law, if only the criterion of popular language were dropped. The *Regulations of Changjwa-ri* are a perfect match with those formal and sometimes clumsy records. The language is overloaded with words derived from the Chinese, even in places where native Korean words could have been used. Moreover, the text is composed by means of syntactic parallelism, another device inherited from the Chinese literary language. The effect is that of rigidity and sometimes even of solemnity.[8] In trying to give weight and power to the *Regulations of Changjwa-ri*, the authors profited from the prestige which the Chinese literary language and Chinese vocabulary have always enjoyed in Korea, even after the promulgation of a suitable Korean alphabet in 1446. The Chinese literary language was the vehicle used in spreading those elements in literature, thought, and politics which were considered to be superior by those Koreans who were in a position to learn to handle the intricacies of the Chinese literary language. Even after

---

[5] Vid. Jakob Grimm/Wilhelm Grimm, *Deutsches Wörterbuch*, bearb. v. Alfred Götze und der Arbeitsstelle des Deutschen Wörterbuches zu Berlin, Bd. 14, 1. Abt., 1. Teil, Leipzig: 1955, Sp. 1171; Gluckman, *Ideas and Procedures in African Customary Law*, p. 9; Burmeister, *Vorarlberger Landsbräuche*, p. 61.

[6] Vid. Paul Gehring, "Um Weistümer", *Zeitschrift der Savigny-Stiftung für Rechtsgeschichte, Germanistische Abteilung*, Bd. 60, 1940, p. 265; Karl Kollnig, "Probleme der Weistumsforschung", *Heidelberger Jahrbücher*, hrsg. Universitäts-Gesellschaft Heidelberg, Bd. 1, Göttingen/New York/ Berlin: 1957, pp. 15, 18, 24, Nachdr. *Deutsches Bauerntum im Mittelalter*, hrsg. Günther Franz, Wege der Forschung, Bd. CCCCXVI, Darmstadt: 1976, pp. 398, 402, 412.

[7] Vid. Burmeister, *Vorarlberger Landsbräuche*, pp. 27s.

[8] The authors of the *Regulations* did not always conform to the niceties of Chinese grammar. For instance, when marking a conditional clause, they tended to use the temporal "when" (*si* 時) instead of a common conditional particle. The author of this study has tried to preserve some of this ruggedness of the documents in his translations of these and other peculiarities, to the detriment of a smooth English text. Thus, in the instances just mentioned he has always translated by "when", where "if" would have been the correct word.

the traditional Chinese culture lost its impact on Korean society, elements of the ancient literary language of the Chinese continued to be used in cases where something important had to be transmitted, and it is for this reason that the language of the *Regulations* is so little imbued with elements characteristic of the daily speech of the common folk. In one instance the obsession with Chinese vocabulary and the desire to elevate the language of the village documents to far above the level of daily speech led the authors to render a purely Korean term, for which there is no Chinese equivalent, by means of Chinese characters. The term could have been rendered more conveniently by the Korean alphabet. The authors thus produced an interesting specimen of phonographic use of Chinese characters in contemporary Korea.[9]

Customary law can neither be conceived of as an antipole of recorded law, nor of recently observed law, nor of a law written down in formal and sometimes awkward language.[10] Neglecting the oppositions discussed above, Dr. Pospíšil, in his turn, thinks of customary law as being opposed to what he calls authoritarian law. By authoritarian law he means rules which have been forced upon their subjects by some legal authority, without having been considered just and proper by the majority of the society. In the course of time, however, those subject to the rules may have found them to be intrinsically rewarding. They may have started thinking obedience to them to be necessary and have ceased to regard them as something enforced upon them against their own wills. As soon as a majority in a society regards the rules to be binding in that sense, originally authoritarian law has ceased to be authoritarian and has turned into customary law. The mental process by which authoritarian law is changed into customary law is called internalization.[11] Thus, Dr. Pospíšil defines customary law as follows: "By customary law . . . will be meant a law that is internalized by a social group."[12] The validity of customary law is based

---

[9] Vid. Appendix 3, note 10 of this study.

[10] Of course, anybody is free to regard any of these attributes as essential to customary law. But in doing so, his definition would become incompatible with those of contiguous fields of law, which in turn would compel him to undertake a far-reaching re-definition of law and legislation.

[11] Vid. Pospíšil, *Anthropology of Law*, pp. 193-209.

The attempts at defining customary law which have been discussed so far are largely those which have already been listed in Dr. Gilissen's introductory essay to *La rédaction des coutumes dans le passé et dans le présent*. Those readers who want to obtain more information on the contents of the definitions and on their sources should refer to this essay. The present review of the concepts will be left as it is, because it is not the aim of this discussion to make a contribution to the theory of customary law, but to make use of elements of such theories in order to be in a position to evaluate the place of the *Regulations of Changjwa-ri* and similar texts within the legal and political framework of Korea.

Dr. Gilissen's notion of customary law — and that of colleagues having contributed to his symposium — is largely determined by experience with African legal systems. The contributors think of customary law as a set of traditional rules of a given society, which in its

on a consent upon its necessity, the *opinio necessitatis* of the commentators of Roman law. Reference to it by some legal authority would neither generate its validity nor, on the other hand, invalidate it as customary law; it would only, according to the general concept of law, confer upon it the status of law. Therefore, a decision of a legal authority which is based on customary law cannot be considered to be a creation of law, but a kind of restatement.[13] If rules such as the *Regulations of Changjwa-ri* had been internalized before they were recorded, the act of drafting and enacting them could not deprive them of their quality as customary law and turn it into non-customary law.

Dr. Pospíšil went a long way to arrive at his concept of customary law. One wonders why he did not take the short cut leading him directly to the nineteenth century work by Georg Friedrich Puchta (1798—1846). Puchta's concept of customary law derives from a comprehensive concept of law as such, which in turn is not entirely an invention of Puchta's. He distinguishes sources of law (*Rechtsquellen*) from sources of legal knowledge (*Rechtserkenntnisquellen*). The former category comprises laws resulting from legislation, observances flowing from juridical scholarship, and what Puchta calls the natural congruence of conviction ("die natürliche Übereinstimmung der Überzeugung"), which neither relies on promulgated laws nor on scholarly tenets. There are three sources of legal knowledge, *viz.* documents (*Urkunden*), scholarly systems of legal thought, and the laws actually applied in life. According to these two sets of sources, Puchta distinguishes three kinds of law, *viz.* promulgated law, the law of the jurists, and customary law. Both the recognition and the application of customary law pose several problems when the law in question can be found in no other source of law than the "natural congruence of conviction" or when it is documented in no other source of legal knowledge than the observances of a social group.[14] Puchta repeatedly states

origin is opposed to rules of European origin which have been laid upon those societies by their colonizers. By way of analogy, the *Regulations of Changjwa-ri* could easily be fitted into this conceptual framework, if we emphasized their opposition to the legislation of the modern Korean state, a legislation which is deeply imbued with modern European and American concepts and terms.

Vid. John Gilissen, "La rédaction des coutumes dans le passé et dans le présent", pp. 23-26.

[12] Pospíšil, *Anthropology of Law*, p. 196.

[13] The term "restatement" seems to have acquired a technical meaning first in American law, meaning "... a systematic, analytical, and comprehensive account of a branch of the law which is unwritten or to be found in a variety of sources, or which has diverged in application by different courts".

Vid. Gluckman, *Ideas and Procedures in African Customary Law*, p. 13 (note 2); Etienne Gutt, "Le *Restatement of American Law* au XXe siècle", *La rédaction des coutumes dans le passé et dans le présent*, pp. 185-196; Anthony N. Allott, "The Recording of Customary Law in British Africa and the Restatement of African Law Project", *loc. cit.*, pp. 197-232.

[14] Vid. Georg Friedrich Puchta, *Das Gewohnheitsrecht*, Erster Teil, Erlangen: 1828, photomech. Nachdr. Darmstadt: 1965, pp. 78-81 *et passim*.

that from among the laws actually applied in life no other provisions deserve the name of customary law than those common observances that flow from a "natural congruence of conviction". These observances he calls *Sitte*, and he distinguishes *Sitte* from *Gewohnheit*, which he considers to be mere individual habits based on nothing but an individual's conviction of the feasibility or necessity of habitually repeating some act. Since *Sitte* is considered to grow from collective convictions, an individual's *Gewohnheit* can neither create *Sitte* nor customary law. The distinction between *Sitte* and *Gewohnheit* equally implies that mere repetition of some act is no sufficient proof of its being a manifestation of customary law. Since mere repetition is no proof of customary law, the mere age of an observance, as documented by repetition, is not proof of customary law, either.[15]

Even if Puchta's concept of customary law had no other merit than that of being simpler than Dr. Pospíšil's, it would already deserve being preferred to the latter's as a guideline in discussions of customary law. Both authors certainly have some things in common. Dr. Pospíšil's "internalization" seems to coincide with Puchta's "natural congruence of conviction", both in matter and in the rank these ideas occupy in the two concepts.[16] In one instance, Dr. Pospíšil's view is more precise than that of Puchta, *viz.* in distinguishing legally relevant custom from other, non-legal custom. This certainly is an important distinction which Puchta failed to make in an explicit way. In other respects, however, Dr. Pospíšil falls far behind Puchta. With regard to the so-called requirements of custom, for instance, there are more than just *opinio necessitatis*. Puchta found it necessary to devote almost 100 pages of his book to the discussion of those various requirements.[17] The most debatable point in Dr. Pospíšil's discussion of customary law, however, is the opposition between customary and authoritarian laws. This opposition is introduced in a way which suggests a certain genesis of customary law. Law promulgated by — authoritarian — political leaders and decision-making bodies appears to be the primary and, implicitly, the only source of all law. Historical evidence, for instance that displayed by Puchta, will easily serve to refute this view.

We shall leave the discussion of customary law as it is. For we have to ask ourselves whether there is any concept of customary law at all which is suitable for a historian of law whose concern is Far Eastern agrarian societies. Both Puchta and Dr. Pospíšil have to rely heavily on states of mind to decide whether some law is a customary one or not. Yet, the historian of Far Eastern rural

[15] Vid *ibid.*, pp. 167-180.

[16] However, it is not the mental process of "internalization", but the result of it that makes some law a customary one. Such a view is certainly in line with Dr. Pospíšil's reasoning, and it would have been better if he had chosen a term emphasizing the final mental state instead of the one emphasizing the process, as "internalization" does.

[17] Vid. Georg Friedrich Puchta, *Das Gewohnheitsrecht*, Zweiter Teil, Erlangen: 1837, photomech. Nachdr. Darmstadt: 1965, pp. 24-119.

law will hardly find any evidence of past "internalizations" or "natural congruences of conviction". This is mainly so because the people immediately concerned are hardly in a position to record their convictions, and those who could well do so are usually not interested in rural affairs. From among all the requirements to be fulfilled by customary law, the historian of Far Eastern rural law will hardly have the chance to check more than those which are related to outward phenomena. What the investigator will then find is a set of long-standing rules, something seemingly close to the *consuetudines* of Roman law.[18] Yet, such long-standing rules cannot necessarily be said to be the outward manifestations of customary law, because they may well lack a common conviction as their base. As has already been said above, the investigator will normally be unable to decide whether such rules are congruent with common convictions or not, because he is unable to confirm the existence and nature of those convictions. However, such positive proof is absolutely necessary. For the fact that some law is not found in government legislation or is not derived from juridical theories does not allow for the conclusion that it is rooted in "natural congruences of conviction". In villages, for instance, it may well be that such a rule owes its existence to an authoritative command of some living village leader. Or, as a command issued by some earlier personality, it is stubbornly kept in the codes or otherwise transmitted in the hope of having it again realized in the future. In Changjwa-ri village laws, there are examples of rules which have been upheld for a considerable length of time, but which do not seem to have ever been applied. Of those older laws which we can consider to have been applied at some time, some may well have been "internalized" and thus been congruent with common convictions, but that congruence may have been lost in the course of time. Whatever the case may be, the investigator cannot be relieved of the task of positively proving that some law is based on the "natural congruence of conviction", before he can call it a customary law.

This state of things leaves us with a severe dilemma. We would either have to change the concept of customary law so as to make it already applicable to those provisions which simply rate as long-standing ones. This, of course, would be a severe deviation from, and simplification of, a rather well-developed theory of customary law. Or we would have to altogether drop the idea of applying the concept of customary law to the non-government and non-jurist laws of an East Asian rural past. The present author feels that there is no other way than the latter.

What we can do here is to enumerate all those of Changjwa-ri village laws which can be said to have appeared at some time before the period under investigation here and to have more or less continuously been observed since then. Although age and continuous application cannot be considered as

[18] Vid. Puchta, *Gewohnheitsrecht*, Erster Teil, pp. 91-104.

sufficient proofs of their being customary laws, both qualities, to a certain degree at least, urge upon us the idea that they are customary ones. However, the present author does not consider it to be a recommendable procedure if the tests of age and continuous application were now successively applied to any single provision of the *Regulations*. The question will be answered as a matter of course, when the provisions are discussed in greater detail later in this study.

Here, the author will briefly comment on those provisions that will later be dealt with in a manner by which the question of their potentially being customary laws will not be answered in an explicit or implicit manner.

All provisions concerning the sanctity of the sacred places in the village can be considered to be old ones, because the very conduct of the village festival itself is an old habit.[19] Besides, the present state of these places shows that they are deliberately cared for by the villagers. It was related by the villagers that about thirty years ago, somebody was expelled from the village because of severe misbehaviour. This shows that at least the sanctions relating to exclusion from the village society under certain circumstances of unlawful acts was valid well before 1952.[20] There are many provisions in the *Regulations* which call for respect from the young people for the old people in the village.[21] Such virtues undoubtedly stem from the once strong influence of Confucianism[22] and are deeply rooted in the Korean population. The same is true with regard to the existence of mutual benefit associations.[23] Likewise, the ways of joint farming mentioned in the *Regulations*[24] are said to have been practised since a long time ago.

The questions concerning age and the continuous application of provisions are much more difficult to answer with regard to the provisions calling for the avoidance of gambling and excessive feasting and trying to urge the villagers to be economical in the conduct of wedding and mourning ceremonies.[25] They may have been promulgated at least as far back as the middle of the Japanese period. However, we have serious doubts as to their genuine acceptance, and hence actual application, among the villagers, because many of the rules run counter to inveterate habits of the rural Korean population, and they may figure as "authoritarian" law only which has not been transformed into real customary law. Conclusions concerning the approximate date of the promulgation of those provisions can be drawn from the existence of the Society for the Promotion of Folk Customs of Changjwa-ri, which has existed at least since 1932/33.[26] This

---

[19] Vid. Arts. 8(3), 28(3), 29(2); Document V; chapter 7 of this study.
[20] Vid. Art. 31.
[21] Vid. Arts. 8(4), 9(3,5), 19, 26.
[22] Vid. Appendix 2 of this study.
[23] Vid. Art. 9(1,2).
[24] Vid. Arts. 7(14), 8(1), 28(2), 29(1,3).
[25] Vid. Arts. 7(1-5), 27(6,7).
[26] Vid. Document I.

society may well have been the agent in spreading those ideas. Although, at present, nobody in Changjwa-ri seems to have any memories of the past activities of that society, they may be reconstructed from other evidence. The idea of "promotion of folk customs" seems to have been particularly widespread in the so-called model villages (Sin.-Jap. *mohan buraku*, Sin.-Kor. *moböm purak* 模 範 部 落) of those days.[27] There, "promotion of folk customs" meant less the revitalization and promotion of folklore than the promotion of frugality in family ceremonies, money-saving, neatness in daily life, avoidance of gambling and drinking, and punctuality. These virtues are roughly the same as those which appear in the *Regulations*. Societies were established in many of the villages, which under the leadership of some central personage (*chūshin jimbutsu, chungsim inmul* 中 心 人 物) made the promotion of customs their main concern or at least one of their aims.[28] Even in rural associations of that time which were primarily concerned with other activities, the promotion of folk customs used to figure as one of their lateral aims, as documents to be discussed later will show.[29] The Society for the Promotion of Folk Customs of Changjwa-ri may have been just one of them, although Changjwa-ri is nowhere listed as a model village, and villagers do not remember their place to have enjoyed that position in the Japanese period. Still, one has to take into consideration that concepts and institutions often emerge as manifestations of a *Zeitgeist* rather than as the results of authoritative planning, and thus may be found even in places where they were not implanted by any conscious and explicit act of any authority. This is the more likely in the case of Changjwa-ri. Since it is situated on the coast and was well known for its seaweed during — and even before — the period of Japanese colonization,[30] it would be surprising to find that the lives of its inhabitants were not thoroughly moulded by the impact of Japanese rural policy, which reached even to places much less exposed to Japanese intrusion.

Hence, there is reason to believe that some parts of the *Regulations of Changjwa-ri* had been accepted and observed as internalized, binding norms

---

[27] Model villages were places inhabited by Koreans, who, spurred on by Japanese "advisers" sent to Korea, excelled in the promotion of agriculture, education, self-government, moneysaving, and improvement of "customs". They were granted allowances by the Governor General after having accomplished outstanding performances in these fields. The number of model villages is given as 257 in the year 1931.

Vid. *CS*, vol. 2, pp. 129, 163-173, 287-294.

[28] Vid. *CS*, vol. 2, pp. 169, 177s, 182s, 185-187, 197, 201-204, 207, 213, 214, 220s, 227, 228, 237, 240, 243, 248, 249, 250-252, 271, 274s, 279, 280s, 286s.

[29] Vid. note 32 of this chapter.

[30] Organized cultivation of seaweed started about 100 years ago. This and the importance of seaweed culture in the period of Japanese occupation as well as Japanese involvement in it can be studied by means of the *Collection of Papers Concerning Affairs on the Coast*.

well before the year 1952. Others, although dealing with "custom" can hardly
have been more than "authoritarian" law.

It has already been said in the preceding chapter that the truly peculiar
feature of the *Regulations of Changjwa-ri* is the claim to deal with the village as
an integrated body corporate. Therefore, the really interesting question is not
whether single provisions can be considered to be customary law or not, but
whether the whole of the *Regulations* as the manifestation of the presumed will
of an integrated village society can be regarded as customary law. Remaining
within the confines determined by the material itself, we should be able to
adduce the existence of village codes preceding the *Regulations* or the existence
of village agencies such as a village assembly or a village committee,[31] before
suggesting even as little as the possibility of the whole village code being
customary law. As a matter of fact, both the existence of village codes and that
of representative formal village agencies prior to 1952 is denied by the villagers
themselves as well as by people living outside the village of Changjwa-ri. Thus,
neither the norms regulating the rights and the proceedings of village assemblies
and village staff nor those calling for the subjugation of individual and
corporative activities under the decisions of the village as such can be called
customary law.

Models of the Regulations of Changjwa-ri

Even if there were no tangible precedents to the *Regulations of Changjwa-ri*
in the village itself, the authors, when drafting the text in 1952, must have had
something in mind which they considered to be a model both in content and
form upon which they could write a village code deemed to be suitable and
proper under the conditions then prevailing in Changjwa-ri. Or else there must
at least have been various stimulations arising from scattered sources, which the
authors of the *Regulations* made into a whole. Here again, for lack of other
evidence, one has to refer to the *Zeitgeist*, which so often makes people do things
they are not conscious of.

The period between the retreat of the Japanese in 1945 and the end of the
Korean War was a time of continuous political and economic instability. This
meant struggle for survival, and there was no leisure for musing on new modes
of life and for trying to realize them with any prospect of durable success. Thus,
it was only the Japanese period which the authors of the *Regulations* could refer
to when they set about restoring order to their village life. Indeed, the very

---

[31] The *Village Articles of Changjwa-ri on Wan Island,* reproduced here as Document VII,
should not be regarded as such a proof, because they are rather a draft of the *Regulations of
Changjwa-ri* than a separate village code on their own.

compound of *kyuyak* (Sin.-Jap. *kiyaku*) in the Korean name of the *Regulations* will immediately turn our attention to that period. There is a set of 23 codes, collected in vol. 2 of the *Settlements of Korea (Chōsen no shuraku* 朝 鮮 の 聚 落), which carry the same element in their names and which have many things in common with the *Regulations of Changjwa-ri*.[32] All of these codes were in force in either the model villages mentioned above or in so-called immigrant villages (Sin.-Jap. *imin buraku*, Sin.-Kor. *imin purak* 移 民 部 落).[33]

Out of these 23 codes two can be considered to be true village codes immediately comparable with the *Regulations of Changjwa-ri*.[34] The decisive point here is that both these two codes from the Japanese period and the *Regulations* conceive of legal subjection in the same way. People become subject to the code by being born in the village or by moving into it. There is no true choice of membership.[35] In other words, membership of what appears, by the name of the codes, to be a society of volunteers (*kai, hoe* 會) is identical with "citizenship" of the village, and this society, seemingly composed of volunteers, is, in reality, identical with the village it is in force in. It is this kind of compulsory membership, as it were, which is the main reason for the assumption that those two texts from the period of Japanese occupation and the *Regulations* belong to the same category.[36]

In the second place, it is the scope and substance of the contents of those codes which put them close to the *Regulations*. The basic concern is with proper conduct, such as the whole range of family conduct, *i.e.*, above all, respect towards superiors in age and status, loyal fulfilment of duties owed to the state, such as taxpaying, harmonious relations among neighbours and with the rest of

[32] These codes are listed as nos. 1, 2, 8, 10-13, 15, 19, 26, 27, 31-33, 35, 36, 38, 41, 45, 47, 50, 55, and 58 in the bibliography of this study.

[33] Most of the immigrant villages were inhabited by Japanese farmers who either came to Korea on their own and started a new life here as owner-farmers (*jisakunō, chajangnong* 自 作 農) or as tenant-farmers (*kosakunō, sojangnong* 小), or else were "invited" to Korea by the notorious Far Eastern Colonization Joint-Stock Company (Tōyō takushoku kabushiki kaisha 東 洋 拓 殖 株 式 會 社). The immigrant movement came to an end in the year 1927, and by 1930 there were only 27 Japanese immigrant villages extant in Korea. Vid. *CS*, vol. 2, pp. 8-17.

[34] These are nos. 11 and 47 in the bibliography of this study. Two other codes, viz. nos. 19 and 27, will not be considered here, because they concern immigrant villages, of which the conditions are only of marginal importance with regard to the whole of Korea.

[35] Vid. *Sŏkkong-myŏn Tangwŏl-li shinkōkai kiyaku*, Arts. 32s (= *CS*, vol. 2, p. 220); *Haesŏng-myŏn Changhyŏn-dong kinrō-shōrei-kai kiyaku*, Arts. 2, 6 (= *CS*, vol. 2, p. 245).

[36] Subjects of the *Regulations of Changjwa-ri* are "the inhabitants". This term signifies all of the people of Changjwa-ri, including those who do not make farming their main source of income, and excluding farm labourers only. It is said that at present there are ten to twelve farm labourers in the village at one time. These are the people who appear as employees and as tenants of houses and rooms in Arts. 32s or as "enclosed families" in Document XIII.21(a). Their groups are not considered as households of their own, and together with the very young and the very old people in the village they are reduced to a minor status.

the villagers, frugality in ceremonies, punctuality, neatness of private homes as well as of village lanes. It is on such a mentality that welfare is expected to grow and to be strived for by more matter-of-fact measures. Compulsory "membership" and the wide scope of village activities based on a deep concern with proper conduct are the two most outstanding features of the two codes from the Japanese period as well as of the *Regulations of Changjwa-ri*. Four other texts from among the 23 codes must be excluded from the category of genuine village codes, because they only correspond to the first of the two requirements, *i. e.* compulsory membership, but not to the latter. Their purviews are identical with the territories of the places they are in force in, but their hold on the villagers is only a partial one in the sense that these four codes regulate single aspects of village life only, such as cattlebreeding, moneysaving, or the cultivation of rice, instead of covering the whole of village life.[37]

It must have been something in the line of those two village codes dating from the period of Japanese rule that has consciously or unconsciously guided the authors of the *Regulations of Changjwa-ri*.[38] However, it would mean jumping to conclusions to say that there could have been no points of reference dating from a time prior to the period of Japanese occupation. Parallels can easily be recognized between the *Regulations of Changjwa-ri* and the texts collected by Mr. Gillet, such as the *Regulations of the Tai Tong Kei [taedonggye* 大 同 契 *]* in *Kwang Choo* [Kwangju 廣 州] or the *Regulations Used in the Ye Choong Kei [ijunggye* 里 中 契 *?] and By-Laws.*[39] The emphasis on virtue and proper conduct in the *Regulations of Changjwa-ri* is already discernable in those earlier texts.[40] Of course, some of the demands of earlier times have lost much of their impact, due to wide-ranging changes in life, and others have been adapted to modern conditions. Thus, for instance, the loyalty to the king of the early texts has been turned into loyal service to the country in the *Regulations of Changjwa-ri.*[41] Yet, the omnipresent emphasis on virtue is the same. It is interesting to note that Mr. Gillet attributed the origins of his codes to "conditions of pronounced lawlessness". Both in the earlier days and in the year 1952 the experience of disorder and moral depravity furnished the

[37] These are nos. 33, 36, 41, and 55 in the bibliography of this study.

[38] It is a remarkable fact that out of the 23 codes only two deal with the village as a corporation. Others are concerned with single aspects of rural life only, and in most cases do not make membership of the associations compulsory. No less than 13 codes deal with the promotion of one or several branches of agriculture. These are the texts listed as nos. 2, 12, 13, 15, 26, 32, 33, 35, 41, 44, 45, 55, and 58 in the bibliography of this study. Four texts are related to the promotion of the spirit of mutual help and general morality, *viz.* the nos. 11, 19, 45, and 47. Two have to do with the promotion of education and the operation of schools, *viz.* the nos. 36 and 50. One can be rated as belonging to both the first and second categories, *viz.* no. 45.

[39] Vid. Gillet, "The Village Gilds of Old Korea", pp. 14-25.

[40] Vid. *Regulations of the Tai Tong Kei in Kwang Choo,* in Gillet, *op. cit.,* p. 15; *Regulations Used in the Ye Choong Kei,* in *loc. cit.,* pp. 29s.

[41] Vid. Arts. 1, 6(1,4,10).

incentive for establishing village rules and for making the eradication of "bad habits" the basic concern.[42] Furthermore, it is interesting to note that respect for the elders in the village is commanded both in the *Regulations Used in the Ye Choong Kei* and in the *Regulations of Changjwa-ri*. The latter text, in correspondence to the *Regulations of the Tai Tong Kei*, provides even for the reservation of particular seats at assemblies for the village elders.[43] Another feature common to all three texts is that all of the three societies appear as penal jurisdictions, for on each page of the codes presented by Mr. Gillet one finds provisions concerning punishments for various wrongdoings and violations of general morality, in particular defilement of the name of the village.[44] Parallels extend even to minute details. Thus, all three texts provide for punishment of absence from village assemblies.[45] Likewise, expulsion from the village is the severest punishment in all of the three texts.[46] The repair of roads is another item common to all of the three codes, and so is the preservation of forests, together with punishments to be inflicted upon those who illegally fell trees.[47]

The historical background of the *Regulations of Changjwa-ri* can be further elucidated by materials and observations pertaining to a kind of village organization called village association (*tonggye* 洞 契), great village association (*tae tonggye* 大 洞 契), or association of the great union (*taedonggye* 大 同 契). Unfortunately, none of the investigators of such organizations has reproduced full texts of the regulations of the village unions, but instead they have contented themselves with publishing abstracts of their contents. Therefore, it is difficult to ascertain which are the differences from, and which the parallels with, the *Regulations*, and the results of present research do not allow for any far-going conclusions. From the materials of nine such village associations, which were collated by Dr. Kang Chang Kyu (Kang Ch'anggyu 姜 昌 奎), it appears that membership includes all households of the village and that it is compulsory. Another feature which suggests close parallels between those village associations and the body constituted and manifested by the *Regulations of Changjwa-ri* is the concern with the mainte-

[42] It is of great interest to observe that the same desire for the eradication of "bad habits" was one of the motives for the recording of customary law in many parts of the world, both in the past and the present. It seems to have been more the desire of the authorities than that of the people immediately concerned, and this again throws some light on the question of whether rules such as the *Regulations of Changjwa-ri* can really be regarded as having altogether sprung from the wishes of the peasants.

Vid. Gillet, "The Village Gilds of Old Korea", pp. 41s; *Regulations of Changjwa-ri*, Arts. 1, 9; Burmeister, *Vorarlberger Landsbräuche*, pp. 47s.

[43] Vid. Gillet, *op. cit.*, pp. 16, 24; *Regulations of Changjwa-ri*, Arts. 9(5), 19, 26.

[44] Vid. Arts. 26s.

[45] Vid. Gillet, *op. cit.*, pp. 15, 24, 25; *Regulations of Changjwa-ri*, Art. 28(1).

[46] Vid. Gillet, *op. cit.*, pp. 18, 19, 25; *Regulations of Changjwa-ri*, Art. 31.

[47] Vid. Gillet, *op. cit.*, pp. 18, 23s; *Regulations of Changjwa-ri*, Arts. 7(8), 8(1), 29(3), 30.

nance and increase of what may somewhat superficially be called village property. The two village associations studied by Professor Yang Hoesu 梁 會 水 , however, do not concern the property of the village and thus the whole of village life, but relate to single aspects only, such as the extension of community aid in cases of marriage and mourning and the organisation of community work. Moreover, observations made in 1943 by Professor Suzuki Eitarō 鈴 木 榮 太 郎 and others by Dr. Kang Ch'anggyu suggest that such village unions kept aloof from general village administration, leaving out the very concerns which figure so prominently in the *Regulations of Changjwa-ri*.[48] Thus, village associations and the like are far from being simple and uniform kinds of societies, and it is in part only that parallels can be discerned between them and the *Regulations of Changjwa-ri*. It is obvious that the ways leading from those older unions — some of them claim an age of about 120 years — to corporations like the one affirmed in the *Regulations* are not straight and even. We need much more careful investigation of much more material, before we can be sure of the nature of that relationship.

The attempt to determine the proper place of the *Regulations of Changjwa-ri* and their relation to precedents is made even more difficult by the fact that the *kye*-element in the names of those former unions pushes us one step further back into history. This *kye*-element suggests some relationship between those village associations and the like on the one hand and associations on the other which have, since long ago, also been known by the name of *kye*. These latter *kye* were voluntary unions and used to cover a smaller range of activities than most of the village associations seem to have done. Somehow, the names and the operating principles of such singular and voluntary unions must have been transferred to the compulsory village associations, but nothing of this process can be said to be known in detail, and even the characteristics of the smallscale mutual benefit associations, as they have been called in this study, are a matter of dispute.

Therefore, although parallels in matters of detail, even very close and surprising ones, can be detected between the *Regulations of Changjwa-ri* and the texts collected by Mr. Gillet and others, we need not, in search for precedents, go back further than the period of Japanese rule over Korea, if we emphasize the universality of concerns as the main characteristic of the *Regulations*. It is only in those few texts from the Japanese period — and possibly in the *Regulations*

[48] Vid. *CS*, vol. 1, p. 601; vol. 2, pp. 256—265, 280s; *Han'guk nongch'on sahoe tapsagi*, comp. Suzuku Eitarō, pp. 57, 58—60,'65, 70, 110s; *Han'guk nongch'onŭi ch'ollak kujo*, comp. Yang Hoesu, pp. 431s; *Kyega idong nongŏp hyŏptong chohabe mich'inŭn yŏnghyang. Ch'ungch'ŏng pukto ch'ilsibo idonge taehan chosa*, comp. Kang Ch'anggyu, [Ch'ŏngju:] Sangdang inswaesa, 1969, pp. 44, 52, 53, 65, 66, 68, 69, (Kang Chang Kyu, *The Influence of "Ke" Societies Upon Ri-Dong Agricultural Cooperative Association*, [ed.] Economic Planning Board, Republic of Korea/United States Agency for International Development to Korea, [Ch'ŏngju:] Choong-Puk National College, 1969, pp. 66, 76, 78, 91, 92, 94, 96, 97, 98).

Used in the Ye Choong Kei — that we find such a firm determination to co-ordinate the whole of what happens in a village and to subject it to the decisions of the village as such. Even if we turn to matters of form and presentation, we recognize the texts from the Japanese period, rather than any earlier regulation, as precedents. For the clear-cut disposition of the *Regulations of Changjwa-ri* and the comparatively precise, "juridical" wording are features lacking in the texts of the village associations prior to the beginning of this century.

CHAPTER 5: THE COMMUNITY

The Egalitarian Community Ethic

Having emphasized the diversity of allegiances in a village and having become roughly aware of the potential obstacles in the way towards village integration, an investigator of Korean villages may all too easily lose sight of a deeply rooted propensity of villagers towards co-operation and accomodation which tends to neglect the boundaries of kin groups and voluntary associations. Where goods are scarce, where people have to be satisfied with what they can obtain by their labour in the fields and waters, and where technical facilities for the production of surplus goods are lacking, everybody is ultimately dependent on everybody else, whether he likes it or not. The isolation of a village in economic and social matters will always generate intimate neighbourly relations among the villagers. They will strive to maintain them, not always through fondness of the neighbours, but at least for simple economic necessity. This is the situation most Korean villages have experienced until very recently. Changjwa-ri is no exception to the rule, its situation being but slightly different from that of most other Korean villages by the trading opportunities seaweed has offered. Those who have experienced living in smaller communities, particularly Korean ones, will remember the extremely complex net of mutual obligations by which the members are tied to each other. Of course, there occur sharp rifts between people, and malintegration as well as considerable differences in wealth among the households are as common in Korean villages as anywhere else. Yet, there seems to prevail an equally strong recognition of the necessity of retaining outbursts of temper and avidity as well as of not pushing particularistic allegiances too far. People are aware of the permissible limits of inequality in wealth, influence, opinion, and temper, and any disregard of them can be suicidal, because anybody suffering under it at some time can retaliate at another. Being obliged to observe rules of reciprocity, accomodation, and co-operation under the conditions of thrift and limited possibilities of development, the villagers, regardless of differences in wealth and influence, are equals. Therefore, this kind of village ethic may be called an egalitarian one.

Experiences such as the ones just described have dealt a blow to the common picture of Korean society. It has long been a habit among observers of the Korean scene to portray Korean ethical principles, beliefs, expectations, and behaviour patterns as being almost exclusively oriented towards, and determined by, lineage. The impression thus created is one of a clear-cut hierarchical system of rank and authority, which is mostly called "Confucian". With regard to rural Korea, however, observers have become increasingly aware of the existence of the ethical and behavioural system outlined above. It is opposed to the authoritarian one by emphasizing such virtues as mutual assistance across lineage boundaries, co-operation among neighbours, accomodation, and inaggressiveness. Within the latter system, the esteem in which a person is held and his influence are dependent on education, popularity, and success in mediation rather than on genealogical rank and age. Thus, two systems, a more authoritarian one and a more egalitarian one, are both entangled with, and opposed to, each other. It is a widely held view among sociologists and anthropologists of Korea that the dominance of either system in a village is correlated to the number of so-called *yangban* lineages and the ratio between them and the number of commoner households. In villages inhabited by one or two *yangban* lineages and only a few commoner households, the *yangban* are not only comparatively unrestrained in maintaining the old virtues of respect to elders and lineage solidarity, but even the commoners will be more inclined to imitate the ideational and behavioural standards of the *yangban* households. In such villages, community solidarity and the readiness to accept and promote innovations are little developed or even entirely missing. In villages, however, where there are several *yangban* lineages and/or where they are outweighed in number by the commoner households, the *yangban* will find it harder to extricate themselves from co-operation within the village and from village egalitarianism.[1]

Dr. Vincent Brandt, anthropologist and author of a book on Korean village life, made the conflict and the interaction of the two ethical systems the very topic of his elaborate study. His emphasis is not on the formal and explicit lineage-oriented ethic system, but on what he calls an egalitarian community ethic. The latter is the prevalent mode of organization in his village. It promotes such informal values as reciprocity, hospitality, and generosity, and generates a variety of informal groupings cutting right across conventional lineage and household boundaries, such as convivial men's groups or *ad hoc* labour groups. Furthermore, it demands correct dyadic relations and makes the more traditionally oriented *yangban* households of the village include other people in the conduct of traditional lineage ritual.[2]

The point which matters here is that the egalitarian community ethic did make people transcend the lineage boundaries, but it nowhere led to true village solidarity, not even an occasional one. The rallying points of interest and action

---

[1] Vid. J. E. Mills, *Ethno-Sociological Reports of Four Korean Villages,* Seoul: U. S. Operations Mission/Korea, 1960; *Han'guk nongch'onŭi sahoe kujo,* comp. Yi Man'gap, pp. 86-104; Pak/Gamble, *The Changing Korean Village,* pp. 18, 39s, 183, 185s, 189s, 194s, 199s; *Tongjok puragŭi saenghwal kujo yŏn'gu,* comp. Kim T'aekkyu, ed. Silla Kaya munhwa yŏn'guwŏn, [Taegu:] Ch'ŏnggu taehak ch'ulp'anbu, 1964, pp. 175-203 *et passim;* Brandt, *A Korean Village,* pp. 8-11, 26s.

[2] Vid. Brandt, *A Korean Village,* pp. 229, 230-240.

are, besides the kin groups, more or less fugitive and informal peer groups, neighbourhoods, and boat crews, but never the village. Dr. Brandt does not relate a single event which involved the village as a whole and showed it as acting in unison. Nor does he point at objects which were shared by all the villagers alike, regardless of individual wealth, rank, age, or sex. The groups, mentioned above, were fugitive and informal, and not a single one comprised a substantial portion of the village populace.[3] Of course, this experience does not invalidate the statements concerning the impact of the egalitarian community ethic on village life. The experience only confines the expectations of subsequent investigators of other villages, particularly of the people interested in legal matters. For although a good deal of the authoritarian and exclusive ethic emphasizing kin solidarity and integration of exclusive clubs and associations may be compensated in many villages by an egalitarian community ethic, the latter does not necessarily go all the way to melting the households and clans into a formal and durable village community. It does not even produce many communities below the village level which present themselves as objects of legal studies. For our concept of law allows for rating only those communities as being susceptible to legal considerations which claim some degree of durability and formality.

The point is of no little importance here. As has already been said before other authors who have written on Korean villages, in particular scholars of the older generation, have shown a tendency to equate their villages with the German *Dorfgenossenschaft*.[4] Dr. Karl Siegfried Bader has explained why this term should not be applied indiscriminately to any kind of neighbourly cooperation, if it is not to lose all its meaning. Dr. Bader has suggested that the term should only be used with regard to those more advanced types of communities where co-operation is no longer left to *ad hoc* decision and does not merely rely on more or less fugitive allegiances, but is firmly rooted in a ground of established rights and duties which remain untouched by the whims of individuals and *ad hoc* groupings. The *Dorfgenossenschaft*, and even more so the notorious *Markgenossenschaft,* are thus distinguished from the simple and more "primitive" rural vicinity, which owes its integration largely to the same conditions as those which produced the egalitarian community ethic in Korean villages.[5] Therefore, it is more appropriate to compare Dr. Brandt's Sŏkp'o —

---

[3] Dr. Brandt frequently refers to his observation that the egalitarian community ethic has not penetrated the cognitive level of the villagers. When asked what they consider to be right and just, they will reply in terms of the hierarchical and formal ethical system, although in daily life they tend to deviate from it. Therefore, the conditions prevailing at Dr. Brandt's Sŏkp'o could not adequately be portrayed by reference to the explicit values maintained by the villagers, but only by a detailed decription of the actual behaviour.

Vid. Brandt, *op cit.*, esp. pp. 144-183.

[4] Vid. Chapter 1, note 8 of this study.

[5] Vid. Bader, *Dorfgenossenschaft und Dorfgemeinde,* pp. 5, 9, 10, 38-62, 116-138.

and probably most other Korean villages, too — to Dr. Bader's vicinity than to anything else. The classification of a Korean village as a *Dorfgenossenschaft* should only be the result of detailed investigation of its social and economic structure, but never an *a priori* supposition.

At first sight, Changjwa-ri can be expected to be closer to a village community of the *Dorfgenossenschaft* type than Sŏkp'o. More than at Sŏkp'o, an authoritarian ethic maintained by families descending from the former *yangban* class is thought to be absent from village life. As has already been said above, there are not so-called *yangban* households at Changjwa-ri. Indeed, the authors of the *Regulations* displayed some concern for the village as such. Prosperity of the village was the aim to be achieved by conscientious observation of the *Regulations*. This implied economic stability for all inhabitants, the eradication of "evil practices in society" and the preservation of "fine customs and good manners".[6] The authors of the *Regulations* were mindful of maintaining a good reputation for the village. Individual misbehaviour was conceived of as being directly harmful to the "name of the village".[7] Village solidarity was to be reinforced by making the preservation of sacred places and the natural beauty of the place a common task of the villagers.[8] Such avowals were clearly modelled upon phrases known from regulations of rural associations and villages of the Japanese period, and we are inclined to simply discard them as meaningless vestiges of those days. However, it would be all too easy to deny the reality of community solidarity only because such formulae appear to be somewhat peremptory rhetoric.

Village Property

If the term "village community" is to have any sense, such a community should have its roots in jointly held and jointly used objects. Whereever goods are rare or expensive, people will grant access to them to all villagers of the vicinity alike, because exclusion of even a single person would mean a serious disruption of the system of neighbourly obligations and would threaten the existence of individuals and households and possibly entail retaliation in other walks of life. It is normal under such circumstances that people do not only enjoy common usufruct of such objects, but also hold each other responsible for the preservation of them. Therefore, around scarce and expensive goods, they will tend to develop a system of common use and collective responsibility. The

---

[6] Vid. Arts. 1, 9.

[7] Vid. Arts. 4, 26, 27(1,8).

[8] Vid. Art. 8

concept as well as the objects themselves may be called village property or common property.[9]

Expressions implying a notion of village property nowhere occur in connection with arable land, woodland, and waters, with the exception of the sacred places of the village. Moreover, it is interesting to note that except for some measures, a pair of scales, and the village well[10] none of the village-owned objects is directly related to the daily work in the fields and houses. The question in what sense, if in any, tracts of soil, woodlands, or waters can be called village property will be discussed in the following sections of this chapter. Here, we shall deal with movable objects only, because it is only they which are explicitly associated with expressions implying the concept of village property. However, even those objects do not belong to the village in the sense that the village as a body corporate, and nothing but the village, has the exclusive or final say in

[9] The term "property" is not particularly suitable, although in Document II and in Art. 17(3) of the *Regulations* the villagers themselves use expressions which seem to imply a modern Western notion of property. As a right to objects, property is an absolute privilege of a person by which he is entitled to exclude anybody else from the use of these objects. Yet, this is not the way objects are dealt with in Changjwa-ri, and the term "property" will be used here only for lack of a more convenient and suitable one. Conditions like those prevailing in Changjwa-ri are adequately circumscribed by Dr. Bader as follows: "Die ... archaische Stufe rechtlicher Gestaltung der Sachherrschaft geht auf Nutzung, nicht auf ein ‚absolutes' Recht an der Sache. Wenn man danach forscht, wem die Sache ‚gehört', lautet die Frage: ‚Wer hat die Sache zu nutzen?' Nutzung aber ist teilbar. Sie kennt verschiedene Dichte, läßt Teilung in Schichten zu, fördert geradezu Gemeinsamkeit in der Rechtsausübung und damit gemeinsame Sachbeherrschung. ... Ebenso muß aber das Streben nach einem abstrakt gedachten Gesamteigentum der Genossenschaft versagen, weil danach von der Genossenschaft gar nicht gefragt wurde und bei Mangel an abstrakten Denkformen nicht gefragt werden konnte. Kein älterer Nutzverband ... hat sich je mit der Frage abgemüht, ob [er] ‚Eigentümer' sei, sondern immer nur um mehr oder minder ausschließliche Nutzung gerungen."

It is regrettable that hitherto almost nothing has been published on Korean concepts of property and usufruct. In a chapter entitled "The Korean People and Their Property Rights", Dr. Pyong-Choon Hahm (Ham Pyŏngch'un 咸 秉 春) has made an attempt at demonstrating that the concept of property as a right incorporated in government law is largely disregarded by the Koreans, just as other written laws enacted by the government are. However, more than disregard for strict and "bookish" property rights this article bears evidence of an uncertainty, prevalent at least among government officials, as to whether the property rights should be enforced by government agencies or whether their pursuit should be left to the proprietors themselves. The questionnaires drafted by Dr. Ham and the responses received do not only seem inadequate to prove his basic assertion, but what is more serious is that they do not allow insight into the character of the property rights actually observed in Korea.

Vid. Bader, *Dorfgenossenschaft und Dorfgemeinde*, pp. 11s; Hahm Pyong-Choon, *The Korean Political Tradition and Law. Essays in Korean Law and Legal History,* Royal Asiatic Society, Korea Branch, Monograph Series, no. 1, Seoul: 1967, pp. 187-204.

[10] Scales and measures seem typically to appear among the objects considered to be village property, for they are also mentioned as such with regard to the village investigated by Dr. Cornelius Osgood.

Vid. Arts. 10, 28(5); Document XIII.5(e); Cornelius Osgood, *The Koreans and Their Culture,* New York: 1951, photomech. repr. Tokyo: 1954³, p. 54.

what can and will be done with them. A discussion of the village's relation to the so-called village property will provide a first insight into the nature and degree of village integration. Yet, before commenting on that matter, we shall shortly review the objects themselves.

Many of the objects which figure as village property are closely related to the conduct of the village festival. In the village, there are a beautiful and very valuable set of musical instruments, dresses, and some scrolls which are displayed at the village shrine. The villagers, being aware of their value, keep inventories of them, always meticulously recording the transmission from one keeper to the other and the names of the witnesses attending the procedure.[11] The sacred places of the village, such as the shrine of the tutelary deity, the trees and bushes surrounding it, the Archery Arbour, and the Plum Altar should also be regarded as common village property.[12] They are entrusted to the conscientious care of the villagers who are not allowed to let cattle graze at those places, or fell trees, or gather fuel there.[13] Moreover, there are several objects which are essential for the proper conduct of the village administration or which are used in receptions the village is obliged to prepare when visiting government officials are expected. This category of village property includes writing utensils, some office furniture, strawmats, awnings, flags, brassware, and, of course, the documents of the village. These objects, together with the musical instruments mentioned above, are carefully handed down from one keeper to the other, mostly the village heads.[14]

Actually, all of the objects mentioned above are held not by the village, but by one or the other of the mutual benefit associations or some other group which this author's informant likewise called by the Korean name for mutual benefit association, viz. kye.[15] The objects have been manufactured or purchased by some particular association, and they are primarily meant to be used by that group's members only or to be hired out to others for money. When people who are not members of an association owning one or the other of those objects want to use them, they have to pay a charge for the use of the facilities (sayongnyo 使 用 料). At present, the fee amounts to between W 500 and W 1000 a day for set of objects, brassware, strawmats, awnings, and musical instruments in particular, which are mainly used in wedding and mourning

---

[11] Vid. Documents I-III. IX-XII.

[12] For the Archery Arbour and the Plum Altar vid. chapter 7, note 10 of this study.

[13] Vid. Documents V, VI; Arts. 8(3), 28(3), 29(2).

[14] Vid. Documents X-XII, XIII.1.

[15] Here, the term kye is employed to mean just any co-operative group of people. It thus applies to any kind of smaller union of people who join hands to achieve some aim in common, and not only to mutual benefit associations in a narrow sense. This usage of the term kye is another instance of the rather vague nomenclature which confuses the investigator of the Korean rural scene. In nature, this usage is similar to that of the term maŭl discussed above on pp. 13s of this study.

ceremonies. However, when they are to be used by, or for the sake of, the whole village, an association has to place them at their disposal without charge.

Thus, a considerable part of the so-called village property in reality is the property of some association or other within the village. On the other hand, an association's claim to exclusive usage and its desire for monetary profit have to yield to the superior demands of the village when the property of some association is to be used in connection with village pursuits, such as the village festival or the entertainment of visiting government officials. By keeping a watchful eye on the transmission and maintenance of the objects, the village authorities do not only serve the village's interest, but that of the other villagers as well, who may rent them from the owner association. The village thus has a double interest in the orderly maintenance of the objects, *viz.* that of a potential user and that of a guarantor. However, the particularistic interests of single associations and their members do not allow the village to own property of its own and to appear on an equal, if not superior, footing with the owners. The recording of the objects as village property and the recording of their transmission are, of course, to be taken as means of enhancing their value in the eyes of the villagers, but these recordings have equally well to be regarded as efforts to make the village appear what it really is not, *viz.* a superior body corporate endowed with rights of its own.

Ownership of the Forests

Ownership of woodlands is a source of constant bewilderment on the part of observers and apparently on that of the villagers as well. It is particularly in this area of village economy that little information can be extracted from written material. Everything depends on a long-term actual observation of the habits. What has been rendered as "woodlands" or "forests" in the translation of the documents hardly reminds us of the dense and large forests of soaring trees we can find in Central Europe or in other parts of the world. Korean "forests" are hardly more than tiny patches of lean trees and bushes covering parts of a hillside. In Korea, dense forests will only be encountered in the vicinity of royal graves and Buddhist monastries. The Koreans use to blame the desolate state of their woodlands on the foreign invaders, Mongols, Japanese, and Manchu, who have several times harassed their country in the course of its history. They usually forget to mention the destructive lumbering by their own government over many centuries as well as the constant drain of wood caused by the peasants, who for lack of other heating material had solely to rely on the woodlands.

The state of the woodlands on Wan Island must have been a particularly bad one for quite some time. The *Writings From a Heart Bent on Tending the People*

(*Mongmin simsǒ* 牧 民 心 書) by Tasan Chǒng Yagyong 茶 山 丁 若 鏞 (1762—1836) contain a detailed survey of the problems and practices concerning forestry in his day and a poignant criticism of official malpractice in that matter. To illustrate his point, Tasan chose Wan Island as an example. This choice was not a matter of chance, for having been a sympathizer of Catholicism, Tasan was banished to live in South Chǒlla Province in 1801, from where he was to return in 1818 only. Most of the time he spent in the vicinity of Kangjin, and therefore he is almost certain to have visited Wan Island and witnessed conditions there.[16] Tasan reports that there were several officials stationed on Wan Island, both civil and military ones, who made considerable private profits by selling timber, notwithstanding the threat of severe punishments. He continues that if one really were to punish them, between four and five thousand blows with the big rod would have to be dealt out on that tiny island. Even if official malpractice could be stopped, there would remain the heavy demands put on the woodlands from too many sides. Timber was needed in the construction of palaces and in shipbuilding as well as for the making of coffins and agricultural tools. Moreover, salt-makers and potterers relied on the forests of the island, and finally there were the fuel-gathering peasants. As long as timber as a commercial good promised to yield big private profits, the severests of laws would be of no avail in stopping the malpractice, and the devastation of the woodlands on Wan Island would continue.[17]

In view of such prolonged destructive lumbering, it is no wonder that protection of the woodlands is again and again impressed upon the people of Changjwa-ri as one of their foremost duties. The topic figures prominently in the protocols of the village meetings, too.[18] In one article in the *Regulations*, a distinction is made between village owned forests, jointly owned forests, and privately owned forests.[19] Besides, county forests and province-owned forests are mentioned, and at one point we read about a county forest co-operative.[20] Such distinctions suggest five kinds of forest owners within the territory of the village, *viz.* individuals, groups of individuals within the village, the village itself, the county, and the province. However, realizing the desperate need for wood and the unavoidable coercion towards accomodation and restraint under the dictates of the community ethic, we doubt whether anybody is ever in a position to observe such neat legal distinctions in daily life. We can easily imagine how the pressing scarcity of wood could quickly wipe out all juridical limitations. The real "owner" would then be one who succeeds in grabbing as

---

[16] Vid. *Jimmei jisho*, ed. Chōsen sōtokufu, Keijō: 1937, pp. 4s.

[17] Vid. *Mongmin simsǒ*, k. 11 (= vol. 3, pp. 442s, pp. 86-88).

[18] Vid. Arts. 7(8), 29(3); Document XIII. 2(c), 5(d), 10, 14(a), 18(c), 19(h), 20(b,c).

[19] Vid. Art. 29(3).

[20] Vid. Document XIII.18(c); Art. 17(2), 31.

much of the material as possible, whether in an open or clandestine fashion. Something of this kind of lawlessness is always in the air of Changjwa-ri. This is the reason why the village installed a forest ranger to watch the woodlands, and why appointments to the post and the question of remuneration so frequently appear on the agenda of village meetings.[21]

Besides fighting imminent lawlessness in matters of forestry by caring for efficient guarding of woodlands, the village also provides an ingenious legal device for easing tension. The prohibition in Art. 29 (3) of the *Regulations* of exploiting the woodlands pertains to the felling of trees only. This implies that all other kinds of usufruct, such as gathering fuel or camellia fruit, are not limited to the respective owners, but are open to all villagers. Even the felling of trees is implicitly allowed to all villagers if it happens in province-owned forests and if the wood is used for agricultural tools.[22] Limitations in ownership would therefore mean limitations in felling trees, but not in gathering fuel. This assumption does not only agree with what the present author was told by his informant, but is further substantiated by entries in the protocols of village meetings. Here, illegal use of forests is not only again associated with felling trees, but the term "village-owned forests" is in two out of four cases replaced by the term "village forest".[23] Moreover, the villagers are said to have used the terms "village-owned forests" and "jointly owned forests" interchangeably, when the distinctions were still valid. Indeed, if the woodlands are primarily viewed as sources of fuel, which is needed by all villagers alike, the distinctions of ownership become meaningless, and the forests are altogether village property. Then, it is only natural that even so-called individually owned forests become the concern of the whole village, as happend in 1961. At that time, entrance even into privately owned forests was regulated by the village and thus taken out of the hands of private owners. The only limitation to indiscriminate common use of woodlands which then remained valid was that certain periods of time had to be observed for fuel-gathering.[24]

In other words, ownership of forests is not an absolute one. No "owner" can lay exclusive claim to the whole of the fruits the forests yield. He has to tolerate intrusion of others into his property at least when it comes to gathering fuel and camellia fruit and, in one instance, the felling of young trees to make agricultural tools. In order to comprehend this kind of usage in a single term, we have to coin the new terms of "intensive" and "extensive ownership". The pattern of the use of woodlands practised in Changjwa-ri is only one more example of a habit which, in the exploitation of forests, seems to have been

---

[21] Vid. Arts. 18-20; Document XIII.4(a), 5(d), 6, 10, 16(a), 17(a), 19(g).
[22] Vid. Art. 30.
[23] Vid. Document XIII.5(d), 10(a), 18(c), 22(a).
[24] Vid. Document XIII.20(b,c).

followed in other parts of Korea as well.[25] At the same time, it is a fine illustration of the egalitarian community ethic discussed above and this might give some flesh and blood to the otherwise arid description of this phenomenon. It it interesting to observe that in fairly recent government legislation such old habits are still taken into account. In the Law on Forests (*Sallim pŏp* 山 林 法), promulgated on December 27th, 1961, with revisions dating from September 2nd, 1963, and January 1st, 1971, rules concerning the exploitation and preservation of village forests are established which provide for associations comprising both "owners of forests" and "people of the region" represented by household heads. Here again, "owners" and non-owners are made to join hands in matters of forestry.[26]

A few words have still to be said about the jointly owned forests and the forest association. Ownership of woodlands which are not definitely given to some individual or corporation is usually obtained by bidding and paying an "application fee".[27] People who do this are organized in a forest association, which holds the woodlands of its members as joint property. Since entrance into the forest association requires some money on the side of the applicants, membership is a fairly exclusive privilege. Yet, as has been said above, ownership primarily means the rights to lumbering, and any adverse effects of this exclusiveness are mitigated by the right of all to gather fuel. Under the system of extensive and intensive ownership it is only natural that the forest association should have a word to say in the appointment of the forest ranger, who otherwise is an officer of the village, and should equally well decide on matters concerning the whole of the woodland within the territory of the village, and not only on those of their association property.[28]

It should be added here that this system of forestry exploitation formally came to an end at Changjwa-ri in the year 1962. The "privatization" of forests brought an end to that collective usufruct and responsibility described above. But still, the village did not altogether abandon its collective control of the woodlands within its territory.[29]

[25] Professor Mun Chŏngch'ang 文定昌 and Professor Yang Hoesu both use the term *iphoe* 入 會 to circumscribe these conditions of forest use. It should be noted that this term neither occurs in the daily speech of the peasants, at least not in this sense of jointly exploiting woodlands, nor does it appear in source materials. It is a Korean rendering of a binomen originally used in Japan. It is read there as *iriai* ("to enter an association") and means the village as a forest exploitation community.

Vid. *Han'guk nongch'on tanch'e sa,* comp. Mun Chŏngch'ang, Seoul: Ilchogak, 1961, pp. 188s; *Han'guk nongch'onŭi ch'ollak kujo,* comp. Yang Hoesu, pp. 380s (note 1); *Han'guk kodae sahoewa kŭ munhwa,* comp. Yi Pyŏngdo, p. 28; Kaisaku Kumagai, "On the Formation of a Customary Law on *Allmende* in Japan (*iriai*)", *The Osaka University Law Review,* no. 20, Ōsaka: 1973, pp. 1-9.

[26] Vid. *Sallim pŏp,* Art. 57.

[27] Vid. Document XIII.19(h).

[28] Vid. Art. 19; Document XIII.20(c).

[29] Vid. Document XIII.22(a).

The Use of Seaweed Grounds and Fishery

In both the *Regulations* and the protocols of the village meetings entries pertaining to this topic are more numerous than those concerning forestry, but they are less informative. It is evident, however, that the use of the coastal waters around the island for seaweed culture and fishing is not different from that of the woodlands.

Almost everywhere along the coast of Wan Island one will find wooden sticks of about a man's hight protruding from the shallow waters, which mainly serve to deliminate the confines of seaweed grounds and fisheries. The term *ŏjang* 魚場 rendered as "fishery" in the translation of the documents originally meant an area of shallow water fenced in by wooden pailings or stone fences. These fisheries, in fact, are traps, for during the periods of high water the fish are thrown into them, and after the tide has ebbed away, the fishermen conveniently catch the fish trapped between the pailings or stone fences.[30] These traditional contrivances have eventually been replaced by modern fishing equipment such as nets and boats. The present author is uncertain as to whether the old arrangements concerning fisheries are still meaningful under the conditions of modern fishing techniques, and he has therefore rendered the expression *kŏn hong* 建洪 , which originally meant the fencing in of fishery of the *ŏjang* type, by the sufficiently vague expression "placing fishing equipment".

The seaweed grounds and fisheries are distributed among the villagers by means of a combined system of bidding and drawing lots. Bidding, when it is successful, is at the same time an application for admission to a club of seaweed ground and fishery holders. Each member of this club has to pay a certain share of his due upon entrance into the club and will discharge the rest of it at some later date. When bidding and admission are complete, the grounds which are at the disposal of the association are distributed among its members by drawing lots. Entrance into this group is not affected by individuals, but by households. In order to be rated as a household eligible for admission, a young man and his family must have lived seperately from his father's house for at least half a year before bidding time.[31] Since the members of this group are the beneficiaries of the arrangement, they also bear the responsibility of keeping the grounds in good order, for which purpose some men are selected and some money is earmarked.[32]

---

[30] There is a painting of such a fishery by Tanwŏn Kim Hongdo 檀 園 金 弘 道 (1745—1816?), which figures as no. 22 in the series of Tanwŏn's genre paintings recently reproduced and published by the T'amgudang 探求堂 in Seoul as *Tanwŏn p'ungsok toch'ŏp* 風 俗 圖 帖 *(Korean Custom Pictures by Tanwŏn)*.

[31] Vid. Document XIII.2(g), 12(a,e), 13(a,b,e), 19(h).

[32] Vid. Document XIII.12(d,e).

On the whole, this arrangement among the fishing part of the village people is not different from that of the forest association. In fact, the club is a seaweed and fishing association, although the term nowhere occurs in the documents. Again, membership of this *de facto* association is an expensive affair, because the amounts to be paid at the bidding are considerable. Besides, the association is eager to maintain its exclusiveness, for the *Regulations* contain a provision which prohibits secret planting of seaweed not legalized by the entry into the *de facto* seaweed and fishing club.[33] On the other hand, this seclusion of a group within the community is somehow compensated for. Firstly, the association wants to preserve a certain degree of equality within its own ranks. Early and individual growing and collecting of seaweed may yield extra financial gains, and therefore the collecting of seaweed is only allowed after the announcement to do so has been issued.[34] Secondly, most of the so-called guarantee fund, *i.e.* the amount of money brought together during the bidding, forms part of the village income, by means of which certain expenditures are covered which are of an advantage to the village as a whole. Thus, to a certain degree, even those villagers who are not involved in seaweed cultivation and fishing will indirectly profit from the ventures of the seaweed and fishing association. We even learn about one case where the fishermen are singled out to pay school expenses for the benefit of the whole village.[35] This is another attempt at making the extra gains of a single group of villagers available to the whole village.

The role of seaweed cultivation and fishing in the village economy deserves some further comment. Usually, Koreans are a little disdainful of fishermen and all other people who live from the sea. This prejudice is largely shared by the rural population, who would always prefer farming to any other rural occupation. Fishermen are not as much tied to the cycle of the seasons and the ensuing behaviour patterns as farmers are, and therefore, they are often regarded as being lazy, untidy, boisterous, untrustworthy, and "uneducated".[36] None of these judgements seems to prevail at Changjwa-ri. The villagers explicitly make the rearing of oysters — which is mostly left to the women — and the promotion of fishery aims of the village community.[37] The importance of sea-bound occupations is further enhanced by the fact that cancellation of the right to seaweed grounds and fisheries ranks among the severer kinds of punishment inflicted by the village upon wrongdoers. This section is frequently mentioned in the village protocols, too.[38] The readiness to accept innovations and the degree to which these innovations are incorporated into community life in Changjwa-ri are remarkable.

[33] Vid. Art. 7(14).
[34] Vid. Art. 29(1).
[35] Vid. Document XIII.19(d).
[36] Vid. Brandt, *A Korean Village*, pp. 60-66.
[37] Vid. Art. 7(14,15).
[38] Vid. Art. 31; Document XIII.9(c), 12(e), 14(b), 15(c), 18(b), 19(h).

The Common Fund

Returning to phenomena which are more immediate manifestations of the community ethic than the joint use of seaweed lots and fisheries, we have to take into consideration the fact that the villagers do not only jointly use certain objects and lands, but that they also have to bear a joint responsibility for those objects and have to care for their preservation and development. To achieve this end, they maintain a village fund and a scheme of common undertakings. Payment into the village fund and participation in the village enterprises are considered to be duties of each household in the village. The actual conduct of the activities and the expenditures from the village fund are subject to the decisions of a village committee regarded as acting in the name and on behalf of the whole village.

The subjects of the village fund and the village enterprises are very complicated, both in matter and in terminology. For the expenditures from the fund and common undertakings are also meant to serve ends which transcend the simple and elementary concerns of the innermost village life. Some of the income and an unproportionally high amount of the expenditure are related to purposes which have been grafted upon the community in the wake of modernization and increasing government influence. These purposes do not concern the cycle of daily farm work, the division of fields and forests, and the festivities of the simple folk. A large part of what is paid from the village fund, or accounted for by the common undertakings, thus belongs to the sphere of commune life and will be discussed in chapter 8 of this study.

The disparity in the distribution of the village expenditure is already evident from terminology. In the *Regulations of Changjwa-ri,* so-called village expenses are juxtaposed to school equipment expenses and miscellaneous fees.[39] Thus, village expenses are only a part of the whole of what the village pays. The present author's informant and the other villagers use a convenient terminology of their own to further subdivide the section labelled village expenses. They distinguish village administration costs (*iunyŏng pi* 里 運 營 費), social entertainment costs (*kyoje* 交際 *pi*), and reception costs (*chŏptae* 接待 *pi*), the latter category being largely identical with the miscellaneous fees of the "official" classification of the *Regulations.*[40] The costs rated as school equipment expenses and miscellaneous fees clearly belong to the sphere of commune life. Again, large parts of the village administration costs and social entertainment costs

[39] Vid. Art. 11.

[40] Another classification of village expenditure, used both in the *Regulations* and in the protocols, distinguishes between ordinary expenses and extraordinary ones. This distinction, however, concerns the manner of accounting only, and it is not congruent with any of the categories described above.

Vid. Arts. 22s; Document XIII.3(c), 4(c,d), 7(c,d), 14(a), 19(c), 21(a,b).

within the village expenses in the technical sense have nothing to do with the immediate concerns of community life. This suggests how little of the village expenditure may really go into community life.

Before proceeding with the description of the community expenses in greater detail, we have to say a few words about community income. The sources of income and the ways of procuring it are nowhere described in the *Regulations*. We can tell from the protocols of the village committee meetings, however, that most of it seems to be obtained by means of apportionment. Whenever the need for raising money or goods arises, a "rank paper" is drafted, and each of the households in the village is assigned to one of the ranks according to its wealth. The richest households will rank first and will have to pay the most. After having assigned the households to the ranks, the amount to be raised is distributed among the different ranks.[41] The number of ranks differs according to the occasion. We read about papers containing thirteen, eleven, five, and three ranks. Only two of the rank papers have been transmitted to us, and from them, we have also learned the exact amounts spent to cover the regular village administration expenses for the year 1956 and those for the construction of a health centre.[42] In one case, the whole sum to be paid is apportioned not to the village households, but to one section of the village population only, *viz.* the fishing community.[43] The only deviation from this pattern of raising money and goods occurs in connection with the remuneration of the village officers and, once, in connection with the financing of the village festival. As far as the documents are explicit on this matter at all, their remunerations are not to be collected by apportionment. Instead, each household is expected to pay the same amount.[44] It is interesting to observe that the drafting of rank papers and the amounts to be apportioned do not always seem to have been left to the choice of the village. For in connection with the village administration taxes reference is made to a standard rank paper issued by the township authorities which should be followed.[45] Obviously this paper contains some guiding figures as to the number of ranks, the characteristics of the households to be assigned to them, and the amounts to be collected.

Another portion of the village income flows from the regulation violation fines which have to be paid by those who damage village property or offend against the village regulations and from the confiscation of spot goods.[46] Again,

---

[41] Vid. Document XIII.3(a,b), 4(d), 5(b), 7(a), 8(b), 15(c), 16(b), 18(d), 19(b).

[42] Vid. Document XIII.3 (Enclosure), 16(b).

[43] Vid. Document XIII.19(d).

[44] Vid. Document XIII.4(b), 8(b), 9(a).
The procedures mentioned in Document XIII.13(d) and 16(a) may be viewed as exceptions.

[45] Vid. Document XIII.8(b).

[46] Vid. Documents I; VII. Pledge, Record (1-5, 7-9); Arts. 28-30, 33; Documents IX; X; XIII.7(b), 9(c), 12(e), 18(b,c), 20(a,b), 24(g,h).

another portion of village income consists of the amounts to be paid as fines by those who in this way buy themselves free from the commune labour (*puyŏk* 夫 役).[47] Finally, some contribution to the village fund may come from the so-called guarantee funds, which consist of the sums collected when bidding for seaweed lots and fisheries. Nothing is said in the documents about any formal and universal obligation of the seaweed and fishing associations to yield part of their funds to the village. Yet, in view of the power of an egalitarian community ethic which does not allow any villager to become extremely wealthy at the expense of others, it is hard to imagine that the members of the seaweed and fishing communities do not in some way or other contribute to the financing of village enterprises and maintenance of village property.

Among the expenses incurred by, and for the sake of, the community those figuring as "expenditure for village administration"[48] are certainly of paramount importance. They include the remuneration for the three most important village office holders, *i.e.* the village head, the forest ranger, and the village beadle, and possibly for minor office holders as well. The whole of such remuneration is often summarized as "wages for [village] service".[49] Besides, money is spent to buy writing materials and to cover "assembly expenditure", which probably means the payment for food and drinks served during village assemblies.[50] Finally some money has to go into the repair of the village office once in a while.[51] Most prominent among the other elements of village expenses, *viz.* the "social entertainment costs", are the expenses of the village festival.

A third category of village expenditure has somehow escaped the attention of the present author's informants, but occurs fairly often in the protocols of the meetings of the village committee. This category includes payments made for goods purchased, such as lamp oil, or for the materials used in the repair of roads and paths and for the preservation of the woodlands.[52] Besides, some money used to be given to the young men of the village summoned into military service to cover their travel expenses between the village and their garrison. However, this practice was stopped in 1957.[53]

In the *Regulations of Changjwa-ri* mention is made of a common aid fund and of indemnifications to be made to people who have suffered damage to, or loss of, their property.[54] This could be understood as another kind of village

[47] Vid. Art. 28; Document XIII.7(b).
[48] Vid. Document XIII.3(c), 4(c), 7(c,d), 8(b), 12(b), 14(a), 19(b,c), 21(a,b).
[49] Vid. Arts. 18, 34; Document XIII.4(a,b), 6, 8(b), 9(a), 10(b), 11(b), 13(d), 15(c), 16(a), 17(a), 19(g).
[50] Vid. Document XIII.4(d), 8(b), 21(b).
[51] Vid. Document XIII.4(d), 19(e), 23.
[52] Vid. Document XIII.4(d), 14(a).
[53] Vid. Document XIII.4(d), 8(a), 12(c).
[54] Vid. Arts. 9(6), 31.

expenditure. Yet, in none of the documents is anything said about giving such kinds of aid. Extending help to people who have incurred losses and damages to their property or are otherwise in distress is such a natural feature of Korean community life that the leading personalities of Changjwa-ri never seem to have felt it necessary to put decisions of that kind on the agenda of village meetings or otherwise to take notice of such acts as peculiarities of village life. Provisions as those quoted above only add to the somewhat hollow verbosity of the *Regulations*.

There is one instance of the village stipulating the salaries of farm labourers. Other sources than the text make us believe that the salaries are not really paid from the village fund, but by the households that profit from the farm labourers' work. Thus, the salaries cannot be considered to be village expenses. The stipulation of farm labourers' salaries by the village is an attempt both to limit an exceedingly high flow of cash and goods from the village and to insure an adequate share of the labourers in what is available at the place. For some farmers, particularly the more well-to-do ones, usually are in need of labourers, and they may thus be enticed to offer higher salaries than they can actually afford to pay and thereby attract labourers away from other households. By stipulating the salaries, the village tries to remove a menace to the economic equilibrium of the place. From the passages in the documents dealing with farm labourers we incidentally learn that there are three kinds, *viz.* those hired for the whole year, probably constituting the "enclosed families" already mentioned in chapter 2 of this study, those hired on a day-to-day basis, and the itinerant farm labourers. With the exception of the first, who are paid in cash only, those belonging to the latter two categories are paid partly in kind, partly in cash.[55]

Common Undertakings

The authors of the *Regulations of Changjwa-ri* went to great lengths to establish a series of duties which have to be obeyed by all villagers alike. Their effort resulted in a curious agglomeration of postulations of moralistic and economic orders, calling for village unity in thought and action. A number of the attitudes and actions called for are oriented towards the nation and the government and will be left out of consideration at the present stage of the study. Others are meant to be of immediate concern for the village. There are calls for co-operation in "the foundation and operation of democratic institutions", "utmost effort in educating the children", co-operation in "disciplining the youth", maintenance of peace and order, performance of rites,

---

[55] Vid. Document XIII.2(a,b).

and extension of help to those in military service.[56] Other exhortations envisage cuts in expenses associated with wedding and mourning ceremonies and congratulatory banquets. Such ceremonies should be made frugal, and people not immediately concerned or not invited should stay away from them and not provoke the hosts to issue invitations to unwanted guests.[57] In other provisions, the people of Changjwa-ri are summoned to observe "humanism" and righteousness and restrain private desires, lest the "name of the village" be defiled and human relations be disturbed. Likewise, it is considered to be a neglect of propriety to leave the house without having put on outer garments.[58] These often vague and high sounding principles are contrasted by several matter-of-fact provisions. Protection of woodlands is one of them, and so are the exhortations to increase agricultural yields, to rear cattle and swine instead of rabbits and sheep, and to care for health and hygiene.[59]

Only a few of these required efforts left traces in the village protocols. It is obvious that some of the provisions are in the line with an already observed community ethic and, thus, they neither needed confirmation by the village regulations, nor did they ever appear as a topic of discussions at village meetings. With regard to other expectations, however, we are led to the conclusion that they simply did not coincide with the aspirations of the villagers and thus did not stimulate concerted action. We have noticed already that accommodation and co-operation are strong in such economic matters as forestry and seaweed cultivation. It is again in the field of economics that the calls for united action meet with some response. For instance, the villagers are summoned to dispose of their goats, in order to avoid damages to the crops.[60] Besides, the efforts to render the social life of the village more frugal are also reflected in the village protocols. There we find several prohibitions to distil liquor, to trade with bread and sweets within the village, and to own tobacco.[61]

In the period under investigation here the village community practised a kind of collective farming at the village level known as *ullyŏk* 울력 .[62] Farming in rice-cultivating areas such as the southern half of the Korean peninsula is characterized by a demand for great numbers of farm labourers for limited periods of intensive farming. Normally, wealthier households are unable to meet such requirements from among their own people. Therefore, villagers often try to organize collective farming such as *ullyŏk*. One or more males of

[56] Vid. Art. 6(2,3,7-9).
[57] Vid. Art. 7(1-5).
[58] Vid. Art. 27(1-4).
[59] Vid. Arts. 7(8-15), 10, 27(5), 28(3,5).
[60] Vid. Document XIII.9(b).
[61] Vid. Document XIII.9(c), 14(b), 15(c).
[62] The word is often spelt 운력 , which suggests a Sino-Korean binomen such as 運力 "revolving power".

each household of the village join hands to form a working group which successively does the farm work in the fields of each household.[63] It is interesting to observe that *ullyŏk* is nowhere mentioned in the village documents, which again proves how little the written documents are really concerned with the routine of peasant life there.

Ullyŏk has meanwhile ceased to be practised spontaneously in Changjwa-ri and thus can no longer be regarded as a real community affair. In Korea, any mode of collective farming organized at the village level has always been a cause of resentment. Its degree depends on the differences in wealth as expressed in landed property. Less wealthy households can do their farming by themselves,

---

Here again, we meet with a considerable confusion in nomenclature. In dictionaries, *ullyŏk* is usually translated as "joint effort" or "co-operation" in general; it is thus not related to any specific mode of collective farming. According to Professor Kim Kwangŏk 金光億 , *ullyŏk* is the voluntary and unpaid joint work of villagers building houses and restoring and cleaning gravesites, whereas in a set of terms discussed by Professor Dr. Hae Young Lee (Yi Haeyŏng 李 海 英), sociologist of Seoul National University, it does not appear at all.

It is worth while having a look at the set of terms which Dr. Yi discussed in the cadre of his contribution to a conference on tradition and change in Korea held on September 1st-6th, 1969, in Seoul. He talked about *p'umasi, ture* 두레 , *koji* 고지 , and *nalp'ump'ari* 날품 파 리 . As has already been explained in note 22 of chapter 3 in this study, *p'umasi* is a kind of co-operation in which human labour is lent in exchange for either human labour, cattle, or machinery within a group of neighbours or kin. This kind of mutual help is found in almost all Korean villages. The standard pattern of *ture* is similar to that of *ullyŏk* at Changjwa-ri. However, in *ture* wages are required from the households benefitting from the work of the *ture* group. The wages are not paid to the individual workers of the *ture* group, but to a village fund. *Koji* means a pattern of collective farming where human labour is offered in exchange for grain or money which the one offering his labour has obtained before in times of need. *Koji* can therefore be characterized as a scheme of indemnification between two or more households by means of an offer of labour in exchange for monetary or food relief obtained before. *Nalp'ump'ari* finally means farming with the help of daily hired labourers paid off in money or grain.

Of these modes of collective farming, *ture* is the only one which is practised at the village level. In this regard, the *ullyŏk* of Changjwa-ri is similar to *ture*, but the term itself does not seem to be known to this author's informants. Likewise, they denied that payments were made to the village fund on the occasion of collective farming. It should be added here that the awnings and strawmats sometimes mentioned in the documents were also used, besides their other purposes, during the collective farmwork. The strawmats were used as seats, and the awnings protected the peasants from wind and sunshine during the periods of rest of the working group.

Vid. "Han'guk nongch'one issŏsŏ nodongnyŏk tongwŏnŭi hyŏngt'ae punsŏk", comp. Kim Kwangŏk, *MIH*, no. 6, 1973/74, p. 169, note 6; Documents X-XIII; cf. *Han'guk nongch'on sahoe tapsagi*, comp. Suzuki Eitarō, pp. 65s, 112-115; *Han'guk nongch'onŭi ch'ollak kujo*, comp. Yang Hoesu, pp. 384-386.

[63] The important part which collective work used to play in the processes of grain cultivation in Korea becomes evident from Dr. Osgood's description of the various stages of these processes.

Vid. Osgood, *The Koreans and Their Culture*, pp. 65-75.

because their fields are few and small. To them, involvement in collective farming often only means working for the benefit of others without much hope of getting anything in return. Nowadays, collective farming on the village level is on a steady decline, because an ever increasing number of people tend to leave the villages and move to the towns and cities. Therefore, the number of people available for collective farming has been declining for some time already. In the fifties already, the village of Changjwa-ri heavily relied on farm labourers, who can well be regarded as replacements for the local labour force that had guaranteed the practice of collective farming in former times. Today, collective farming in Changjwa-ri, like almost all other collective enterprises organized on the village level, is inspired and guided by the village officers or by the local government authorities, and it is thus close in nature to the commune labour to be discussed in chapter 8 ot this study.

CHAPTER 6: COMMUNITIES AND OTHER GROUPS WITHIN THE VILLAGE

Preliminary Remarks

Nobody would hesitate to regard the village community of Changjwa-ri as something similar to, or even indentical with, the *Dorfgenossenschaft* as conceived by Dr. Bader. There is a strong determination to handle the innermost affairs of the village on a basis of near-equality and to maintain an equilibrium of wealth and influence. This concept is alive at least among those who, because of wealth and power, sway their village fellows. Nevertheless, the community has been restricted in many ways, and its state has always been a precarious one. Within the last decennia in particular, its basic tenets have increasingly become incompatible with the powers and values underlying the sweeping changes in the economic and social orders of the nation. Industrialization is offering opportunities of living in urban areas to an increasing number of people, and they make use of them, because life in towns and cities seems to be much more varied and pleasant than in the countryside. Where the spirit of enterprise and competition is encouraged, people are less ready to unite with others to accomplish tasks which do not promise immediate individual profits. Even such a remote place as Changjwa-ri seems to have experienced the changes at an early date. We have noticed already that the pattern of collective farming known as *ullyŏk* seems to have declined as early as the fifties, due to the movement of people to towns. Likewise, we have mentioned the "privatization" of woodlands, which again deprived the community of much of its material base.

However, the instability of the community and its predictable decline are not only due to powers from outside the village. Some of the forces outweighing potential community strength issue from the village itself, and they manifest themselves as groups within the village. Some of these groupings have long been an integral part in Korean village life, and, inasmuch as they thwart a successful and continuous operation of the village community, the weakness of the village, too, is a traditional one. These smaller groups within the village tend to require much of the material means and the affections of the villagers to the detriment of any larger organization. It can be assumed that in many cases the development of a genuine village community has been impeded from the very beginning, because too much of the peasants' means went into the smaller groups. What in the case of Changjwa-ri may be viewed as forces divesting a once strong village community of much of its power, has elsewhere been an element obstructing the very rise of a community.[1] The comparatively small amounts of goods and money involved in the ventures of those smaller groups are no proof to the contrary. Most Korean farmers have hardly more than they need for their bare subsistence, and cash in particular is notoriously lacking. Therefore, any spending on purposes other than eating and drinking is always a serious drain on the resources, small as the amounts may be.

An understanding of village life and an adequate evaluation of the village community in particular largely depend on the knowledge of such groups within the village. Since their impact is of an economic order, it is impossible to judge upon their effects without having statistical data at hand, which show how much of the means of the villagers goes into such groups and how much is directed towards community enterprises. It is here that a statistical survey would really be helpful. Yet, as the present study is more concerned with the nature and the basic issues of village life than with the actual developments of a single case, the author will restrict himself to briefly surveying the kinds and operational modes of such groups within the village. It has to be left to future investigations into Korean village life to deal with the relationship between the village and the groups within the village and to concentrate on this topic when computing statistical data.

Some of the groups within the village have been initiated by the villagers themselves and have been operated according to rules which have been developed among the rural populace over many centuries. They rely on principles similar to those discussed above under the headline of community ethic. As far as basic tenets are concerned, these groups are in no way different from the larger village community and thus can be called communities within the community. Others among the associations owe their existence to government policies. They can be met with in all Korean villages, although they are not always welcomed by the villagers. Our attention here is called to those bodies and rules that affect the joint use and the preservation of woodlands, which have appeared above as the province of the village community and as a cornerstone of a developed community life. Any interference with usages concerning forestry would mean a blow to the material base of a village community, as it has developed around the joint use of woodlands, and the maintenance of such habits has been its main rationale.

Mutual Benefit Associations

Nine groups in Changjwa-ri appear to be somehow related to each other in character, for they all have the *kye*-element in their names. Five of them are mentioned in the *Regulations*. These are the forest association, the association

---

[1] The point is further illustrated by the data given in note 21 of this chapter.

for help in marriage ceremonies, that for contributions toward furneral expenses, the association for bier bearers, and that for burial ceremonies.[2] Besides, there is a sun-shade association (*ch'ailgye* 遮 日 契) which is the owner of the awnings[3], a bamboo association (*chukkye* 竹), manufacturing and providing the bamboo poles used in seaweed cultivation, a filial piety association (*wich'in'gye* 爲 親), which is to raise the means for the conduct of birthday ceremonies for older people, in particular the sixtieth birthday (*hwan'gap* 還 甲) parties, and an age peers' association (*tonggap kye* 同 甲), which is to organize and finance picnics and other social events for older gentlemen of the same age.[4]

These mutual benefit associations are the rather modest remnants of a mode of organization and self-help once very popular throughout the whole of Korea. In former times, associations of the *kye* type were not confined to help in marriage and funeral ceremonies, and they did not just occur as groups within the villages either. Their pursuits extended from such simple and innocent matters as the organizing and financing of picnics and banquets to the building of schools and the conduct of local education, to the collective discharge of tax duties and *corvée* labour, to banking, and even to the whole organization of a village community.[5] The *kye* associations did not only comprise parts of a village population, but often united the members of a whole lineage, regardless of their places of residence, or the population of several villages in one area. In principal, membership was voluntary. For a long time in history, such mutual benefit associations seem to have been the only efficient and really popular vehicles of organization of rural life in all its facets, only matched in importance by the clans and lineages. In a way, authors are right in claiming them to have been the characteristic feature of traditional social and economic life in rural Korea.

Admidst the bewildering variety of pursuits and kinds of extension, we can easily recognize the basic pattern of the *kye* associations. The basic idea is the payment of contributions, either in kind or in money, by its members. The whole of the funds or parts thereof are paid to an association member in case of need, or else are used for the achievement of the aim which the association has set itself. In more developed groups, the expenses of the association or of individual members are not covered by payments from the treasury or by *ad hoc* collections from among the members, but from the interest which has been obtained by lending out the fund to association members or anybody else who

---

[2] Vid. Arts. 7(6), 9(1,2).

[3] Vid. p. 53 of this study.

[4] It is interesting to observe that here again the documents do not fully reflect the reality of village life, for the latter associations are not mentioned in the documents.

The age peers' association may be viewed as the popular and modest version of the club of elder statesmen (*kisa* 耆 士) discussed in Appendix 2, note 14.

[5] The latter aspect has already been commented upon on pp. 45-47 of this study.

was in need of it. Even the pure banking associations fit into the scheme, although they do not specify any single pursuit of their own to be fulfilled by means of the association capital. Here, the collection of capital is an end in itself, and the association is an "abstract" one in the sense that any member or the group as a whole decides on the use of the gain according to the circumstances.[6] Each member of a *kye* association is a benefactor at one time and a beneficiary at another; no one gains, and no one loses, at least not in theory. The concept of the mutual benefit associations is thus another manifestation of the slogan "all for one, one for all", which we have already recognized as underlying the operations of a village community. This is the reason why we can regard mutal benefit associations as being not different in character from village communities.[7]

The majority of the mutual benefit associations which survive in present-day rural Korea as a residue of the once flourishing pattern is concerned with

---

[6] The operational mode of a banking association has been aptly described by Professor Pak Ki-Hyuk.

Vid. Pak/Gamble, *The Changing Korean Village,* pp. 47s.

[7] So far, the most extensive writing on mutual benefit associations has been done by Professor Kim Samsu 金 三 守. By collating source materials and various theories concerning the origins and tenets of mutual benefit associations, Professor Kim has successfully dissected the manifold links, in origin and substance, by which the *kye* are related to guild-like organizations of a religious and social order, to lineage organizations, patterns and organizations of collective farming, friendship groups, the Local Articles (*hyangyak* 鄉 約) of Confucianism, and ways of collective discharge of tax duties. However, his concept of the mutual benefit associations in the narrower sense really appears to be too narrow. There are many association contracts carrying the *kye*-element in their titles, but they are neglected by Professor Kim, because he wants to restrict the use of the term *kye* in such a way as to apply it only to those groupings which operate on an interest-making base. Furthermore, his study is wanting in systematic and historical coherence. Yet, his book, being based on extensive research in source materials, is an unsurpassed pioneer work which will remain an indispensable guide to materials for any future student of the subject.

The present author here wants to list the titles of a few important studies which have appeared after the latest edition of Professor Kim's book was published, or which have otherwise escaped his attention.

Vid. Daniel L. Gifford, "Korean Guilds and Other Associations", *The Korean Repository,* vol. II, [Seoul:] 1895, pp. 41-48; Gillet, "The Village Gilds of Old Korea"; *Han'guk sahoe kyŏngje sa yŏn'gu,* comp. Kim Samsu; *Han'guk nongch'onŭi ch'ollak kujo,* comp. Yang Hoesu, pp. 396-399; Susan Shin, "The *Kye*. A Study of Social Change in Korean Villages", *Papers on Japan,* vol. 4, from seminars at Harvard University, publ., distributed by the East Asia Research Center, Harvard University, Cambridge/Ms.: 1967, pp. 177-214; "Kyejiptan yŏn'guŭi sŏnggwawa kwaje. Kŭ chiptanjŏk sŏnggyŏkkwa kinŭngŭl chungsimŭro", comp. Ch'oe Chaesŏk, *Kim Chaewŏn paksa hoegap kinyŏm nonch'ong,* ed. Kungnip pangmulgwan, Seoul: Ŭryu munhwasa, 1969, pp. 581-599; "Han'guk ŏŏp kongdongch'eŭi sŏngnipkwa chollip yangt'aee kwanhan chosa yŏn'gu. Ŏch'on'gyerŭl chungsimŭro", comp. Pak Kwang-sun, *Kyŏngjehak yŏn'gu (The Korean Economic Review),* ed. Han'guk kyongjehakhoe, no. 19, Seoul: 1971, pp. 118-139; *Nongch'on'gyee kwanhan yŏn'gu. Nonghyŏpkwaŭi pigyorŭl chungsimŭro,* comp. Chang Tongsŏp, [Kwangju:] Chŏllam taehakkyo ch'ulp'anbu, 1973.

marriage and mourning ceremonies as well as with the organization and financing of banqueting parties and picnics among friends and age peers. Most of these mutual benefit associations are organized within villages. Changjwa-ri and its mutual benefit associations fit well into the general Korean scene.[8] Some detailed information could be obtained on the association for help in marriage ceremonies and on that for contributions towards furneral expenses. The contributions by means of which the funds are formed are determined by the association members both with regard to kind and amount of contribution. Although such details may be altered during the time of existence of an association, the contributions usually consist of grain. Upon entrance into the association, each member pays one *mal* 斗 [9] of washed rice, and he will have to pay two *toe* 升 [10] in each of the subsequent years. The two associations differ from each other with regard to the kind and amount of payments made to their members when they are in need of it. A member of the association for help in marriage ceremonies has as his due a certain amount of cotton, one bag (*kamani* 叺)[11] of washed rice, one jar (*tok* 독)[12], of the size of one *mal*, of distilled liquor, and five baskets (*tongu* 동 우)[13] of bean sprouts. A member of the association

---

[8] A survey of rural co-operatives and mutual benefit associations conducted by Dr. Kang Ch'anggyu of Choong-Puk National College (Ch'ungbuk taehak 忠 北 大 學, Ch'ŏngju 清 州 , has yielded statistical material showing that between 52% and 70% of the associations surveyed belong to the category of marriage and burial associations, the others being distributed among four other categories. Dr. Kang has reproduced some of the regulations of such associations, and so has Professor Yang in his book on the structure of Korean villages.

Another very popular kind of benefit association is a type of banking club which lends money for short terms and usually exorbitant interest to non-members. Bishop Rutt called it a "quickly-get-rich-money-club". This kind of *kye* is mostly organized by women, and since it is most popular in towns and cities, it does not strictly fall within the province of a study on rural Korea.

Vid. Richard Rutt, *Korean Works and Days. Notes from the Diary of a Country Priest*, ed. Royal Asiatic Society, Korea Branch, Rutland, Vt/Tōkyō: 1964, pp. 92-95; *Han'guk nongch'onŭi ch'ollak kujo*, comp. Yang Hoesu, pp. 432s; *Kyega idong nongŏp hyŏptong chohabe mich'inŭn yŏnghyang*, comp. Kang Ch'anggyu, pp. 12: table 2-5, 47 (Kang, *The Influence of "Ke" Societies Upon Ri-Dong Agricultural Cooperative Association*, pp. 28: table 2-3, 70).

[9] One *mal* equals 18.039 1.

[10] One *toe* equals 1.804 1. *Toe* as well as *mal* also mean types of vessels the capacities of which correspond to the dry measures mentioned here.

Vid. *Han'gugŭi nonggigu*, comp. Kim Kwangŏn, Minsok charyo chosa pogosŏ, publ. Munhwa kongbo pu/Munhwajae kwalliguk, no. 20, Seoul: 1969, pp. 329s, plates nos. 408-412.

[11] The word is related to the Japanese *kamasu*, and the seemingly Chinese character, too, is of Japanese origin.

[12] The term usually refers to much larger vessels.

Vid. *Han'gugŭi nonggigu* comp. Kim Kwangŏn, pp. 260s, photos nos, 308-310, 312.

[13] Professor Kim Kwangŏn gives *tonguri* 동우리 as the standard name.

Vid. *op. cit.*, pp. 285s, photos nos. 347-349.

for contribution towards funeral expenses will get one bag of washed rice, one jar of distilled liquor, three rolls of hemp cloth, and one mourning flag. One is probably correct in assuming that the filial piety association and the age peers' association operate on more or less the same basis. The other clubs, *i.e.* the association for bier bearers, that for burial ceremonies, the sun-shade association, and the bamboo association differ from the other two. The latter fraternities do not make their gain by lending out grain for interest, but by hiring out objects or offering manpower, in return for which money is expected to be paid at the rates mentioned above.[14]

When trying to determine the role these mutual benefit associations play in Changjwa-ri, we shall have to emphasize their independence from the rest of the village community. The only bond which ties them to the larger village community is the provision that the draft of association contracts is subject to the approval of the village community.[15] This is obviously meant as a device to check undue financial burdens which may be put on the villagers by the mutual benefit associations, but we have never heard of this provision as having been discussed and realized at a meeting of the village committee. Not only is the membership of the associations small,[16] but they do not contribute anything to the welfare of the village community. In this regard, the associations concerning marriage and mourning ceremonies are markedly distinguished from the forest association. As far as every villager is entitled to enter the woodlands to collect fuel, the care of the forest association for its association forest is at the same time a contribution to the general welfare of the village. In contrast to the marriage and mourning associations, the forest association is linked to the whole of the village community and in part will be considered an agency of the village community. The same could be true of the *de facto* associations of the fishermen and seaweed cultivators, and this is the reason why the latter associations are not discussed in the present chapter, but have instead been dealt with in the preceeding one. The mutual benefit associations, on the other hand, are profit-seeking clubs which have the collective profit of their restricted membership in mind. This tenet is in no way affected by the habit of lending mainly to members, and to non-members only when a member appears as guarantor. Even profiteering practised on members may help to increase the assets of the association as such.

---

[14] Vid. pp. 53s of this study.

[15] Vid. Art. 17(6).

[16] With regard to membership, too, the mutual benefit associations of Changjwa-ri agree with the majority of associations in other Korean villages, where the number of members is said to be between 11 and 20. In Changjwa-ri, the associations have between 10 and 20 member households.

Vid. *Kyega idong nongŏp hyŏptong chohabe mich'inŭn yŏnghyang,* comp. Kang Ch'anggyu, pp. 46: table 3-7 (Kang, *op. cit.,* pp. 68s).

Secondly, we have to take into account the fact that mutual benefit associations are not limited in duration. The members of the associations in Changjwa-ri profess that an association may be dissolved when the aim has been achieved, *i.e.* when each member household has obtained a payment, and that in such a case a general assembly of the members will have to decide on an even distribution of the remaining assets. However, no dissolution of an association ever seems to have occurred, at least not for the professed reasons. Likewise, nobody in the village seems to be able to remember the dates of the foundation of any of the associations. In the case of the death of a man representing a member household of an association, his son or grandson may inherit the rights and duties of membership. Moreover, every association provides for the admittance of new members.[17] Such provisions definitely prove that changes of membership are not considered to mean the foundation of a new association or some other kind of renewal. In this respect associations such as those in Changjwa-ri differ widely from the clubs of former times, when the existence of an association always seems to have been inseparably linked to the life of its members. Instead, the associations of today are meant to outlive any of their members. They are corporations leading "lives" of their own, which are independent of the lives of their members. As corporations we can regard them as being on an equal footing with the village community. We observe therefore a variety of communities within one and the same small territory. They all claim endless duration, whatever the differences in size and assets may be.

Thirdly, the very existence of such marriage and mourning associations suggests the expenses involved in such *rites de passage*. In the past, foreign travellers never failed to give expression to their surprise at the elaborate ceremonies observed on such occasions, even by less well-to-do people, and the costs associated with them.[18] The habit of spending fortunes on marriage and burial ceremonies has not ceased in modern times, and since such comparatively sumptuous functions, which usually exceed the means of a single household, continue to be observed, the mutual benefit associations as devices to cope with such expenses are continued, too. It is highly interesting to observe that the majority of the mutual aid associations, investigated by Dr. Kang between the years 1966 and 1969, had been established after the military coup of May 16th, 1961, although the new regime ordered all associations to be disbanded because

---

[17] In Changjwa-ri, upon entrance into an already existing association the new member household has to make a contribution which equals the ideal share each other member household holds of the assets of the club at the moment of the new entrance.

[18] Vid. John Ross, *History of Korea, Ancient and Modern. With Description of Manners and Customs, Language and Geography*, Paisley: without date, pp. 311-315, 317-320; Isabella Bird Bishop, *Korea and Her Neighbours. A Narrative of Travel, With an Account of the Recent Vicissitudes and Present Position of the Country*, New York/Chicago/Toronto: 1898, pp. 114-118, 286-291.

of their disruptive effects on rural society! A lot more of these *kye*, established before 1961, simply seem to have ignored the government order and continued their operations.[19]

A lot of money and contributions continue to flow into marriage and burial ceremonies and, consequently, into the mutual benefit associations related to these rites. In spite of considerable disapproval among the farming populace, the habit does not seem to have lost much ground so far. To get an impression of the situation, we again refer to Dr. Kang, who by his survey found out that, firstly, among the few people who showed discontent with the *kye* system as a whole the majority were members of the kind of mutual benefit association which is under discussion here. Secondly, the reasons given for their discontent were the waste and the extravagancy of the ceremonies,[20] which are further increased by the exorbitant interest charged on the loans.[21] In Changjwa-ri, however, the interest charged on the loans is less detrimental to the peasants, for the normal rate of interest is said to amount to 20 % only. Adverse effects on the household economy are further diminished by the already mentioned limitations imposed on the payments to be given to the member households.

Still, the existence of the associations is no mean curtailment of the growth and vitality of both the individual households and of the village community.

[19] Vid. *Kyega idong* . . ., comp. Kang Ch'anggyu, pp. 35: table 3-1, 37s (Kang, *op. cit.,* pp. 55, 58s).

[20] Dr. Kang was surprised to find that 84 % of the association members questioned by his staff approved of the existence of mutual benefit associations, although they were otherwise well aware of the debts and other contrarities usually associated with *kye* membership. Dr. Kang ascribes this stubborness to an inveterate conservatism, which in his opinion leads to accepting the obvious drawbacks of the associations as part of a natural order. A foreign observer, however, wonders whether the rural co-operatives, which are so warmly advocated by Dr. Kang as replacements for the mutual benefit associations, did not fail to offer a better alternative in financial matters, and whether "modernization" on the whole did not fail to provide alternatives to marriages and burials as events around which a Korean peasant's thought centers and which are almost the only occasions for feasting and relaxation in a hard life. The rural people may well haven chosen their *kye* system as the lesser evil; they are familiar with it, and it may not have appeared to be more untrustworthy than co-operatives and "modernization". Such suppositions are confirmed by the severe shortcomings of the rural co-operatives as described by Professor Pak Ki-Hyuk.
Vid. *Kyega idong* . . ., comp. Kang Ch'anggyu, pp. 63s: tables 4-5, 4-6, 83s: tables 4-17, 4-18, 85: table 4-19, 86-135 (Kang, *op. cit.,* pp. 89s, 118s, 120, 121, 122-177); Pak/Gamble, *The Changing Korean Village,* pp. 40s, 175-177.

[21] Dr. Kang demonstrated that associations are instrumental in rural usury. The assets of 91 % of the associations surveyed are increased by lendings on excessive interest. 93 % of the grain lending associations charge interest between 40 % and 50 % for a six month term. Of the *kye* lending out cash, 76 % charge between 60 % and 84 % for interest. Under these circumstances, associations cease to be self-help agencies, because the exploitative thrust is turned against their own members, 51 % of all *kye* lending to their members only.
Vid. *Kyega idong* . . ., comp. Kang Ch'anggyu, pp. 56-58, 61: table 4-4 (Kang, *op. cit.,* pp. 82-84, 85s, 88).

Realizing the fact that Korean farmers are usually short of surplus money which could be spent on things other than the daily needs, any part of the small amounts available which is put into such associations is immediately subtracted from other ventures, such as those of the larger village community. Secondly, the existence of those mutual benefit associations clearly marks the limits of the village community in terms of people. Since the mutual benefit associations are the clubs of the poorer part of the village population, and since they generally prevent contributions from that group of the villagers from flowing into the community, the existence of the *kye* proves that the village community, in fact, is an affair of the more well-to-do peasants only. The insistence of even the poorer peasant households on celebrating marriages and mournings in the traditional sumptuous fashion helps to maintain that split within the village and, implicitly, the limited scope of activity of the village community.

Other voluntary groupings within the village are intended to be less durable than the mutual benefit associations are, and they cannot be conceived of as being equally deeply rooted in the social and economic structure of the village. They emerge whenever an occasion requires it, but they do not necessarily disappear when the aims they were established for are achieved. Koreans are known to be fond of forming groups whenever some pursuit starts claiming attention. However, this propensity towards uniting and doing things together is less due to a simple, emotional enjoyment in company and joyful co-operation than is often believed. Instead, it is promoted by the desire to include as many people as possible in any kind of decision-making and action and to take into account as many points of view as there may be, or at least to pretend to do so. Here, the same considerations are at work as will be detected when studying the operational principles of the village administration in chapter 10 of this study. Guided by the desire to diffuse responsibilities, Koreans will hardly ever delegate new tasks to an already existing grouping and thus widen its competences, when the new tasks are similar to the ones of the old group. Instead, they will establish a new group, at the same time continuing the old one and diverting its activities to quite a different field. It thus happens that many spontaneous associations in villages and elsewhere outlive the rationale of their creation. In an effort to preserve the once established rights of the members of such a group to participation in decision-making, they are often granted representation and participation in the general village affairs and thus become an informal ingredient of the social and political structure of the village.

In Changjwa-ri, only two specimens of this type of voluntary association found their way into the documents. The one was the Fine Customs Society, to which was later entrusted the repair of the village well.[22] The other one was an action committee which had been established to handle the repair and

---

[22] Vid. Document XIII.5(e).

enlargement of Ch'ŏnghae School and the establishment of a health centre there.[23] Its activities did not end at that, for long after the task had been accomplished, when the repair of the village office was on the agenda, the action committee appeared as a group of its own side by side with the group of neighbourhood heads, the group of "interested people", and the administration committee of the village.[24]

Other Groups

Most of the other groups within the village are covered by the term "corporations within the village".[25] In the period under discussions here, this category included a Women's Club (*puin hoe* 夫 人 會), meant to familiarize the women of the village with new housekeeping techniques and childrearing practices,[26] and a village section of the Korean Red Cross (*Han'guk chŏksipcha sa* 韓 國 赤 十 字 社). These two groups are mentioned as the only significant ones of this category existing at that time.

In addition, we have to mention the 4-H-Club of the village. In 1962, the youthful members of the 4-H-Club were to replace the former forest association as far as its task of guarding the woodlands was concerned.[27] In the amendments to the *Regulations* drafted in 1964, these youthful members appear as the "advance-guard" of the village and the main agency in educating the youngsters and preparing them for their future tasks as trustworthy villagers and faithful subjects.[28] The 4-H-Clubs started as Korean chapters of the movement of the same name that had originated around the turn of the century in the United States of America. After World War II, considerable contributions of livestock and seeds were sent to the Korean clubs by their American counterparts. The 4-H-Clubs were made into more formal institutions, organized on a nation-wide scale by the Law on Agricultural Instruction (*Nongsa kyodo pŏp* 農 事 敎 導 法) from 1957. Their particular aim was to recruit so-called volunteer leaders in agricultural matters, who were to break up the traditional pattern of village leadership. With the Law on Village Development (*Nongch'on chinhŭng pŏp* 農 村 振 興 法) from April 1962, the 4-H-Clubs were turned into an almost exclusive affair of the rural youth and

---

[23] Vid. Document XIII.5(b), 16(b), 22(b).

[24] Vid. Document XIII.23.

[25] Vid. Arts. 17(1), 24.

[26] The rather modest status Women's Clubs held in the years under consideration here has been illustrated by Professor Pak Ki-Hyuk.
Vid. Pak/Gamble, *The Changing Korean Village,* p. 43.

[27] Vid. Document XIII.22(a); Pak/Gamble, *op. cit.,* pp. 45s.

[28] Vid. Document XIII.24(f).

were put under the youth section of the Village Development Bureau. Young people between the ages of 13 and 24 were to become members of the clubs, which from then onwards were not only to care for the promotion of cattle-breeding and the introduction of a wider choice of crops, but were to promote a comprehensive re-education of the 4 H, *viz.* head, heart, hand, and health, in order to generate new modes of rural life. The decisions mentioned above were a quick reaction in Changjwa-ri to this new government policy.[29]

The county forest co-operative mentioned in Art. 17(2) of the *Regulations of Changjwa-ri* calls for a more elaborate explanation. Neither the *Regulations* nor any other documents tell us any details about it, and therefore it is difficult to ascertain what this co-operative was like in the period under discussion here. The very term "co-operative" (*chohap* 組 合) makes us search for the beginnings of such co-operatives in the period of Japanese occupation of Korea. For it was in that period only that co-operatives began to appear under that name, which is a Sino-Korean rendering of the Japanese *kumiai*. As early as 1904, the first series of so-called rural societies (Sin.-Kor. *nonghoe*, Sin.-Jap. *nōkai* 農 會) came to be established in Korea. Sometimes, they were not called societies, but co-operatives. These rural societies seem to have mostly been initiated by the Japanese authorities and to have been operated by Japanese farmers in the so-called immigrant und model villages. Their aim was to bring about an increase in agricultural yield by improving manufacturing methods in household industries, such as silkworm raising, cotton planting, and husbandry.[30] With the Decree on Rural Societies in Korea (*Chōsen nōkai rei* 朝 鮮 農 會 令) in January 1926, they were brought into a strict hierarchical order, the various levels of which coincided with those of the general administration. Only the societies dealing with husbandry and those concerned with forestry were kept out of this system of hierarchically arranged rural societies (Sin.-Kor. *kyet'ong nonghoe*, Sin.-Jap. *keitō nōkai* 系 統 農 會). The co-operatives belonging to these two branches of agriculture continued operating on the lowest levels of the adminstrative hierarchy only, *viz.* in the counties and on islands.[31] These facts allow the conclusion that even at the beginning of the Japanese period there existed forest co-operatives on the county level. Husbandry and forest co-operatives became incorporated into the hierarchically arranged system of agricultural societies in March 1933 only. At that time, the assets of the former county forest co-operatives were transferred to the provincial branches of the Korean Forestry Co-operative (*Chōsen shinrin kumiai* 朝 鮮 森 林 組 合).[32]

---

[29] Vid. *Sae maŭl undong. Kŭ iron'gwa chŏn'gae,* comp. Hongbo chosa yŏn'guso, publ. Munhwa kongbo pu, Seoul: 1972, pp. 193-198.

[30] Vid. *Han'guk nongch'on tanch'e sa,* comp. Mun Chŏngch'ang, pp. 9-43.

[31] Vid. *ibid.,* pp. 44-50.

[32] Vid. *ibid.,* pp. 59s.

This is the last bit of safe information that it was possible to obtain on the subject with regard to conditions prior to the year 1961. We are entirely left in the dark as to what a county forest co-operative could have meant to the authors of the *Regulations* in 1952. Political and legal conditions seem to have still been so troubled in those years that only eye-witnesses of village life in those days are likely to be able to tell exactly what it was like and what co-operatives meant.[33] An attempt at restoring order in matters of agricultural co-operatives was only made as late as the year 1957, when the Law on Agricultural Cooperatives (*Nongŏp hyŏptong chohap pŏp* 農 協 同 組 合 法) was promulgated. A similar attempt with regard to forestry was made even as late as 1961 by the Law on Forestry.

Still, even in those troubled years the authorities seem to have managed to keep a hand on the treasured woodlands, or at least they tried to do so. For otherwise, the authors of the *Regulations* would not have mentioned a county forest co-operative and the village would not have been obliged to pay its expenses. In trying to keep the forestry affairs of their jurisdiction under control, the authorities continued a practice which had come to them as a legacy of the period of Japanese rule. For instance, the appointment and removal of heads of rural societies on the county and islands levels rested with the provincial governors. Likewise, the regulations of such societies required the approval of the authorities.[34] It seems that in later years the county heads and the island magistrates themselves held the posts of co-operative heads in their areas of jurisdiction. Therefore, management of the co-operatives on the lowest levels can be said to have been part of the general administration.[35] This pattern was in part resumed by the forestry legislation of 1961. According to the Law on Forestry, the establishment and the regulations of village forest associations require the consent of the authorities and the registration at government offices. The grip of the authorities on village woodlands was further tightened by the provision that village forest associations as a whole had to be members of the forest co-operatives organized on the county level.[36]

It was thus only at the beginning of the sixties that a county forest association again acquired some discernable shape. Besides demonstrating that the forest co-operatives of the Republic of Korea were not much different in character from their predecessors of the Japanese period, this later legislation

---

[33] The turmoil of those days, as it was reflected in matters of agricultural co-operatives, can be told from Professor Mun's description of the embezzlements and other irregularities which occured at the central headquarters of the co-operatives, and from his account of the fight for priority between the agricultural and the credit co-operatives, which led to the final dissolution of agricultural co-operatives in April 1951.

Vid. *ibid.,* pp. 265-267.

[34] Vid. *ibid.,* pp. 46s: 4(f,g), 5, 6.

[35] Vid. *ibid.,* p. 59.

[36] Vid. *Sallim pŏp,* Arts. 61-64, 72.

throws some light on the village forest association discussed in the preceding chapter, and on the nature of government interference in village affairs. If that forest association was ever a real association of volunteers having united to establish a community, it could legally have been so only between the years 1945 and 1961. The legislation on forestry matters of 1961 and thereafter positively proves that a village forest association, even if it was established on a voluntary base, has since then largely been determined by decisions made on the superior county level. This may well have been the case even before that time, as the existence of a county forest co-operative in 1952 suggests. The *kye*-element in the name of the forest association is delusive, because it suggests free choice and freedom, which have not been granted in reality. If the forest association ever succeeded in conducting its affairs on a basis of self-determination and freedom, it could only do so by circumventing government interference. It seems as if the preservation of a village community and of communities within it is more a result of a fight against the law than an affair protected by law. The establishment of government-inspired groups within the village and the absorption of voluntary associations into superior units are the two means to establishing government control of the villages.

An Attempt at Evaluating the Community

The legislation on forest co-operatives and forest associations thus illustrates those among the factors minimizing the growth of village communities which come from outside the village. However, it has not been the objective of the above considerations to generally condemn the *kye*-type associations and government policies towards the villages as being detrimental to the village community, and to implicitly laudate the village community as a panacea curing the evils of rural life. As the distinction of villages along the lines of *yangban* and commoner households may already have suggested, there is nothing like "the typical" Korean village. Therefore, the effects of communities within the village and the government policies can be expected to be different under different circumstances. Judgement on village communities, associations, and government policies are to be limited to single cases only, at least at such a preliminary stage as has been attained up to now in the investigations of Korean villages. If there should be anything criticized in the government policies, it is the inflexible approach to complex situations. Furthermore, such judgements are out of place here, because they would mean straying across the boundaries of the present study. They would have to be based on ample factual evidence of village economy and the values maintained by the peasants, which the present author is not able to give.

However, dealing with the general differential factors in village life, two instances should be remembered, if we want to judge on the merits and drawbacks of the village community. As has been said above, it is rather an exclusive affair. The lists of participants in meetings of the village committee and the like do not, in total, contain more than seventy names in twelve years. When looking at the protocols of the year 1957, with the regard to which documentation is particulary rich, one notices that not more than 26 men had the final say in village affairs in Changjwa-ri, *i.e.* about 25 % of the household heads. Basically being an arrangement among the wealthier members of the village population on the joint use of property, a village community can be expected to include only a number of the villagers in other places as well. It is easy to imagine that such conditions may reach a stage where the community becomes an obstacle to the development of the rest of the village people.

Secondly, the village communities have hitherto shown a strong tendency towards isolation. In the remote past as well as in more recent decades, the neighbouring village has hardly meant either a challenge to one's own doings or an incentive to co-operation in a wider area. In Korea, one would hardly find any territorial union which owes its existence and coherence to initiatives emanating from the local populace itself. Instead, such a union will always be due to government acts. Therefore, the Korean rural scene by and large is one of atomized communities which have the government authorities as their only point of reference for either friendly or inimical reactions.[37] Since economic improvement often requires large-scale co-operation, the isolationist attitude of the village community would often have impeded such improvements, if the government had not interfered. The forest association's membership of the county forest co-operative, for instance, inevitably brings the village of Changjwa-ri into contact with other villages or parts thereof, and inevitably brings about some kind of accommodation and co-operation in a wider area. Of course, such a transgression of the narrow confines of the village world is not a

---

[37] In this respect, Korean villages seem to differ markedly from their Japanese counterparts, at least from those of earlier centuries. The difference becomes obvious from a study and translation, made by Professor Dr. Dan Fenno Henderson, of 50 specimens of what he calls "village contracts" of the Tokugawa 德川 period (1600—1867). In a substantial number of these pieces, it is the villages, as bodies corporate, that appear as contractors of other villages. The agreements concern matters of common water usage, use of some area as commons of two villages, settlement on common lands, rental of a mountain by one village from another, various agreements on, and guarantees of, inter-village loans, and multi-village co-operation in attempts to prevent the opening of new fields in the commons as well as in supervision of corvée labour to be delivered at a post station. No document of this kind of obviously spontaneous village-to-village co-operation seems to have been discovered in Korea so far.

Vid. Dan Fenno Henderson, *Village "Contracts" in Tokugawa Japan. Fifty Specimens with English Translations and Comments,* Asian Law Series, [ed.] School of Law, University of Washington, no. 2, Seattle/London: 1975, pp. 43-50, 66-75, 85-87, 93-95, 115-118, 126-128, 179-187.

voluntary one. The villagers do not directly unite and do not act of their own free will, but their contacts are mediated by their villages and the corporations they belong to. Furthermore, what may finally result as co-operation is not really negotiated, not even among the corporations concerned, but is commanded and supervised by the government. Thus, if there were no government, there would be no co-operation among villages, and nobody could enjoy the benefits such wider co-operation often produces. Yet, even if we concede the benevolent effects of government action in many cases, we equally well have to take into consideration the often disastrous results in other places or in other than economic walks of life in the same locality. It seems that there is no smooth and uniform solution to the problem of interaction between village community and government, because the rural scene in itself is far from being uniform. Witnessing the fact that government action often does not produce any benefit for the population, even where open corruption and malpractice have not been the reasons for the failure, we again have to ask the question whether nation-wide uniform legislation is the right answer to the challenge.

CHAPTER 7: THE VILLAGE FESTIVAL

Admidst the manifold restrictive pressures the village community must have been experiencing for a long time already, the village people of Changjwa-ri have imperturbably held fast to the most colourful manifestation of village solidarity, *viz.* their village festival. Being of a religious and mental order, it has largely remained unaffected by the political and economic vicissitudes and has hitherto withstood the cultural inroads of modernization. It is both a visible manifestation of the community spirit, otherwise divested of most of its modes of expression, and an annual revival of it. The festival is one for the whole village, and each household in the village is expected to make its contributions to the fund by means of which the festival is financed and to share otherwise in its conduct. These are the reasons why a chapter on the village festival is to conclude a survey of the village community of Changjwa-ri.

Those features of the festival shall be explained here that are essential to an understanding of the references to it in the *Regulations of Changjwa-ri* and in other documents. The considerations concerning its place in village culture will be left to Appendix 2 of this study. The village festival of Changjwa-ri has been studied in great detail by Dr. Yi Tuhyŏn. Although his approach is that of a cultural anthropologist, his account of the festival may well serve the present purposes. Therefore, it will be summarized here in as detailed a manner as necessary for the convenience of those who are not in a position to read Dr. Yi's article themselves.

The deity worshipped at Changjwa-ri is regarded as the tutelary spirit of the village, on whom the welfare and the peace of the whole place depend. Unlike the deities worshipped in most other village festivals in Korea, the one in Changjwa-ri is not a more or less amorphous spirit residing in some conspicuous natural object, such as an old and tall tree or a bizarre rock, but a deified human being.[1] The tutelary spirit of Changjwa-ri is called Great General Song (Song

---

[1] The metamorphosis of human beings, fictitious or real ones, into tutelary spirits of localities is not a familiar feature in Korean folk-religion. An investigation into the traditions of the village festivals of 88 localities in Korea, conducted in the mid-thirties of this century, shows that only 16 of the spirits can be traced back to distinct human beings. (The authors of the investigation did not include the tutelary spirits of the village of Hahoe 河回 in North Kyŏngsang Province [Kyŏngsang pukto 慶尙北道], who are likewise deifications of human beings.) They became the tutelary spirits of the places, either because they once rescued the local populace from a plight and are thus memorized as benefactors, or because they acquired a reputation as paragons of loyalty and devotion. All of the other deities are either devoid of any definable shape or are simply thought of as old "men" or "women". They are

taejanggun 宋大將軍). There is some confusion as to the identity of the
man who is supposed to have been the incarnation of the spirit.[2] Older people in
the village believe it to have been Chang Pogo, the younger and more educated
relate this name to a certain Song Ching 徵 or Song Chin 津 .[3] The histories
written on command of, and published by, the government contain no
information on him, but he is believed to have been a military leader involved in
the insurrection of the Three Patrols (*sam pyŏlch'o* 三別抄) in 1270-73.[4] It is
said that General Song showed commiseration for the starving people of the
region; he plundered some ships which were carrying tribute rice, and
distributed the rice among the local populace. After his departure from Wan

---

usually credited with the rescue from epidemic diseases, and accordingly worship is said to
have started after such a crisis.

    Vid. *Burakusai,* comp. Murayama Chijun *et al.,* Chōsa shiryō, ed. Chōsen sōtokufu, no. 44
(Chōsen no kyōdo shinji, part 1), Keijō: 1937, photolithogr. repr. Min'gan sinang charyo
ch'ongsŏ, publ. Wŏn'gwang taehak minsokhak yŏn'guso, no. 2, [Seoul:] 1971, pp. 201-213,
esp. 201, 202, 203s, 207-212; *Han'guk kamyŏn'gŭk (Korean Mask-Dance Drama),* comp. Yi
Tuhyŏn, written under the sponsorship of the Ministry of Cultural Affairs and Public
Information, Bureau of Cultural Properties, Seoul: Han'guk kamyŏn'gŭk yŏn'guhoe, 1969,
pp. 159-164; Frits Vos, "De traditionele vormen van dramatische kunst in Korea", *forum der
letteren,* Jg. 1972, no. 4, Amsterdam: 1972, p. 22.

   [2] Vid. "Wando-ŭp Changjwa-ri tangje", comp. Yi Tuhyŏn, pp. 433-436.

   [3] The relation between Song Ching and Wan Island is substantiated by an entry in an
encyclopedia from the early Yi period. There, Song Ching appears as a prodigious archer, but
there is no indication of his lifetime or of other achievements of his. The story is repeated twice
in township gazetteers (*ŭpchi* 邑誌) from the end of the Yi period. Of course, although
these various entries do not prove the authenticity of the version told today, they bear evidence
to the considerable age of stories which establish a relationship between Song Ching and Wan
Island.

    Vid. *Sinjŭng Tongguk yŏji sŭngnam,* k. 37.19a.1s (= p. 657a); *Kangjin-hyŏn yŏng-ŭp-chin
chi,* "Kojŏk cho"; *Kangjin-hyŏn yŏji sŭngnam,* "Kojŏk cho".

   [4] After having helped to eliminate the ruling Im 林 clan and to restore full power to king
Wŏnjong 元宗 (1260—1274), the Three Patrols turned against the king, when they learnt
about his complete submission to the Mongols. The rebellion broke out on Kanghwa Island
(Kanghwa-do 江華島), on June 20th, 1270. Soon afterwards, the insurgents moved south
and established their headquarters on Chin Island (Chin-do 珍), from where they controlled
the southern coastal waters of Korea. Continuously raiding and pillaging the smaller islands
in that part of the country, they sometimes penetrated far into the interior. The looting was
temporarily brought to an end when government troops succeeded in capturing Chin Island in
July 1271. The rebels were forced to retreat to Cheju Island (Cheju-do 濟州島). There, they
continued their activities, until the insurgency was crushed by the seizure of Cheju Island in
June 1273.

    A detailed account of the rebellion, with extensive notes and a survey of the institution of
the patrols, has been given by Professor Dr. William Henthorn. It is interesting to observe that
the view expressed in the historical records, talking about raids and looting, differs from that
of the popular traditions of the region as in the case of the one underlying the village festival of
Changjwa-ri.

    Vid. Henthorn, *Korea. The Mongol Invasions,* pp. 173-193, 226-235.

Island, the people started venerating him as a heavenly spirit in commemoration of his benevolence.[5] Dr. Yi Tuhyŏn believes that in the traditions of the local people Chang Pogo and Song Ching have been blended into one cultural hero who, at some time, started being worshipped as benefactor of the people and guardian deity of the village. The worship of General Song, once practised in many places on the island, at present is alive in Changjwa-ri only.[6]

[5] Vid. *Ch'ŏnghae pisa,* comp. Kim Sonam, Pusan: Nongch'on kyemong munhwasa, 1955, pp. 15s, quoted in "Wando-ŭp Changjwa-ri tangje", comp. Yi Tuhyŏn, pp. 434s.

[6] As in the case of Song Ching and the insurgency of the Three Patrols, the local people's appreciation of Chang Pogo differs widely from that of the historical records. In a tale about Chang Pogo which has been transmitted in Changjwa-ri until the present day, it is not the condemnation of a traitor and insurgent which finds its expression there, but the love of, and pity for, the man. In that tale, Chang Pogo's death is ascribed to a particularly vile ruse. Yŏm Chang 閻長 , the man who is said to have assassinated Chang Pogo, and Pogo entered into a competition as to who would be the first to fly to a rock off the shore and hoist a flag there. When Chang Pogo had changed into a pheasant and Yŏm Chang into a falcon before starting off for the flight, the falcon grabbed the pheasant and killed it. In order to remind people of this atrocious deed, a rock off the shore of Changjwa-ri is still called Pheasant Reef (Kkat'uriyŏ 까 투 리 여).

This tale is curiously reminiscent of the story told about the fight for the throne between King Suro 首露 of Karak 駕洛 (trad. dates 42—562) and his rival T'arhae 脫解 , in the course of which both men were transformed into birds. The motif of bird fight also occurs in a version of the foundation myth of Koguryŏ. Part of that myth deals with a competition between the River Earl (Habaek 河伯) and Haemosu 解慕漱 , son of the Heavenly Emperor (Ch'ŏnje 天帝). Haemosu wants to marry Yuhwa 柳花 , and before getting permission to do so, he has to enter a magical competition in the course of which River Earl and Haemosu three times change into pairs of animals, and in all three cases, each of the two animals is hostile to each other. One of their transformations is into a pheasant (Habaek) and an eagle (Haemosu), and the eagle kills the pheasant. This part of the myth is found in its more elaborate versions only, *viz.* in the "Lay of King Tongmyŏng" (Tongmyŏng-wang p'yŏn 東 明 王 篇) and in the "Treatise on Geography" (Chiri chi 地 理 志) of the *Veritable Records of King Sejong (Sejong sillok* 世 宗 實 錄).

The version mentioned above is an effort to combine the proper foundation myth of Koguryŏ, in which Chumong 朱蒙 plays the central part, with the myth of Tan'gun 檀 君 . By ascribing divine origin to Koguryŏ, this fabrication served to enhance the prestige of Koryŏ, which considered itself to be the legitimate successor of Koguryŏ. It is evident that this complex version of the Koguryŏ foundation myth was particularly popular during the Koryŏ period, but it seems to have originated in a time prior to it. For in his "Lay of King Tongmyŏng", Paegun sanin Yi Kyubo 白 雲 山 人 李 奎 報 (1168—1241) quotes "Fundamental Records" (pon'gi 本記) of a — lost — *History of the Old Three Kingdoms (Ko Samguk sa* 古 三 國 史) as his source. The tales of bird fights between Yŏm Chang and Chang Pogo, Suro and T'arhae, Haemosu and Habaek may thus be considered to have originated in about the same period. The motif seems to have been fairly widespread in Korea, and the story told in Changjwa-ri is a distant remembrance of it.

Vid. "Tongmyong-wang p'yŏn", p. 45 (Yi Kyu-Bo, "A Lay of King Tongmyong", transl., annotated Richard Rutt, *Korea Journal,* ed. Korean National Commission of UNESCO, vol. 13, no. 7, Seoul: July 1973, p. 50, lines 80-99); *Samguk yusa,* k. 2, "Karakkuk ki", p. 110; "Tongguk kunwang kaeguk yŏndae pyŏng sŏ", p. 52; *CWS: Sejong sillok,* k. 154, 4a.8-5a.3,

In order to ensure General Song's everlasting benevolence, the villagers present offerings to his spirit and every year beg for his favour again. There is a small straw-thatched shrine on a tiny island called General's Island. This island lies about 300 m off the shore of the village, and it is there that the yearly offerings are made. The interior of the shrine is empty during most of the year. Only when the day of the sacrifice draws near, do the villagers put a table into the shrine on which they place a tablet declaring it the seat of General Song's spirit. On the day of the festival, they display the offerings on the same table, such as rice cakes, fruit, a pig's head and claws, vegetables, rice, and rice-beer (*makkŏlli* 막 걸 리). During the rest of the year, we only find the usual attributes characteristic of the sacred places of Korean folk-religion. They are the so-called "prohibition ropes" (*kŭmjul* 禁 줄), *i.e.* straw-ropes stretched between two or more trees to mark off the sacred precincts, and scrolls[7] suspended from the pillars of the small shrine. The shrine itself is surrounded by luxuriant, beautiful camellia bushes, pagoda trees, bramble bushes, nettle trees, and calebasse trees, which form a grove at the top of General's Island.

The village festival takes place around the night after the fifteenth day of the first month according to the lunar calendar.[8] This is the first full moon night of the new lunar year and it marks the beginning of spring. Hence, it is the appropriate occasion to turn to the spirits for a plentiful harvest, for peace, and a lucky new year. On the evening of the fifteenth day, the peasants' band starts playing its music. The people join them in dancing and drumming, and there is much agitation in the village. The band will stop playing around midnight, but will re-appear around 3 o'clock in the morning, touring the village to wake up the people. Then, the male adults of the village gather on the shore in order to walk to the shrine of General Song on General's Island. For at that early morning time, it is low tide, and the way to General's Island can be covered on foot. Before that larger group of villagers set out for their walk to the island, those directly responsible for the sacrifice have already gone to General's Island, in order to accomplish the last preparations there. There is the steady

esp. 4b.7-14 (= vol. 5, pp. 683s; *Chōsen keizai shi,* comp. Paek Namun, Keizaigaku zenshū, vol. 61, Tōkyō: Kaizōsha, 1933, pp. 24-30); Kurakichi Shiratori, "The Legend of the King Tung-ming 東 明 , the Founder of Fu-yü-kuo 夫 餘 國 ", *Memoirs of the Research Department of the Toyo Bunko,* no. 10, Tōkyō: The Toyo Bunko, 1938, pp. 1-39; "Wando-ŭp Changjwa-ri tangje", comp. Yi Tuhyŏn, p. 434; "T'arhae chŏnsŭng ko. Chŭgwiŭi chujirŭl chungsimŭro hayŏ", comp. Kim Yŏlgyu, *Kim Chaewŏn paksa hoegap kinyŏm nonch'ong,* ed. Kungnip pangmulgwan, Seoul: Ŭryu munhwasa, 1969, pp. 483-494; *Han'guk minsokkwa munhak yŏn'gu,* comp. Kim Yŏlgyu, Seoul: Ilchogak, 1972², pp. 102-106, Frits Vos, *Die Religionen Koreas,* Die Religionen der Menschheit, hrsg. Christel Matthias Schröder, Bd. 22.1, Stuttgart/Berlin/Köln/Mainz: 1977, pp. 31-37.

[7] The texts of the scrolls are reproduced as Document III in this study.

[8] The subsequent description of the festival has largely to be based on Dr. Yi's article. The present author's experience was limited by the fact that bad weather prevented a full display of the festival when he went to Changjwa-ri in 1970.

accompaniment of the vigorous farmers' music (*nongak* 農 樂), which from that time on will continue almost without interruption until the afternoon. The sacrifice begins at sunrise exactly — the doors of the shrine facing east — when the shallow waters around the myriads of rocky islets start glittering in the sun. The ceremonies reach their climax when the address[9] is read to the spirit of General Song, the wishes of the population are presented, and the villagers inside the shrine and outside of it bow to the spirit. Having accomplished the ceremonies, the men squat down in front of the shrine to enjoy the food and drinks, which before were on the table inside the shrine, and many other delicacies prepared for the occasion. Stimulated by the rather strong rice-beer, the peasants' band resumes its music, and after a tour of the island, the men will go back to the village, this time by boats which in the meantime have arrived from the village.

Back in the village, the procession heads for two huge and bizarre cypress trees (*chamaecyparis obtusa*) at the northern and southern entrances to the village, in order to show reverence to the spirits residing there, and then turn to the village well. These trees are the places called Archery Arbour and Plum Altar[10] in the *Regulations*. Reverence to the trees and the village well is an element of folk-religion in the festival of Changjwa-ri which it has in common with most village festivals in Korea. This ritual of the festival is somehow separated from the otherwise more dignified and sophisticated ceremonies. Still, it is an integral part of the whole. For the very position of the trees at the entrances to the village indicates that the spirits thought to reside there are equally well conceived of as tutelary spirits of the place, and reverence to them is necessary in a festival devoted to the worship of village guardian deities. Having finished the procession, the villagers spend the rest of the day in banqueting and drinking. Sometimes, a village assembly follows in the evening.

The village festival requires a lot of preparatory work and charges in kind and money. Both the work and the charges are a common concern of the villagers, which makes the conduct of the festival a genuine community affair. We have already mentioned the musical instruments and dresses used during the shrine festival. We have also referred to the fact that three parts of the village alternately have to repair the roof of the shrine. Mention was also made of the raising of contributions to cover the festival expenses by means of an apportionment. The immediate preparations for the functions and certain other tasks associated with the actual conduct of the ceremonies are entrusted to several villagers. There are a master of the sacrifice (*cheju* 祭 主) and his wife, a steward (*chipsa* 執 事), and an intendant (*yusa* 有 司). Besides, the presence of the village head is required in most ceremonies. The master of the sacrifice and his wife are responsible for the general preparations of the food and drinks.

---

[9] The text of the address is reproduced as Document IV in this study.

[10] For explanations of these names vid. pp. 140-143 of this study.

The preparations take place in the house of the master of the sacrifice. They begin about ten days before the date of the shrine festival. Of all the villagers, the steward and the village head are the only people allowed to enter the shrine. There, the steward reads the address to the spirit of General Song, and the village head presents the wishes of the villagers.

We do not know much about the qualifications required of those officeholders, nor are there distinct rules for their selection. They do not necessarily seem to be identical with the people at the top of the Fine Customs Society or any of the other associations within the village. Their selection does not seem to be subject to any formal rule, and thus is very likely to be made within that contiguous flow of opinion which is so characteristic of village affairs. Dr. Yi says that these office-holders are either chosen from among the well-reputed people in the village or that sometimes people in distress volunteer for those posts. The master of the sacrifice and his wife — and probably the other office-holders as well — strictly have to observe purity, and for twelve days before the festival have to take baths in a spring in the mountains before dawn. If anything unclean happens in the houses of the selected office-holders, such as the birth of a piglet or an outburst of insanity, the person concerned has to be changed for somebody else.[11]

[11] Vid. "Wando-ŭp Changjwa-ri tangje", comp. Yi Tuhyŏn, pp. 438, 440s.

CHAPTER 8: THE COMMUNE

The Government and the Rise of the Commune

The preceding discussion of various aspects of the village community has prepared the ground for an evaluation of the village as a commune. The underlying idea is that the commune should eventually replace the village-centred community, but that this process does not necessarily entail the weakening of village integration and co-operation. In contrast to the contents of chapter 6, we shall now concentrate on the role that the government plays in the process of the dissolution of the traditional village community.

It would be entirely misleading to think of Korean villages and towns as free communes which are guaranteed certain well-defined rights by the government and which are endowed with material means sufficient to accomplish tasks again to be determined by the community. In Korean rural communes, it is always the local representative of the government who has the final say, as will become evident from a glance at the laws concerning local self-government.[1] Government power is mandatory not only in actual village affairs, but must even be viewed as the main force behind the genesis of the commune. For whenever the people of a village look beyond the narrow horizon of their houses and fields, their festivities, their grievances, and their quarrels, they do so, because the government urges them to do so. This is the rule, and exceptions are hard to find. We have already had the opportunity to point at government mediation in opening ways of supravillage co-operation and co-ordination. The same can be said with regard to the introduction of modern school education, electricity, and many other innovations. Even where changes are due to the initiatives of single far-sighted and enterprising individuals among the villagers, these people will inevitably rely on government officials, at least in financial matters, because in most cases the government will be the only source the money necessary for the intended changes can be drawn from.[2] Government participation does not stop at this, for such steps will affect the innermost core of village organization and destroy most of what we have come to know as the village community. Even where government officials are not over-ambitious in "modernizing" the villages within their jurisdiction and are not intent on destroying

---

[1] Vid. Appendix 1 of this study.

[2] This view and many others expressed in this chapter are shared by the present author with Dr. Yi Man'gap.

Vid. Man-gap Lee, "Rural People and Their Modernization", *Aspects of Social Change in Korea*, ed. C. I. Eugene Kim/Ch'angboh Chee, Kalamazoo/Mich.: 1969, pp. 73, 76s, 81.

the traditional modes of village organization, they can hardly avoid doing so. When village forest associations and fishing guilds are urged to enter organizations of a higher, governmental order, their affairs will cease to be determined by the villagers. In a similar way, "privatization" of woodlands will contribute to the weakening of the traditional village organization.

Inasmuch as the introduction of innovations and the subsequent changes in village economy and organization require new modes of organization, the village turns into a commune and eventually ceases to be a community. It seems to be the characteristic feature of Korean village communes that, firstly, their genesis is closely associated with modernization in the economic field and that, secondly, it is almost exclusively dependent on government action. Since Korean villages seem to have never developed a village-to-village co-operation, they have never developed habits of organizing and financing those enterprises which exceed the powers of a single village. Likewise, having been devoid of such traditions of co-operation, the villages never generated rules which would have been recognized as the "vested interests" of a region and could have served as a safeguard for regional self-government to be respected by superior government agencies. Therefore, the villages in Korea, each for itself, were entirely at the mercy of the government, when, in modern times, the increasing government powers to exercise control over the countryside met with the increasing desire of the villagers to have their economic lot alleviated by modern technical and educational facilities. Furthermore, the government has traditionally been short of officials who were generally familiar with rural conditions and who were able to act in accordance with the peculiar circumstances of a locality. The process of modernization thus helped to create that awkward and typically Korean kind of commune we have today. In the case of Changjwa-ri the rise of the commune finally produced a long catalogue of duties to be borne by the village, but no rights which the villagers could successfully enforce against a reluctant government.

At the same time, it should be noted that the conditions described above have not altogether destroyed village solidarity, although they tend to dissolve a community as *Dorfgenossenschaft* in an economic and legal sense. Changjwa-ri offers some examples of such residual collective behaviour under commune conditions. Instead of concentrating on the inner village life and of regulating the use and preservation of jointly held property, such behaviour is oriented towards the world outside the village and should primarily be viewed as a kind of collective shelter under which the villagers can go into hiding in order to protect themselves from potentially excessive demands.[3] Some of these devices

---

[3] Such motives for community identification are also attested by Dr. Willard D. Keim. Vid. Willard D. Keim, "A Survey of Two Korean Villages to Determine the Attitudinal Aspects of Progressiveness", *Journal of Korean Affairs/Han'guk munje,* ed. Young Hoon Kang, vol. V, no. 3, Silver Springs/Maryl.: 1975, p. 11.

will be discussed in the chapter on village administration, some in the present one. Most of the measures taken by the village can claim a long tradition of their own. Although the shaping of the communes has gained considerable momentum in recent decades as part of the modernization process, their origin is not at all of a recent date, neither are the counter-measures of the rural populace. It will be sufficient to recall to mind that the emergence of *i* divisions was motivated by the desire of the government to obtain better control over the population in the countryside. The villages have been communities and communes from their very beginning. The collective behaviour on the commune level illustrates how a mode of organization originating in the community sphere of village life has been transferred to the commune level, and how both levels have inextricably fused with each other. The collective behaviour thus both results from, and revitalizes, the spirit of solidarity even at a time which does not favour the flourishing of communities. Here again, however, one should not generalize from the case of Changjwa-ri. Yet, it is easy to imagine that solidarity in commune affairs can only grow on community solidarity, which in turn requires over-all favourable village conditions not always met with in Korea.

As the Korean commune is a government-determined affair, an inquiry into the nature of the village commune will lead us right to the core of the relationship between government and village. A last word of warning seems to be in place here, however. The preceding remarks may all too easily suggest the idea of an absolute antagonism prevailing in the relationship between village and government. An oppressive and insensitive government appears to be opposed to an egalitarian and harmonious village community. In fact, neither is the village community an egalitarian and harmonious society, nor are government measures altogether repressive. There has been the opportunity above to comment on the limitations of the community. The community makes sense to the wealthier peasants only, whose fields and forests are so large that they cannot be guarded and tilled by the men of a single household. The people whose fields are smaller can well do without a formal community, and, except in matters of forestry, they can well remain indifferent towards it or may even feel oppressed by it, for instance, when they are summoned to take part in *ullyŏk*. On the other hand, certain government-inspired innovations are known to create greater integration than the village community does. With regard to Changjwa-ri, it suffices to mention the primary school. Dr. Brandt has convincingly argued that the primary school in his village has greatly contributed to the spread of an egalitarian community ethic,[4] and the same may be assumed to be true in the case of Changjwa-ri. What really causes trouble in such ventures is neither the government initiative nor the innovation itself, but the financing and maintenance of such new institutions. The self-protective measures of the

---

[4] Vid. Brandt, *A Korean Village,* pp. 91, 150.

villagers are often only meant to solve problems of that order, and not to simply undermine government actions.

The Preponderance of Duties

The "guidance and superintendence by government and other public offices" seems to be omnipresent at Changjwa-ri.[5] Government surveillance means much more than light-handed and informal watching of what happens in the village. The government authorities may request the convention of village assemblies, and such a request may cancel all the regulations concerning the standing orders of such meetings. This can mean significant interference with the innermost village affairs. In spite of such a potentially heavy preponderance of government initiatives in village affairs, the authors of the *Regulations of Changjwa-ri* tried to portray the relationship between the village and the government as being based on reciprocity. Loyalty towards government instructions and easy acceptance of government slogans are apparently conceived of as repayments for benefits allegedly received from the government authorities. The key term here is "loyal service to the country", implying such things as commitment to the attempts to restore the unity of the national territory and to its defence, at making the national holidays a concern of the family, and at promoting the spirit of democracy.[6] Yet, we do not learn much about the government's commitments to the villagers in this alleged relationship of reciprocity. The only benefits from the government side which occasionally trickle through to the villagers are the so-called supplies. They comprise things which cannot be bought by the villagers for lack of cash, or which are otherwise given to them as a government grant to promote agriculture, such as crude oil for lamps or fertilizers. These goods are given to the village for distribution among the households.[7] However, with a market economy developing, the provision of such goods eventually becomes meaningless, and thus even that slight token of reciprocity on the government side loses its importance.

We could dismiss the declarations of loyalty and submissiveness as mere rhetoric, as we have done before with so many other provisions in the *Regula-*

---

[5] Vid. Arts. 1, 4, 6(6), 12, 15, 17(2).

[6] The term translated here as "loyal service to the country" is *po kuk* 報國 in the *Regulations,* literally meaning "to repay to the country in reciprocity for what has been received before". Professor Dr. Yang Lien-sheng 楊聯陞 has written an instructive article on *po* (Chin. *pao*) as a concept determining social relations among individuals in China. The occurences of the term in the *Regulations of Changjwa-ri* and in Yi dynasty literature serve as an excellent example to illustrate the survival of the concept and its transfer to non-individual relations.

Vid. *Sŏngho sasŏl,* "Insa mun" (= vol. 1, pp. 616s); Lien-sheng Yang, "The Concept of *Pao* as a Basis for Social Relations in China", *Chinese Thought and Institutions,* ed. John K. Fairbank, Chicago: 1957, pp. 291-309; Arts. 1(6), 6(1,4,5,10).

[7] Vid. Arts. 27, 31-33; Document XIII.9(b,c), 14(b), 15(c), 22(b).

tions, if the same kind of unilateral obligation, the same kind of imbalance in duties, did not prevail in the more matter-of-fact dealings as well. When reviewing the details of the commune activities, we shall notice that all the duties lie with the village and none with the government. There is not only no material compensation for duties fulfilled, but also no political one. It is interesting to observe that the villages in Korea are not represented on the decision-making bodies of the lower administrative divisions. The laws of the Republic of Korea do not provide for any such participation and representation,[8] and the *Regulations of Changjwa-ri* do not lay claim to them. When representatives of the village travel to the county seat, they mostly do so in response to a summons from the side of the county office. They may occasionally even state their own ideas and make their own suggestions, but there is no legal or other guarantee that their opinions will really be taken into account.

Yet, it would mean an over-simplification of things, if we regarded the imbalance of duties as a mere manifestation of oppression and exploitation. The fulfilment of many of the duties imposed on the village is not only to the advantage of the government and government-inspired policies, but also to that of the village. First among such duties is the maintenance of Ch'ŏnghae School. The costs associated with it are a considerable burden to the villagers. It is easy to understand that the so-called school equipment costs — or education taxes, as they are once called — figure as a category of their own besides the village expenses, *i. e.* the costs spent on community purposes in the narrower sense, and the miscellaneous fees.[9] The pattern of having some of the school expenses covered by the immediate beneficiaries of a school, instead of charging the public treasury with the whole of the costs, is a normal and legal one in Korea. It is stipulated in the laws that the costs of a school are to be covered in part by contributions from the public treasury, from the household of the self-administrative corporation concerned, from any sources of income of the school itself, and in part from so-called special dues (*t'ŭkpyŏl pugwagŭm* 特 別 賦 課 金), from fees charged to individuals (*susuryo* 手 數 料), and from charges for the use of public facilities (*sayongnyo*). The latter have all to be paid by the people concerned. These various incomes are to cover the costs of the maintenance of the school building and other facilities associated with it, whereas the salaries for the teachers, at least those for primary school teachers, are paid by the government.[10] What school expenses really mean to the villagers

[8] Vid. Appendix 1 of this study.
[9] Vid. Arts. 11, 17(5); Document XIII.19(d).
[10] Vid. *Kyoyuk pŏp* 教育法 , Arts. 68s.
The regulations referred to are amendments from the years 1963 and 1968 of the original law, promulgated in 1949. The provisions thus cover only part of the period under discussion here. Yet, the basic principles of the operation of primary schools in Korea have been largely the same since even before the year 1963. Unfortunately, the present author was not in a position to provide the older versions of the Law on Education at short notice.

will immediately become evident if we take into consideration that the fees and charges may be raised upon a simple payment notice (*nabip kojisŏ*　納 入 告 知 書), which may be issued by the authorities at any time and without previous consultation with the people concerned. Only the so-called special dues are subject to long-term legislation.[11] The school expenses are not only comparatively high, but may strike the villagers like a bolt from the blue and thus add considerably to their financial troubles. Any further expenses associated with the maintenance of the school tend to cause resistance among the villagers. For instance, in 1962, it seems to have been very hard to raise the money for the costs of the windows and doors of the new school building and for the celebration of its opening. In order to get the debts paid, the village committee finally had to resort to coercion by threatening those who were remiss in paying with the cancellation of fertilizer supplies.[12]

Two other facilities should be mentioned here. They, too, owe their existence to large-scale government initiative, but are meant to serve the common weal of the village, and thus have to be maintained, partially or entirely, by the village commune. One of them is a water storage reservoir, the accounts of which have to be settled by the village committee. The other is a health centre, established on the premises of Ch'ŏnghae School in 1958. The latter caused much financial trouble to the village commune, because in 1961, a decision had to be taken to cover the deficiency caused by its maintenance.[13]

Another item among the commune tasks is commune labour. As has already been said in the chapter dealing with the community, the term does not mean collective work in the fields or any other kind of collective farm and repair work which the village community has to decide upon. Like the operation and financing of primary schools, commune labour as a commune undertaking is subject to national law and is by no means left to the decision of the village. According to law, the decisions on the kind and time of commune labour rest with the assemblies of the superior self-administrative corporations. Instead of personally participating in commune labour, an individual may pay a certain amount of money or send another person to replace him. The legislator has allowed the local authorities to either summon the whole of the population of a locality or only parts of it, lest injustice should be created.[14] For all practical matters, commune labour in Changjwa-ri means the repair of roads. This includes repair and maintenance both of the narrow paths running through the

---

[11] Vid. *Chibang chach'i pŏp*　地 方 自 治 法, Art. 128; *Chibang chach'i pŏp sihaengnyŏng* 施 行 令, Art. 51.

[12] Vid. Document XIII.22(b).

[13] Vid. Document XIII.5(f), 16(b), 19(c).

[14] Vid. *Chibang chach'i pŏp,* Arts. 19(4), 129; *Chibang chach'i pŏp sihaengnyŏng,* Arts. 52, 54.

rice-fields of the village and of the large road running through the village and linking it with the township of Wan-do and the mainland.[15]

None among the tasks mentioned so far offers much opportunity for official abuse, at least not in theory, and it would mean jumping to conclusions, if we were simply to discredit the whole system as exploitation. It would require a lot of conivance among quite a number of officials and other people, before long-term profiteering from the money and the work of the simple folks could be achieved. This does not mean that within such a relationship between government and commune embezzlement and other kinds of abuses cannot occur at all. The danger is imminent, but the reproach of corruption cannot solely be based on the pattern as such, but has to be proved in any single instance.

This matter is somewhat different when it comes to the notorious miscellaneous fees.[16] This term covers the third large category of village expenses besides village expenses in the narrower sense, *i. e.* community expenses, and school equipment expenses. Miscellaneous fees can be raised by the authorities on any occasion. There is neither a strict legal base to this habit nor any legal definition of what miscellaneous fees are to be like, and this vagueness of the term suggests various ways of abuse. Anyway, the miscellaneous fees are a heavy and always unexpected burden on the shoulders of the villagers, and this is the reason why all that has to be regarded as miscellaneous fees appears as extraordinary expenses in the documents. On various occasions, the protocols of the meetings of the village committee give us some idea of what has to be understood by miscellaneous fees in Changjwa-ri. Most of them are meant to cover the expenses caused by entertaining officials and other authorities visiting the village.[17] Thus, the protocols list expenses "for receptions in connection with administrative affairs" or "for giving receptions to the heads of government organs".[18] Likewise, receptions had to be given for those who came to the place for "cleaning work", which means desinfection, or who conducted smallpox vaccinations, or drafted population surveys.[19] Reimbursement to be paid to village representatives who had spent money on trips to the county seat is practically of the same order.[20] The military putsch of 1961 had its

[15] Vid. Art. 8(1); Document XIII.2(c), 4(d), 17(b), 19(f).

[16] Vid. Arts. 6(6), 11, 17(2), 20, 27(8).

[17] It has been an old habit in Korea to offer food and drink, even sleeping-places, horses, and money to such official visitors. Village codes from the end of the last century show that the demands of visiting officials had become such a nuisance to the village economy that the village decided to put an end to the malpractice and therefore decided what should be given to the visitors in future times and what not. This malpractice thus became the incentive to draft a village code.

Vid. Gillet, "The Village Gilds of Old Korea", pp. 31s, 42, 43.

[18] Vid. Document XIII.4(d), 21(b).

[19] Vid. Document XIII.4(d), 14(a).

[20] Vid. Document XIII.4(d), 21(b).

faint repercussions even at Changjwa-ri, for in April of that year, some money went into the support of a military police protection society.[21] A rather interesting item figures somewhat bashfully as "allotments in election time". This means money which was given — and probably had to be given — to somebody who ran as a candidate in some election in 1956, as an advance for future benefits promised to be turned to the village in the case of a successful campaign.[22]

Again, there is no proof for the assumption that these levies of miscellaneous fees brought the village near to the verge of economic ruin. The author of this study did not collect any data which could substantiate such a view. He does not even want to imply that things are or were bad in Changjwa-ri. Again, it must be emphasized that the reader should become aware of the possibilities of harmful inroads on village life, in order to understand the general character of the relationship between government and commune. It is for this purpose that the character of miscellaneous fees and other village expenses had to be discussed here.

An Evaluation in Historical Perspective

It is highly interesting to observe what the villagers think about the various contributions and how they actually discharge themselves of the commune tasks. Basically, both the payments of money and the contributions in kind and work are done individually. There is no legal provision calling for corporate village taxes or for villages to act as divisions conducive to the collection of taxes and other fees, or to be responsible for mobilizing commune labour corps. Nevertheless, the villagers in a way consider the sums of individual tax debts as collective village debts. Negligence in payment is not simply an individual fault, but a defilement of the name of the village, and it is regarded as a violation of the village regulations. In one case, it even appears that the taxes of the villagers were really considered to be corporate village taxes to be paid from the village fund.[23] In order to raise the money needed for the establishment of a health centre, it was decided in 1958 to collect an average five *toe* of grain from each household, which was to be hired out for rent. The implication is that the rent was to be used for the establishment of the centre.[24]

The examples given above illustrate how community principles have been transferred to the commune level. The community tenets postulating that everybody has to stand security for everybody else and that rights and duties are

[21] Vid. Document XIII.19(b).
[22] Vid. Document XIII.4(d).
[23] Vid. Arts. 6(6), 27(8); Document XIII.14(a).
[24] Vid. Document XIII.16(b).

to be shared on a footing of equality and equity has thus tinted many of the commune actions. This transfer is by no means of a recent date, and it is a rewarding task to follow its traces back into history, even if the present state of scholarship does not allow for much insight yet.

When looking for earlier examples of collective discharge of debts, we find the habit of freeing oneself from military service by supplying a certain quantity of cotton. This habit is said to have been particularly popular in the latter part of the Yi period. People seem to have resorted to this device to free themselves from other kinds of services as well. It is believed that in order to achieve prompt payment people concluded agreements between each other to jointly raise the quantity of goods and have it ready when it was one of their group's turn to pay. Professor Hatada Takashi 旗 田 巍 holds that this habit led to the formation of *kye*-type associations on the village level called military cotton associations (*kunbogye* 軍 布 契). He even views them as the models of all other kinds of voluntary associations of the *kye* type. Professor Kim Samsu disagrees with him on the latter point, but otherwise acknowledges the existence and importance of such associations. Curiously enough, both scholars provide ample evidence of payments made in cotton to free the payer from military service, but neither of them produces textual evidence of mutual benefit associations which might have served as instruments for providing that cotton.[25] Supposing that such associations — or at least the habit of collective payment as such — did exist, we could take them as early proof of the principle which, in Changjwa-ri, underlies the attitude towards payment: several people unite to extend help to someone of their number and to obtain help in return.

The procedure followed in financing the health centre is also modelled upon precedents from the Yi period. It differs in no way from the manner followed by those mutual benefit associations which raised the means required for the pursuit of their aims by hiring out grain and by acquiring the facilities wanted from the rent.[26]

The collective discharge of commune work on the village level can also claim a long tradition. It was practised in the so-called model and immigrant villages during the period of Japanese rule in Korea, from where it was transmitted to Changjwa-ri. But it is likely to have already been practised during the Yi period,

---

[25] A record of a union which appears to be close in nature to the alleged military cotton associations can be found in the writing of Sunam An Chŏngbok 順 庵 安 鼎 福 (1712—1791). That passage deals with the collective discharge of the duty to provide horses. Vid. *Sunam ch'ongsŏ*, k. 16.35b.7-36b.4, 38b.9-44b.2 (= vol. 1, pp. 365, 366-369); W. R. Carles, *Life in Corea*, with illustrations and maps, London: 1888, p. 262; "Kei", comp. Hatada Takashi, *Seikai dai hyakka jiten*, ed. Shimonaka Kuniyoshi, vol. 7, Tōkyō: Heibonsha, 1968, pp. 110s; *Han'guk sahoe kyŏngje sa yŏn'gu*, comp. Kim Samsu, pp. 92-97, 333-336.

[26] 17 out of 66 codes of Yi times associations explicitly provide for hiring out money or grain for interest to finance the pursuits of the associations.

although there is almost no direct textual evidence to it.[27] During the Yi period, work on roads had its place within the system of *corvée* labour which most subjects owed to the monarchy, besides perhaps other services in the armed forces, or services due to somebody's professional skills.[28] The interesting point is that the conscription unit for this kind of labour service was the household, and not the village. Except for a short summary of tasks in the *Enlarged References to Documents* (*Chŭngbo munhŏn pigo* 增 補 文 獻 備 考), pertaining to early conditions of the wards (*pang* 坊) of the capital only, the construction of roads and bridges nowhere in government documents occurs as a collective village duty. The entry on ward work (*pangyŏk* 坊 役) in the *Rules and Precedents from the Six Statutes* (*Yukchŏn chorye* 六 典 條 例) seems to deal with conditions in the capital only. Besides, it refers to military duties and not to construction work. What Dr. Yi Chongha describes as ward work again is work imposed on the inhabitants of capital areas only and does not concern the bulk of the population of Korea.[29] Even documents which have originated from within the rural populace itself are largely silent on this matter. Hitherto, the present author has found only one literary proof of a concept of village commune work in former times. In a village code of unknown date it is said that those who turn against the fundamental virtues of village life will be excluded from the privileges of the village community, and will be condemned to do "village work" (*iyŏk* 里 役). It is not said what this work is like, but we may conclude that it is mean labour for the whole of the village. Again, this is not commune labour in the sense the term is employed in Changjwa-ri, because it is meant as a punishment.[30] Likewise, the term *riyaku* 里役 employed by Professor Tagawa Kōzō 田 川 孝 三 does not mean village commune labour

---

[27] There is an interesting remark made by Professor Yang Hoesu saying that the construction and repair of roads was considered a "beautiful custom" (*mip'ung* 美風) under Japanese rule. This corroborates an observation made earlier in this study, viz. that such terms in village codes of the period of Japanese occupation are often euphemisms meant to camouflage very unpleasant facts. This usage of *mip'ung* throws an interesting light on similar terms in the *Regulations of Changjwa-ri*.

Vid. Carles, *Life in Corea*, p. 180; Gillet, "The Village Gilds of Old Korea", p. 33; *CS*, vol. 1, pp. 74s, vol. 2, pp. 34, 168s, 188, 197, 209 (Art. 6.4), 213, 238; *Han'guk nongch'on tapsagi*, comp. Suzuki Eitarō, pp. 57, 64; *Han'guk nongch'onŭi ch'ollak kujo*, comp. Yang Hoesu, pp. 400 (note), 431s, 435s; Shin, "The *Kye*", p. 187; Arts. 1, 9.

[28] This labour service in its proper sense is called *yoyŏk* 徭役 by Professor Dr. Yi Chongha 李 鍾 河 . The term does not entirely coincide with the nomenclature of the sources, for there appear other words besides *yoyŏk*, meaning the same thing. *Yoyŏk* has been turned into a generic name to be used for scholarly purposes by Dr. Yi.

Vid. *Chosŏn wangjoŭi nodong pŏpche*, comp. Yi Chongha, Seoul: Pagyŏngsa, 1969, pp. 134-140.

[29] Vid. *Chŭngbo munhŏn pigo*, k. 224.9b8-10b.4 (= vol. 3, p. 616); *Yukchŏn chorye*, Hojŏn p'yŏn, pp. 431s; *Chosŏn wangjoŭi nodong pŏpche*, comp. Yi Chongha, pp. 316-330.

[30] Vid. *Tonghŏn choyak*, [p. 4a-b].

as envisaged here, but is a word which is used by him to circumscribe all village office holders and which should therefore be read *riyaku*.[31] In spite of the almost total silence of the written sources on the construction of roads as village work, this work must have been a widespread practice in the villages of Yi dynasty Korea. It appears once as an item in a comprehensive programme of rural activities, dating from the year 1675. Part of this catalogue is a reaffirmation of earlier government laws on the subject, part of it — in particular the passage where the remark on the roads is found — rather sounds like a recognition by the government of habits which have sprung from the populace itself and are now "legalized" as useful or inevitable practices.[32] Another testimony of a former habit of accomplishing the construction and repair of roads as a village commune labour is found in oral literary tradition. In a version of the puppet show *Play of the Marionette Bride* (*Kkoktu kaksi kŭk* [*norŭm*] 꼭 두 각 시 劇 [노름]), which certainly dates from the Yi period, one of the male protagonists appears as the — incompetent and lazy — organizer of road construction work in his village.[33] We may therefore conclude that village commune labour as work on roads is very likely to have been a standing practice in Yi times and as such has survived until the modern era. Modern legislation in this matter appears to be a continuation of that old custom. We may further conclude that this particular commune undertaking had its origin not in government law, but in the minds of the villagers themselves.

The continuous transfer of community behaviour to the commune level is not a "natural" affair. Yet, it can be assumed to have already occurred in earlier times. The existence of *i* preceded any effect of a community ethic within them. As we know, the *i* were divisions created by the government, and they were meant as instruments of local control. On the other hand, the mutual benefit associations of those days, in which much of the collective village behaviour described in this chapter had its origin, cut right across the borders of human settlements. As far as we can tell from the textual evidence available at present, the vast majority of those mutual benefit associations was organized along the lines of kin and age-peerage. Only about twenty of the association regulations from the Yi period out of an odd eighty available to the present author pertain to mutual benefit associations organized on the village level. And even with regard

---

[31] If not paid for as in Changjwa-ri, holding a village office may well be considered to be a burden, and thus, filling a village office is close in character to *yŏk* as a punishment. By the morphophoneme *yŏk* in the name of the village office holders' work in Changjwa-ri, that work is suggested to be akin to the burdensome commune labour, which carries the same *yŏk* in its name.
    Vid. *Richō kōnōsei no kenkyū*, comp. Tagawa Kōzō, Tōyō bunko ronso, ed. Tōyō bunko, no. 47, Tōkyō: 1964, pp. 732, 733, 738; Document XIII. 4(b), 9(a), 15(c), 16(a).
[32] Vid. *CWS: Sukchong sillok*, k. 4.50a.1-4 (= vol. 38, p. 304 — November 13th, 1675).
[33] Vid. *Han'guk kamyŏn'gŭk*, comp. Yi Tuhyŏn, pp. 416s (act 9).

to those twenty texts, we cannot be sure whether the territorial and social base of the few associations really was identical with the *i*. In other words, the character of the *i* as instruments of control and the development of mutual benefit associations did not converge in the beginning. But somehow, association tenets encroached upon the doings of at least some villages and started determining not only their actions as communities, but also their modes of fulfilling government-initiated commune tasks. We do not know anything about the reasons, the time, and the stages of the convergence; illumination of it will remain one of the main tasks of future inquiries into the legal and social history of Korea.

There have already been several occasions in this study to emphasize that village integration cannot be taken for granted. This chapter provides another one. In the light of the above considerations, the degree of convergence achieved at Changjwa-ri should again better be viewed as an exception rather than as a rule. However, even the rather modest degree of integration shows that the opposition of community and commune is only to be used as a mental device in analysis, and not to be regarded as an appropriate description of the real modes of conduct of village affairs. As far as practical village life is concerned, the intimate link between the two levels brings to light an embarrassing ambiguity. For the more the villagers are accustomed to a disciplined response to the summons of their village fellows, and the more elaborate their means are of smoothly fulfilling their commune duties, the easier it is for the government officials to get the village to do what they want to have done. A well-organized village community may thus be the very cause for the final loss of the little amount of autonomy it has managed to preserve.

CHAPTER 9: THE CRIMINAL JURISDICTION OF THE VILLAGE

In an analysis of village law, we cannot do without throwing a side-glance at that record of offences and punishments which can be called the criminal law of the village. Trifling as many of the wrongdoings and sanctions may be, they deserve our full attention, because the fact that they frequently occur in the documents provides us with another key to the comprehension of general village conditions and village law. Amidst the many curtailments of that little village autonomy that may have been enjoyed, and amidst an increase in number of those village affairs which have come to be determined from outside the village, the criminal jurisdiction of the village seems to stand out as an imperturbable token of its autonomy. Autonomous criminal jurisdiction on the village level is of an older date in Korea, and if there is anything in the village code of Changjwa-ri which we tend to rate as customary law, it would be its criminal regulations. The village tradition of threatening misbehaviour with punishment is quite alive, and therefore § 7 of the *Regulations*, which contains the criminal law of the village, is one of the few parts of the village code which does not seem to be a dead letter. Such a state of things is surprising at first sight, and it calls for an explanation of the reasons why the criminal jurisdiction of the village survives under conditions which are not favourable to village autonomy.

The arrangement of the articles of § 7 of the *Regulations* is determined by the degree of severity of the punishments to be meted out, and not by the character of the offences. The mildest punishment is a reprimand. If somebody does not comply with the reprimands, he has to face a cut in supplies.[1] Next in severity is the collection of agricultural products of the season worth the pay of one day of labour. More severe is the confiscation of commodities and the collection of grain worth twice the pay of a day of labour. If the offender fails to pay in due time, collection will be made by force in both cases.[2] A variation of this kind of punishment is the confiscation of the illegally acquired goods and the subsequent filing of charges against the offenders with the government authorities, if the mischief concerns the woodlands.[3] As to the fourth level, the severest one, the authors of the *Regulations* provided for the suspension of supplies and for the refusal of seaweed lots and of the collection of forest

---

[1] Vid. Art. 27.

[2] Vid. Arts. 28s.

According to information gathered in 1973, the payment of the fines has come to be made in money instead of in kind. The amounts correspond to the wages to be paid to farm labourers and have been set at W 500 for men and W 300 for women.

[3] Vid. Art. 30.

products.[4] Another kind of punishment, *viz.* that of cutting the allowances to be given to the village office-holders, is beyond the normal penal code, because it does not affect ordinary villagers.

There are four categories of offences. The first one comprises a series of offences against morals and decency, such as defilement of the name of the village by indecent behaviour, "intoxication" through self-indulgence, disregard of "human rights", neglect of propriety by leaving the house without putting on outer garments, and disregard of the necessity to "protect" the native place. All these offences are listed under the heading of the severest punishment.[5] Next comes disregard for village enterprises, manifested by absence from village meetings and from commune labour, and harm done to the sacred places of the village and other jointly held property.[6] The third category comprises damages done to the economic equilibrium of the village, either by trying to gain undue individual profit, or by doing harm to other people's property, such as theft or uninvited participation in wedding and mourning ceremonies.[7] The fourth category of offences includes damages done to the government, either by being remiss in the payment of taxes and miscellaneous fees, or by illegally felling young trees in province-owned forests.[8]

These catalogues of offences and punishments are far from being final. Evidence from the protocols of village meetings proves that they are rather taken as guide-lines allowing for the determination of new offences and punishments, when conditions require to do so. The records of offences and punishments have thus changed considerably in the course of years. Actions became punishable which nowhere in the *Regulations* were recorded as offences, whereas most of the offences listed in the *Regulations* are never heard of again in later years. The only exceptions to this rule are four provisions for punishment in connection with damage done to the forests, which again proves how important a rank matters of forestry occupy in the economy and in the minds of the villagers.[9] The series of new legislation started in 1957 with a provision forbidding the raising of goats and urging the villagers to dispose of their animals.[10] In the same year, distillation of liquor was forbidden, and so was the selling of bread and cakes within the village, and the owning of tobacco.[11] In an effort to enhance the prestige of the *Regulations* in 1959, violation of the village code was declared an offence, in a very general manner though.[12] Undutiful

---

[4]   Vid. Art. 31.
[5]   Vid. Art. 27(1-4,9).
[6]   Vid. Arts. 28, 29(2).
[7]   Vid. Arts. 27(5-7), 28(4), 29(1,3), 31.
[8]   Vid. Arts. 27(8), 30.
[9]   Vid. Document XIII.18(c), 20(a-c).
[10] Vid. Document XIII.9(b).
[11] Vid. Document XIII.9(c), 14(b).
[12] Vid. Document XIII.18(b).

behaviour in limited ventures was also threatened with punishment. Thus, it was stipulated in 1962 that all who were entitled to receive supplies of fertilizers, but had not paid their shares of the window and door costs of Ch'ŏnghae School and of the costs resulting from the celebrations of the opening of the new building, should be deprived of their supplies, until they had paid their dues.[13]

It is interesting to observe that the actual punishments the villagers were threatened with are all very close to those of the severest kind as stipulated in Art. 31 of the *Regulations*. For instance, the punishment for raising goats is not just a simple reprimand or a levy of a penalty in kind, but the suspension of fertilizers and other goods for one year, although the raising of goats as an offence is similar in nature to that of the unauthorized raising of rabbits and sheep, or the illegal grazing of cattle dealt with in Arts. 27(5) and 28(4). Distilling liquor is to be punished by the confiscation of tools and goods, the prohibition of growing seaweed, and again the cancellation of supplies for one year. The punishment for this offence, like that for trading within the village and for owning tobacco, is reduced only one year later, by providing for a cancellation of supplies and the right to fishery. The severest punishments are the suspension of supplies and the cancellation of rights to seaweed cultivation and fishery, but expulsion from the village, too, is provided for in one instance.[14] It is only in cases of offence against forestry rights that the punishments envisaged in the protocols are more or less the same as those provided for in the *Regulations*.

Although the record of offences which can be abstracted from the protocols of the village meetings differs in detail from the record in the *Regulations*, the incentives behind the criminal jurisdiction are the same over all the years. The obvious motive behind all of the penal jurisdiction is the avoidance of wastefulness, the commitment of the villagers to economic innovation, and the strict observation of the rules concerning forestry. The criminal code of Changjwa-ri betrays a commitment to modernization and village integration, and its authors did not hesitate to threaten the people with punishments which in most cases are more severe than those originally envisaged, in order to enforce the basic ideas. This preoccupation with matters of economy and village integration makes the provisions calling for observation of decency and morals a subordinate affair. This part of the criminal code heavily relies on exigencies which we first encountered in older village rules, particularly in those of the *tonggye* type. Judging from the few texts available, we can say that most of those provisions are hardly more than exhortations to preserve harmonious relations among neighbours, to show deference to elders, and to avoid violence. Rather than determining single offences in a distinct manner, those older village codes

[13] Vid. Document XIII.22(b).
[14] Vid. Document XIII.18(b).

conjure up an atmosphere of peace and harmony. If they ever enumerate distinct offences, they mostly mention disturbances caused by drunkards, oppression of the weak and young, fighting, quarrels among friends and brothers, and lack of respect for the old people.[15] That part of the criminal code of Changjwa-ri that does not deal with strictly economic matters certainly is a reminiscence of those well-worn commands and prohibitions. Moreover, it seems that the villagers' concept of their village as being under its own jurisdiction goes back to those earliers codes. However, the precise and exacting commands which are proven to be the real core of the village criminal jurisdiction by both the *Regulations* and the protocols derive from concepts of village order for which we have to search in the period of Japanese rule in Korea.

In the light of such observations, we have to ask ourselves in what sense, if any, the criminal code of Changjwa-ri can be regarded as true village law. It certainly is village law in the sense that it is related to the more or less unique conditions of a single village. Furthermore, it is village law, because it is applied to the residents of that village.[16] The exemption of "employees", *i. e.* farm labourers who continuously reside at Changjwa-ri and form "enclosed families", and of the old and young people in the households does not really invalidate it as village law. The exemption pertains to "family conduct" only, for which the household heads are held responsible instead of the actual offender. Likewise, it is a lessor of a house or room, and not an offending lessee, who is held responsible in cases of offence committed by the lessee.[17] These rules read like an attempt at preserving the jurisdiction, limited as it may be, of the patriarchal household heads and at having the village law remain outside the main gates of the houses, as it were. For otherwise, the household heads might not have acquiesced to a village law and might have rather regarded it as too severe a menace to the sway they hold over their houses and kin. Rather than weaken the penal code of the village, provisions like those quoted in the last sentence testify to its strength, which seems to have been on the verge of encroaching even upon the vested interests of household heads. Moreover, the penal code of Changjwa-ri is village law even in the sense that it is adjudicated by a village "court", *viz.* the village committee.[18] To comprehend the meaning of such an order of things, we only need to refer to what Dr. Bader writes about village jurisdiction in medieval Germany, where it could hardly evade the participation of some local overlord.[19] If we transferred that state of things to

---

[15] Vid. *Hongch'ŏn Sŏmyŏn Kuŏm-ni chŭk Yondong Yun pansŏ t'aek iban'gye ch'ŏ,* [p. 7]; *Regulations of the Tai Tong Kei in Kwang Choo,* in Gillet, "The Village Gilds of Old Korea", pp. 14s; *Regulations Used in the Ye Choong Kei and By-Laws,* in Gillet, *op. cit.,* pp. 17, 24s; Gillet, *op. cit.,* pp. 29s, 41.

[16] Vid. Arts. 1s.

[17] Vid. Arts. 32s.

[18] Vid. Art. 27.

[19] Vid. Bader, *Dorfgenossenschaft und Dorfgemeinde,* pp. 350s.

Changjwa-ri, we would have to imagine *e.g.* the county head of Wan-do taking part in sessions of the village court and passing sentences in village quarrels. Nothing of this kind seems to have happened at Changjwa-ri, and this fact further accounts for a considerable degree of independence in legal affairs. The villagers consciously tried not to involve the authorities at all. This becomes obvious from documents dealing with forestry, the nature of which does not tolerate complete official abstention. Yet, even here, the villagers will first try to settle matters among themselves, and it is only after an offender has refused to obey the judgments passed by his village fellows that they will hand him over to the authorities or to the individual owner of woodland.[20]

Misgivings as to the autonomy of village jurisdiction result from the fact that some provisions are related to affairs in which the government, and not the village, must have a main interest, such as dutiful taxpaying and the prohibition of felling trees in province-owned forests.[21] Moreover, the continuity itself of criminal jurisdiction in Changjwa-ri is a surprising phenomenon. Of course, we cannot tell from the documents whether any of the prohibitions and punishments were ever applied on a large scale, and if so, whether they struck the offender in as uncomprimising a manner as is provided for in the code. Yet, it is the determination to do so which counts. This determination is in sharp contrast to what Dr. Brandt reports from his Sŏkp'o. There, the peasants are utterly reluctant to resort to regulations and open charges when they have to deal with an offender. Nobody would risk gaining an enemy by insisting on laws. Safeguarding of personal relations is more appreciated than emphasis on village welfare, the idea of fairness, or operation in accordance with rules. Unanimity, even if it takes some time to achieve it, is preferred to any kind of coercion and division. According to Dr. Brandt, ". . . an impersonal formal system of justice with universal rules seemed highly immoral."[22] There is sufficient reason to believe that the basic values upheld at Changjwa-ri do not differ from those of Dr. Brandt's village. They are intimately associated with the conditions of a small, self-supporting economy, of which Changjwa-ri for most of the time under discussion here is just one more example. We have had several occasions to point out the effects of a community spirit which requires consent rather than division, accomodation rather than self-assertion. Therefore, the repeated emphasis on prohibitions and punishments sounds somewhat incredible.

These considerations, together with the emphasis on concerted action in economic dealings, provide us with the clue to the answer to our initial question as to why the criminal jurisdiction of Changjwa-ri could last as a seemingly autonomous affair. The answer is simply that it is no autonomous affair, or at least, that large parts of it are not. We have recognized traces of an inveterate

[20] Vid. Art. 30; Document XIII.18(c), 20(a,b).
[21] Vid. Arts. 27(8), 30.
[22] Vid. Brandt, *A Korean Village,* pp. 145, 161-163, 197-201.

desire to maintain the peace of the village, to promote harmony among its inhabitants, to care for the forests, and to handle village matters among the villagers themselves, all of which are more manifestations of a community ethic. But we have equally well recognized the propagation of values which transcend the peculiar concerns of a single village, or which do not automatically follow from the ways of village life. Suffice it here to call to mind the provisions concerning taxpaying or the exhortations to modernization and co-ordination of village economy. It appears that some presumably old habits have been transferred to serve ends which are not in the immediate interest of the village, or which at least were not devised by the villagers themselves. In concept, this transformation goes back to the period of Japanese occupation, even if its actual manifestation at Changjwa-ri is of a later date. In this regard, the criminal jurisdiction is placed mid-way between the concerns of a community and those of a commune. These conditions run exactly parallel with those which we have already observed with regard to the village economy. The frequency with which prohibitions and punishments are recorded in the documents allows the conclusion that a penal code must have appeared as a particularly suitable instrument for the imposition of new ends on village life and for the transformation of the village. This is the reason why the authorities tolerated and probably even promoted a village code which otherwise was illegal by the standards of modern Korean government law. The real limitations of autonomy are not undone by the large scope of action which seems to have been left to the village in matters of legal "technicalities", such as the formulation of rules and adjudication. Those responsible for the transformation seem to have been quite confident that things would take the course they wanted them to take, even if they did not seriously interfere. The only question is whether this confidence was based on the readiness of the villagers to absorb the new trends or on their readiness to submit to any authority, either from within the village or from without.

CHAPTER 10: THE VILLAGE GOVERNMENT

The Futility of the Formal Lay-Out

Having discussed the "inner organization" of the village, *i. e.* the material rights of the households, individuals, and corporations, and the corporate rights by which the various groupings are characterized, a few words have to be said about the "outer organization", *i. e.* the persons who see to it that these rights are observed in a proper way, and about the decision-making institutions. According to the *Regulations of Changjwa-ri*, decision on village affairs and representation of the village are entrusted to a general assembly of the inhabitants, a village committee, and a "board of executives", consisting of the village head, the village clerk, and the forest ranger. Thus it seems as if the village was governed by two parliamentary chambers to which a board of executives was made responsible.

However, the authors of the *Regulations* do not seem to have had much faith in the viability of such a system, because they did not devote much space and attention to the details of the operation of those bodies. The carelessness with which the formal lay-out of the village government is treated and the limitations in competence of the formal decision-making bodies soon become evident from the provisions regarding the general assembly of the inhabitants. Firstly, the number of participants is not definitely stipulated; "under normal circumstances " there should be one person from each household who takes part in it. Secondly, the assembly has no right to convene of its own will. Instead, it is summoned by persons who are not members of it, *viz.* the village head or the government authorities.[1] Thirdly, the standing orders are not given any particular attention. There are only provisions defining the rights of the chairman and a provision concerning voting and elections. However, even these scanty provisions are altogether jettisoned when an assembly is convoked by the government authorities.[2] Fourthly, the powers of the general assembly are extremely small. It is granted the right to elect the village head and to vote on bills presented by the village head or the heads of the corporations.[3] Besides, the general assembly is entitled to consider petitions handed in by people other than the village head or the heads of the corporations.[4] None of the executives is in any way answerable to the general assembly.

[1] Vid. Art. 12.
[2] Vid. Arts. 13-15, 19.
[3] Vid. Arts. 19, 15, 14.
[4] Vid. Art. 15.

The village committee seems to be a much more powerful institution than the general assembly of the inhabitants, both with regard to its range of powers and to the power inherent in its decisions. The record of items the village committee has to decide upon clearly shows that its power is to extend to virtually all aspects of village life.[5] There is a strong emphasis on the financial dealings of the village, and this alone seems to ensure a considerable influence on village affairs. The village head is made dependent on the decisions of the village committee in matters of village expenditure, and the village head and the heads of the corporations are obliged to submit the estimates of income and expenditure of the village and of the corporations to the village committee.[6] Moreover, the village committee has a word to say in the establishment and abolition of regulations and association contracts. This right is confirmed three times in the *Regulations*.[7] Besides, the village committee has the right to recommend persons for appointment as village clerk and forest ranger, and it acts as village court.[8] Yet, although they appear to be very wide, the powers of the village committee, too, are very limited. This is due to both its structure of membership and its mode of convention. The village committee is to be composed of six village deputies, who are elected at the assembly of the neighbourhood heads.[9] But since the neighbourhood heads in their turn are commissioned by the village head, upon recommendation of the neighbourhoods, the village head indirectly determines who will become a member of the village committee.[10] Furthermore, the village committee cannot meet on its own decision, but is convoked by the village head.[11] This scheme largely deprives the village committee of its autonomy and turns it into a sort of advisory body of the village head.

The fact of the general disregard for the "technicalities" of the village meetings is substantiated by the evidence we can collect from the protocols of the village meetings. Out of the 24 village meetings of which the protocols are extant, only two come close to what the general assembly should be like according to the *Regulations*, although even these two meetings do not exactly correspond to it either in date or subject matter. After all, the kind of general

[5] Vid. Art. 17.
[6] Vid. Arts. 20, 22.
[7] Vid. Arts. 17(4,6), 24.
[8] Vid. Art. 19.
[9] Vid. Arts. 17s.
The neighbourhoods appearing in connexion with the village government are not necessarily identical with the neighbourhoods as social units, which we have hitherto come to know as solidarity groups. The neighbourhoods figuring in village government are administrative divisions of the village created by the government authorities in collaboration with the village head. There are ten of these neighbourhoods in Changjwa-ri.
[10] Vid. Art. 19.
[11] Vid. Art. 13.

village assembly envisaged by the authors of the *Regulations* is more of a ritual than a strictly political institution. Since it is to be held on the 15th day of the first month of the lunar calendar, it is closely associated with the conduct of the village festival. It is not unusual that such village meetings are held around the time of a village festival in Korea. They are just another social event of the festive days, and it is hard to imagine that any matter-of-fact decisions can be taken on such occasions of joy and pleasure.[12] Basically, the general meetings seem to be hardly more than social gatherings of the men of the village, where the "praise of those of good behaviour and of the meritorious and industrious ones" mentioned in Art. 17(8) of the *Regulations* is one of the main pursuits, and where eating and drinking occupies much of the time. The "sundry expenses for the time of the public village meeting"[13] are for the most part those eating and drinking costs. The intended transformation of a ritual-like function into an important and regular occasion for decision-making does not seem to have succeeded well in Changjwa-ri, for the villagers themselves do not appear to have regarded those general assemblies as occasions for efficient decision-making. Absence from village meetings would not have been punished, if the villagers had liked to participate and had regarded them as opportunities where their own concerns were dealt with.[14]

The little influence the provisions of the *Regulations* have on actual village government and on the thoughts of the villagers is further demonstrated by the deviations in nomenclature of the meeting protocols from the terminology of the *Regulations*. The village committee is called village administration committee wherever it occurs in the protocols.[15] Moreover, the recording clerk is not called village clerk, but village beadle, and on two occasions the older term "ward" is used instead of the formally correct "neighbourhood".[16]

The Informality of the Village Government

Who is really in power at Changjwa-ri, and how are decisions really arrived at? From what has been said in the preceding section, we could be inclined to consider the village head to be the centre of power in the village. He can largely determine the composition of the village committee, and the conventions of

---

[12] In the mid-thirties, it was found out that of a sample of villages celebrating village festivals 29 % held village meetings in connexion with the festivities. The general assembly of the inhabitants of Changjwa-ri is probably similar in character to those meetings called *tonghoe* 洞會.

Vid. *Burakusai,* comp. Murayama Chijun *et al.,* pp. 457-471.

[13] Vid. Document XIII.4(d).

[14] Vid. Art. 28(1).

[15] Vid. Document XIII.3-12, 14-16, 18, 19.

[16] Vid. Document XIII.4(a), 11(a), 16(a), 19(a,f), 20.

both the general assembly and the village committee depend on him. In one instance, he is even considered to be a member of the village committee.[17] Furthermore, he gives instructions to the village clerk, and by drafting the estimates of village income and expenditure, he can largely determine the course village life is to take.[18] The same is true of his right to make known his opinion on education.[19]

Yet, the village head, too, is subject to a variety of limitations and pressures. In the first place, his selecting and commissioning the neighbourhood heads is a secondary step which he takes only after the candidates for the posts of neighbourhood heads have been "recommended" to him by the people of the neighbourhoods. In the second place, both the conventions of the general assembly of the inhabitants and of the village committee are not left to the village head alone, but need the consent of the heads of the corporations. In the third place, the heads of the corporations join him in presenting bills to the general assembly. The bills, in turn, depend on the decisions of the village committee.[20] Fourthly, although the possibility of guiding the village affairs is enhanced by drafting the financial estimates, this privilege does not entail absolute power for the village head, because the final decisions depend on the village committee, of which the village head is only one among several members.[21] Finally, we have to mention here the obligation of the village head to appear, together with the heads of the corporations, before the village assemblies, in order to answer questions and to render account of the administration.[22] Considering the general weakness of the village assemblies, it is hard to imagine that the village head and the heads of the corporations would ever convene a meeting of the village committee, if they were afraid of embarrassing questions and of reprimands. Still, by such questions and reprimands, the village committee may exercise some pressure, not a strictly legal and formal one though, when the questions come as a surprise attack.

The authors of the *Regulations of Changjwa-ri* who have devised the neat, but all too futile two-chamber-system of village government have incorporated into their code the rules by which the village is really to be run. The dealings of the seemingly omnipotent village head are not so much checked by the two village assemblies as by the heads of the corporations on the one side and the heads of the neighbourhoods — or a number of them — on the other. The government of the village therefore is an affair to be conducted by the village head, the heads of the neighbourhoods, and the heads of the corporations, who

[17] The *Regulations* are ambiguous in this matter. According to Art. 18, the village committee consists of those publicly elected at the assembly of the neighbourhood heads plus the village head, whereas in Art. 20 it is explicitly stated that the village committee is composed of no other persons than the village deputies.

[18] Vid. Arts. 20, 22.   [19] Vid. Art. 26.

[20] Vid. Art. 15.   [21] Vid. Art. 17; cf. note 17 of this chapter.

[22] Vid. Art. 16.

are required to act in unison. This lay-out of village government clearly aims at giving an equal share of power to each of the three "pillars". For the greater share of power which the village deputies, *i. e.* six of the neighbourhood heads, seem to enjoy according to the *Regulations*, by being involved in more items of decision-making than any other group, is balanced out by curbing the village deputies' autonomy and by making them dependent on the village head's commission. The power of the village head, in turn, is matched by the restrictions which come from the side of the heads of the corporations. This order of village government again shows that in the eyes of the authors of the *Regulations* the diverging interests and opinions which demand reconciliation are not those of individuals, but those of the two main groups into which each individual is absorbed or should be absorbed, *viz.* the neighbourhoods and the corporations. Moreover, since the submission of young people to older persons is upheld as a virtue in Changjwa-ri, we can safely assume that as heads of neighbourhoods and corporations, let alone as village head, we will meet the more mature gentlemen of the village, and village government will thus be an exclusive affair of the older men.

With some difficulty we have dissected the real order of village government at Changjwa-ri, but we are still left in the dark as to how decisions are actually made. These processes are likely to be of an order which defies codification. The group of older and allegedly more mature men, who hold village government in their hands, is bound by a set of common interests and responsibilities as household heads and by intimate knowledge of village affairs. They know each other too well to need a set of rules for making decisions.[23] We are probably not far from the truth if we imagine village government to be a constant flow of conversation and gossip which by far transcends the few hours of village meetings. Under such circumstances, we are not surprised at the fact that the members of the village committee and the village head are not elected, as the *Regulations* prescribe, but are "nominated . . . upon public oral recommendation".[24] Decisions need not be taken on formal conventions, because they have already been taken before.

[23] The authors who have hitherto written on village government in Korea have concentrated on the problems of leadership and have tried to answer questions as to the qualifications village leaders should have. At present, the author of this study need not comment on their writings, because his concern is with the fact of the informality of village government, and not with actual decision-making.
  Vid. *Han'guk nongch'onŭi sahoe kujo,* comp. Yi Man'gap, pp. 182-204 (Man-gap Lee, "Korean Village Politics and Leadership", transl. Glenn D. Paige, *The Korean Affairs,* vol. 1, no. 4, 1962, pp. 398-412, repr. "The Village Political and Social Structure", *A Pattern of Political Development: Korea,* ed., introd. C. I. Eugene Kim, The Korea Research and Publication, Inc., Series, [Kalamazoo:] 1964, pp. 107-125); "Nongch'on palchŏn'gwa chidojaŭi yŏkhal", comp. Yi Kwanggyu, *MIH,* no. 5 (Im Sŏkchae sŏnsaeng kohŭi kinyŏm nonch'ong), 1972, pp. 151-194; Pak/Gamble, *The Changing Korean Village,* pp. 189-191.
[24] Vid. Document XIII.5(a,c).

The village government of Changjwa-ri lacks precision and formality where in Western eyes precision and formality are highly desirable. But this is not the only aspect worth some consideration. An equally important facet is the desire to include as large a number of people as possible in the process of reaching a consensus. It is on this aim that the whole scheme of village government is ultimately based. Both informality, *i.e.* the neglect of what is written in the *Regulations*, and inclusion of as many people as possible are well illustrated by the protocols of the village meetings. Only two out of the 24 village meetings of which the protocols are available are faithful to the letter of the *Regulations* by being genuine meetings of the formal village committee. In the earlier of the two examples, only the six village deputies and the village head are said to have taken part, whereas in the latter example the village head is counted as belonging to the group of the village deputies and thus as a full member of the village committee.[25] All other meetings are something inbetween the general assembly of the inhabitants and the meetings of the village committee. They clearly manifest the endeavour to enlarge the base on which the village decisions should rest and at the same time to preserve village policies as a domain of certain people. The most interesting feature is the inclusion in about half of the meetings of a group of people who are not provided for at all in the *Regulations, viz.* the "people interested in the matters discussed".[26] The translation offered here of the term *yu chi* 有 志, however, renders only part of the meaning, for this expression does not only mean concern for certain matters, but equally well implies that these people have an intimate knowledge of village affairs and that their word counts, so that their opinions cannot be neglected, even if the people are not members of any formal body or do not hold any village post. A closer look at the lists of participants in meetings would reveal that most of those "people interested in matters to be discussed" have been out of village politics for some time. The device of having the *yu chi* participate in village meetings can be considered a subtle means of sugarcoating their formal exclusion and thus of avoiding bad feelings on either side. Moreover, an even greater number of protocols records the inclusion of all the neighbourhood heads, and not only the six men who as so-called village deputies constitute the village committee.[27] As a consequence, in about half of the records, the listing of participants according to the groups they belong to is altogether abandoned, although the village committee, the neighbourhood heads, and the "people interested in the matters to be discussed" are mentioned separately in the initial sentences of most of the protocols.[28]

---

[25] These two protocols faithfully reflect the ambiguity which is inherent in the rules determining the village head's relation to the village committee.
Vid. Document XIII.2, 6; note 17 of this chapter.
[26] Vid. Document XIII.3, 4, 7-12, 20, 22, 23.
[27] Vid. Document XIII.2(d), 4, 7-12, 15, 19, 20, 22, 23.
[28] Vid. Document XIII.3, 4, 7-14, 21.

Yet, the enlargement of the decision-making body and the effacing of the formal distinctions provided for in the *Regulations* do not lead to the creation of another formal, though unofficial, decision-making group in the village. The enlargement does not imply a real increase in the number of people and does not produce strict formality in the number of participants in village meetings. In all cases, the number of participants recorded in the protocols is smaller than the number we would obtain by adding a certain number of "interested people" to that of ten neighbourhood heads — or six village deputies — and the village head. This may be due to the fact that sometimes one person may have taken part in more than one capacity but signed the protocol only once. Such may be the case in protocols listing more than six names under the heading of the administrative committee or less than ten neighbourhood heads.[29] But in each of these cases, at least one group must have been represented by a smaller number of men than it was allowed to dispatch. The discrepancy becomes particularly obvious in a protocol from 1959, when eleven men were elected to enlarge the formal village committee, but only seven of them signed the protocol of the very meeting they were elected at.[30] Still, none of the discrepancies between the number of actual participants and that of persons obliged or allowed to take part in the meetings seems to have invalidated any of the decisions. Nothing could better illustrate the extreme informality of the village government of Changjwa-ri.

The Position of the Village Head

The inclusion of as many people as possible and the informality of village government can be better understood by considering the peculiar position of the Korean village head. As it is said in the *Regulations of Changjwa-ri,* the village head on the one hand "manages" the village affairs, and represents the village on the other.[31] Since he is probably the person best known to the authorities, it is to him that they will turn when they feel the need to remind the villagers of their commune duties, which, above all, mean discharge of tax duties, payment of miscellaneous fees, payment of all kinds of other contributions, and proper dealings in forestry. The village head is thus confronted with the unpleasant task of drawing money from his village fellows and curtailing their economic powers in many other ways, whereas his loyalties will almost certainly remain with them. The village of Changjwa-ri hardly providing any reason for serious rifts among its inhabitants, the village head's attention will be more occupied with these "representation" duties than with "managing" village affairs and easing

---

[29] Vid. Document XIII.15-20, 24.
[30] Vid. Document XIII.18.
[31] Vid. Arts. 20, 23.

tensions within the village. Dr. Yi Man'gap went even so far as to regard the knowledge of affairs, other than strictly agricultural, and the capacities of negotiation, representation, and co-operation with the government authorities as the main qualifications required from a Korean village head.[32]

The village head is thus caught right in the middle of what may at times become a nerve-racking conflict. On the one side, he is expected by law to extend help to the agents of the government, and on the other side, he is expected by his village fellows to co-operate with them in easing bureaucratic pressures.[33] The position of village head is not always coveted by the villagers, and the desire for personal benefits and honours, which in most cases are the motivations for running for the post, must be very strong to induce somebody to accept the position.[34] In Changjwa-ri, the villagers tried to make the post of village head — and those of the other office-holders — more acceptable by holding out the prospect of remuneration.[35] In one instance, they even went so far as to grant him the whole yield of a certain plot of arable land for a comparatively low rent.[36] The inclusion of many people and the informality of village government may be viewed as other devices to ease the village head's dealings with the authorities. For by consulting as many people as possible, the village head cannot only hope to make a wider range of villagers familiar with the government's wishes and try to persuade the people to comply with them, but he can also hope to better sound out the villagers' opinions on certain issues and, if necessary, to better oppose the government authorities with the unanimous support of the influential people behind him. This scheme of informal village government could thus well serve both parties.

It is in the light of such considerations that the changes of the *Regulations* enacted in 1964 acquire their full significance. The outwardly apologizing tone of the initial sentences of that protocol definitely proves that the changes were to conform to wider government plans, and thus are very likely to have been requested by the local government authorities. The aim was to break up the

---

[32] Vid. *Han'guk nongch'onŭi sahoe kujo,* comp. Yi Man'gap, pp. 194s, 203s (Lee, "The Village Political and Social Structure", pp. 117, 123).

[33] Vid. *Chibang chach'i pŏp,* Art. 147(3).

[34] Besides being a focus of trouble and conflict, the position of village head seems to have carried very little, if any, prestige with it because of the kind of people who filled it. In the *Play of the Marionette Bride,* the position is held by Pak Ch'ŏmji 朴 僉 知, the arrogant, clumsy, and timorous *yangban* protagonist and one of the objects of general disdain and ridicule in the play.

Vid. *Chosŏn yŏn'gŭk sa,* comp. Kim Chaech'ŏl, ed. Kim Chaesŏng, Chosŏn mun'go, vol. 5, part 2, Keijō: Hagyesa, 1939, p. 143; *Han'guk kamyŏn'gŭk,* comp. Yi Tuhyŏn, p. 416 (act 9); *Han'guk nongch'onŭi sahoe kujo,* comp. Yi Man'gap, pp. 194s (Lee, "The Village Political and Social Structure", p. 109).

[35] Vid. Art. 18; Document XIII.4(a), 5(c), 6, 8(b), 10(b), 11(a), 16(a), 17(a), 19(g).

[36] Vid. Document XIII.13(d).

informal, but apparently strong group of influential people who held village government in their hands. Firstly, the village head was no longer to be considered a member of the village committee, and, secondly, the village committee was no longer to necessarily consist of older and influential neighbourhood heads. The members of the village committee were to be elected by the neighbourhoods and no longer commissioned by the village head. Thirdly, the village committee was explicitly said not only to assist the village head, but also to supervise him. Fourthly, too deep an involvement of the village head in the schemings of the village was to be prevented by limiting his term of office to one year.[37] These changes agreed with alterations in government laws enacted in 1961, according to which the village head was no longer elected by the villagers, but appointed by the heads of the superior self-government corporations.[38] In this manner, government law had preceded village law by making the village head an agent of the government authorities and unilaterally emphasizing his role of "reprentative". By further isolating the village head from the other influential people of the village, the changes in village law from 1964 were but a supplementary step. Supposing that the above analysis of the village head's position is correct, those changes in both government and village law did not only expose the village to more direct government influence, but they also prove in an indirect manner the strength of the informal village government of the earlier years.

Village Democracy

In an inquiry into the "outer organization" of Changjwa-ri, we cannot leave out of consideration the assertion that the guidance of government authorities is null and void if it runs counter to democratic development. Likewise, we have to take into account the professed aim of raising the spirit of democracy in the village and the exhortation to co-operate "... in the foundation and operation of democratic institutions".[39] Obviously, the authors of the *Regulations* considered the lay-out of their village government to have been democratic, or at least they hoped village government to attain such a state. An attempt at finding an answer to the question in what sense, if any, the village government at Changjwa-ri can be called democratic, is a task both intriguing and rewarding.

Whenever people use the term "democracy", they cannot entirely divest it of the qualities it was endowed with in the region and the time democracy was

---

[37] Vid. Document XIII.24(a-e).
[38] Vid. *Chibang chach'ie kwanhan imsi choch'i pŏp* 地方自治에 關한 臨時措置 法, Art. 9(3.2).
[39] Vid. Arts. 4, 6(2,5).

born. Even in occasional propagations of "national" democracies, such as so-called "Korean democracy" or "Indonesian democracy", their advocates are always eager either to preserve some of the mechanisms known from the Western models or else to abolish many of the "formalities" and preserve the "spirit" only, by asserting that their type of democracy is representative of widespread attitudes and aspirations among the populace. Thus, even in their attempts at deviation from the models, the advocates of national or otherwise defined democracies still betray their commitment to alien concepts. It is therefore not unfair to evaluate a government that likes to be called democratic by applying to it the standards of democracy as known from its origins. Evaluations of this kind are always likely to cause confusion and misunderstanding, and therefore it is not unnecessary to emphasize that the present author is intent on comparison, not judgment.

Commitments to the Western concepts of parliamentary democracy are not lacking even in such a remote place as Changjwa-ri, as the intention to establish a two-chamber-system may have illustrated. But we have found out already that the professed intentions neither correspond to the real intentions of the authors of the *Regulations* nor to the realities of village government. The ways in which the villagers think of their government lack the two concepts which are basic to parliamentary democracy, *viz.* equality and representation. The general assembly of the inhabitants is not even conceived of as a parliament in a democratic sense, because its participants are neither elected nor are they the representatives of an electorate considered to be composed of free individuals, each of whom has an equal right to share in policy-making in the village by electing and voting. The general assembly is instead a group of men who owe their participation in that assembly to their status as household heads, which in turn is independent of any election. Nor can the general assembly be said to be a true people's assembly, for a provision in Art. 12 of the *Regulations* implies that participation of all the inhabitants of the village is to be taken as abnormal.

The village committee does not fit into the scheme of parliamentary democracy, either. In the first place, it is not all of the neighbourhood heads who belong to the village committee, but only six of them. The village committee thus cannot be called a second chamber of a parliament, in which secondary divisions, *i.e.* the neighbourhoods, are represented on a basis of equality. In the second place, the people of a neighbourhood are not a constituency, and the neighbourhood heads are not truly elected, but are recommended by the people of a neighbourhood and then commissioned by the village head.

Although the village government of Changjwa-ri is devoid of institutions and procedures essential to parliamentary democracy, and although the concepts basic to that kind of democracy have hardly entered the minds of the villagers, the actual conduct of village affairs displays a considerable number of what may be called democratic virtues. The very informality of village government precludes the appeal to rules and regulations. Rather than settle conflicts by applying regulations and by voting and division, the villagers preserve a chance to judge a situation by its singular circumstances, to apply their common sense, and to observe the rules of equity. The key-tone in village government is reconciliation and consent rather than law and voting. This is more than what mostly flows from, or is behind, the formal democratic procedures of the West. It is in this sense, and in this sense only, that the "outer organization" of Changjwa-ri may be called democratic. True, the chance of practising such democratic virtues was given to a small group of villagers only. This probably was the utmost that could be achieved in a society which is not familiar with the concepts of equality and representation basic to Western parliamentary democracy. Instead of discarding the pattern of village government at Changjwa-ri as a manifestation of carelessness and political immaturity, the present author rather appreciates the perseverance by which the spirit of accommodation, so characteristic of Changjwa-ri and other Korean villages, is maintained and even extended to the government of the village.

CHAPTER 11: PROSPECTS OF VILLAGE LIFE AND VILLAGE STUDIES

The preceding discussion of the documents from Changjwa-ri has shown a considerable discrepancy between law and reality. On the one hand, the *Regulations of Changjwa-ri* do not contain much law that is really observed and do not pay due attention to the variety of institutions that really exist. On the other hand, with regard to what they do say and proclaim, there is sufficient reason for the suspicion that it is highly fictitious.

The order of some important domains of village life is altogether left out of the *Regulations.* They do not say anything about the real kinds and number, the statutes, and the operations of the mutual benefit associations, the conduct of the village festival, the true nature of so-called village property, and about collective farming. The terminology concerning village income and expenditure is confusing, and the information on payment of farm labourers misleading. Wherever the authors of the *Regulations* touch upon really crucial affairs, such as the use of woodlands, the forest association, the use of seaweed grounds and fishery, they do so in a rather casual manner. The reader may have noticed that most of the information on such subjects has not been obtained from the *Regulations*, but from the protocols of the meetings of the village committee, from local informants, from observation, or it had to be inferred from general knowledge.

In fact, the authors of the *Regulations* are concerned with something other than recording actually observed village law. Time and again, they conjure up a village society which is based on "humanism", righteousness, and harmonious neighbourly relations. Instead of recording what is to be remembered as really observed village law, they indulge in portraying a village society which is perfectly adapted to the policies of the government and the concerns of the whole nation. Such a "portrait" of a village as an integrated whole which is determined by the concerns of the nation is highly wishful thinking and proves most of the *Regulations* to be mere abstract rules. On several occasions in this study, the author has accounted for his opinion that peasant behaviour which is determined by concerns for "the village" is more the exception than the rule in Korea. Even where it can be observed to a certain extent, as is the case in Changjwa-ri, the values underlying such behaviour are generally not reflected in the minds of the peasants. Wherever a certain degree of village integration is achieved, it does not flow from such consciously maintained abstract values as the *Regulations* want us to believe. Therefore, the very existence of such codes like the *Regulations of Changjwa-ri* proves that they are not very likely to have been initiated by the peasants concerned. The initiators of such village codes should be sought for either outside the village or among those villagers who for some reason are alienated from actual village life. Dr. Brandt has observed that ". . . only the village head and a few others think and talk in terms of such abstractions as village cohesion and solidarity, although similar concepts are used consciously more often in the context of lineage ideology. The importance attached to behaving correctly or at least circumspectly towards individuals in actual situations works out in practice to promote good relations in a wider context. In other words, immediate sociability in face-to-face situations with another individual often takes precedence over group solidarity in the abstract sense of a psychic or emotional bond uniting all inhabitants of the village."[1]

The observations and conclusions as given above can further be corroborated by the scarcity of village codes. As far as can be told today, genuine village codes, which pertain to all walks of village life and to which the inhabitants of a village are subject in a compulsory manner, are rare. Of the codes extant from the Yi period, only 19 can be rated as village codes. The ratio is even worse with regard to the texts dating from the period of Japanese occupation. Here, only two out of 23 samples of regulations are village codes.[2] It follows from the observations made by Dr. Kang Ch'anggyu that only 30 % of the association rules surveyed by him are village codes in the sense defined here.[3]

Besides being largely fictitious, the *Regulations* in part are also superfluous, because they merely reiterate provisions which can already be found in superior government law. In particular, this is true with regard to the regulations concerning taxpaying and the maintenance of Ch'ŏnghae School. It is those fictitious or superfluous provisions which make the *Regulations of Changjwa-ri* more a sample of paternalistic admonitions. It is no wonder that the villagers often seem to have regarded them as something alien to their lives. If they had considered them as rules which really answered the requirements of their lives, they would have liked to take part in village assemblies, and a provision stipulat-

[1] Brandt, *A Korean Village,* p. 161.
[2] For the sake of comparison with the *Regulations of Changjwa-ri,* the review of codes from the Japanese period has been limited to texts bearing the element *kyuyak* (Sin.-Jap. *kiyaku*) in their titles. This procedure may have seriously distorted proportions, because genuine village codes may also be found under titles which do not contain the *kyuyak*-element. As a matter of fact, there are three village codes in the *Korean Settlements (Chōsen no shuraku)* which are not labelled as *kyuyak* or *kiyaku,* but in other respects are quite similar to those two *kiyaku* codes mentioned above. They are called *dōyaku* (Sin.-Kor. *tongyak* 洞 約), thus being similar in name to that village code of Changjwa-ri which immediately preceded the *Regulations.* In other words, the number of genuine village codes dating from the Japanese period will almost certainly appear to be considerably higher, as soon as the investigation is extended to texts other than those labelled *kiyaku.*
Vid. *CS,* vol. 1, p. 601; vol. 2, pp. 256-265, 280s.
[3] Vid. *Kyega idong nongŏp hyŏptong chohabe mich'inŭn yŏnghyang,* comp. Kang Ch'anggyu, pp. 44s: table 3-6 (Kang, *The Influence of "Ke" Societies Upon Ri-Dong Agricultural Cooperative Association,* pp. 65-67).

ing punishment for absence from them could have been omitted. Likewise, re-emphasizing the validity of the *Regulations* would not have been necessary.[4]

We must assume that the local government officials have somehow or other interferred both in the process of formulating the text and in the enactment itself. The interference need not have been a heavy-handed one, and no coercion need have been applied. Yet, interference there must have been, although the formula at the end of the code pretends the *Regulations* to be the result of a free agreement among free villagers, and although no visible traces are left of any government interference in the text itself. Considering the ingrained habit of submission to authoritative command and admonition, which is a legacy of Korea's Sinicized, "Confucian" past,[5] the authors of the *Regulations* can be imagined to have reacted at even the slightest hints or even to have met impending government desires halfway. On the whole, the *Regulations* fit into government policies on the countryside in a surprisingly smooth way, whether the authors of the *Regulations* wanted it or not, and whether they were aware of it or not. This is the reason why the authorities fostered or at least tolerated the penal jurisdiction of the village and the establishment of a whole village code, although village legislation was — and still is — illegal by the standards of modern government law. In general, the inner affairs of a Korean village are difficult to observe, let alone to control, by an outsider. Normally, an official dispatched by the government is neither familiar with the conditions of a particular place nor with rural affairs in general. Therefore, he will normally have to be satisfied with an uninterrupted flow of taxes, miscellaneous fees, and other contributions. He will not bother with the affairs of a tiny village as long as everything remains calm, at least on the surface. He will not only tolerate village codes such as the *Regulations of Changjwa-ri*, but will even welcome them. There are overtones of repression and domestication in the *Regulations*, and if villagers succeed in maintaining order among their fellow villagers, it may also help to achieve the commune ends the government is mainly interested in. The "guidance and superintendence by the government and other public offices" is thus supplemented by the submission of the common villagers to the men who constitute the informal village government. A village code like the *Regulations of Changjwa-ri* is not a manifestation of a village's determination to handle its own affairs and to ward off government interference, but a more or less direct help to government authorities in controlling some locality. In spite of this professed tendency to submit to authoritarian guidance, the village does not seem to have been ready to accept the "guidance and superintendence by the government and other public offices" in the beginning. The formula rarely occurs in the *Village Articles of Changjwa-ri on Wan Island*. This seems to have

---

[4] Vid. Art. 28(1); Document XIII.9(d).

[5] Remnants of the "Confucian" past in Korean village culture will be discussed in Appendix 2 of this study.

been the reason why the *Articles* were quickly replaced by the *Regulations of Changjwa-ri*.

In view of the rather domesticating character of the *Regulations*, we are reluctant to call the whole of their provisions customary law. It is hard to imagine that villagers will continuously submit to the double coercion exercised by village elders and government authorities and thus "internalize" the rules ensuing from submission. True, there are some provisions that follow examples set in the period of Japanese occupation or in even earlier times, and they can surely be called old. Yet, they are not necessarily "internalized" and thus customary. To say the least, most Koreans harbour considerable resentment against the Japanese, and the grudge may easily have been transferred to a Korean rural policy which all too often followed in the footsteps of the Japanese, as can be told from the legislation on forestry, for instance. Yet, there does exist some kind of customary law in the village, only the *Regulations* do not record its contents, they only hint at the fact of its existence. The village festival, the patterns of collective farming, and the ways of using seaweed grounds and fisheries, where custom is strongest, are hardly dealt with in the *Regulations*. The authors of this code, having been preoccupied with quite different things, acknowledged observation of such habits in passing only.

There is enough reason to assume that other village codes will not be all too different in character from the *Regulations of Changjwa-ri*. After all, they all pertain to societies which were created as administrative tools and which are apparently considered to be something artificial even today. Therefore, students of Korean villages who rely on such village codes as their main research material can hardly expect to obtain immediate insight into the economy and the social life of a village. However, as documents revealing something about the relationship between government and village, they will be a rewarding object of research. The degree of autonomy and, hence, the amount of really observed customary law contained in a village code may vary from place to place. The strength of village autonomy will always depend on the weakness of government authorities, which in its turn is determined by the general political conditions of the nation and also by the geographical conditions of a locality. Peasants do not seem to be doomed to submission in all circumstances.[6] We may thus expect graduation and variation. We must not all too hastily consider the *Regulations*

---

[6] With regard to East Asia, the question of whether peasants are generally unable to create durable organizations of their own has recently been raised again by Professor Irwin Scheiner. He has studied the problem in some detail with regard to conditions in the Japan of the late 19th century. Preferring the more conspicuous events in history, he has concentrated on the conditions preceding and following peasant rebellions, and he has given little or no attention to daily life.

Vid. Irwin Scheiner, "The Mindful Peasant. Sketches for a Study of Rebellion", *Journal of Asian Studies*, vol. XXXII, no. 4, 1973, pp. 579-591.

of Changjwa-ri as a typical specimen of Korean village law in all respects before many more codes have been reviewed. Before generalizing on the subject, it is necessary to obtain more information on the conditions under which such codes were drafted, on the persons who drafted and enacted them, on their motives for doing so, and on the modes of co-operation between villagers and government authorities. Such data has to be gathered from a great many places, and the pursuit of such inquiries will remain one of the main tasks in the future study of village codes and the realities associated with them.

The review of the documents from Changjwa-ri may have taught us yet another lesson. Besides collecting data of the kind just mentioned, students of Korean village life should turn their attention more towards the sub-village communities and associations than has hitherto been the case in most of the studies on Korean villages, where inquiries into the social hierarchy and leadership qualifications figure so prominently. The strength and independence of communities within the village and mutual benefit associations are the reverse side to the weakness of village integration. Therefore, an evaluation of village integration and, implicitly, of the prospects of rural economy, society, and culture will heavily depend on insights into the kinds and distribution of wealth within the village, into the formation of communities and other groups as associated with different layers of wealth und prestige, and into the size of the resources and the ways of their going into one or more of the local communities and associations, including "the village".

Largely being a record of what the government and perhaps a few villagers wanted the village to be, the *Regulations of Changjwa-ri* anticipated conditions which were to become reality only in the years subsequent to the period under observation here. It is easy to imagine that in the fifties and early sixties, the village community managed to maintain much of its vigour, notwithstanding continuous attempts at enlarging the range of commune duties. The nature of government impact has changed since then. This seems to be less due to the present regime's view of what proper government should be like than to the increased powers of a modern state to enforce its demands. This increase is due to changes in communication facilities and technology. The eclipse of the small community is in sight. For whatever protective measures the village of Changjwa-ri and others have developed, they were adequate only in protecting the villagers from excessive tax demands and other smaller and occasional encroachments from the side of the authorities. But they are doomed to fail when a government proceeds with large-scale land-reclamations, with the building of huge water reservoirs and industrial plants, and with the resettlement of people, all of which are projects under way in many parts of the country. In Changjwa-ri, the change of the "village office" into the office of the village agricultural co-operative, which occurred as early as 1966, was the token of the new age. General village administration seems to be in the same hands as the affairs of the village rural co-operative. As a commune, the village has been transformed into a production unit.[7]

This shift in emphasis is both a return to, and a deviation from, earlier patterns of rural control. For on the one hand, the government wants to use the villages in as strict a manner as instruments of local control as it tried to do in Yi times. But the emphasis no longer lies on political and police matters, but on economic pursuits. Devoted to the achievement of economic goals and the growth in GNP, the government tries to replace the community by a production unit obeying the commands of growth and modernization. Again, the author has to point out that he wants to abstain from evaluation and criticism of such policies. This is not because he is afraid of pronouncing criticism, but because he is well aware of the many favourable side-effects which follow in the wake of this transformation. The real question, however, seems to be whether such policies can really achieve their main ends in the way they are often enforced. Many cases are known of villages where the people finally refrained from pursuing ventures they had originally agreed to, because the emphasis on material incentives, on individualism, and on growth as such as well as harsh guidance turned to threaten the material equilibrium of the village and the accord among the villagers.[8] People who enthusiastically celebrate the annual growth in GNP and set about, among other things, sacrificing the village community and all it is based on as an evil on the way towards a "modern society" do not always seem to know what they are talking about.

Given the generally increasing government influence on rural affairs in Korea, students of Korean village life should in the future devote more attention to the so-called community development (*chiyŏk sahoe kaebal* 地 域 社 會 開 發) than has been necessary up to now. Here, a word of explanation is in place as to why this author has almost entirely abstained from discussing community development.[9] Community development reached its first heights in the period under discussion here, and it seemed to have the potential of profoundly changing the appearance and the inner fabric of Korean villages. Community development was — and is — inspired and guided by government agencies. In a proper evaluation of community development the author would have had to divulge varied and often incompatible government policies, which in turn would have gone far beyond the limits of a study which is mainly

[7] This policy has a striking parallel in an attempt by the North Korean government of the year 1958 to make the villages co-terminous with rural co-operatives.

Vid. Robert A. Scalapino/Chong-sik Lee, *Communism in Korea,* part II: The Society, ed. under the auspices of the Center for Japanese and Korean Studies, University of California, Berkeley, Berkeley/Los Angeles/London: 1972, p. 809.

[8] A striking example of that kind of reaction has been reported by Dr. Brandt.

Vid. Brandt, *A Korean Village,* pp. 192-195.

[9] The very few traces community development left in Changjwa-ri in the period under discussion here have been mentioned on pp. 76s of this study.

concerned with conditions at the "grass-roots" level. This author was further prevented from commenting at large on community development by the fact that community development in the course of time has generated a rather large bulk of literature which is often hidden in out-of-the-way periodicals and thus not easy to get hold of.[10] Moreover, the little of the writing on community development the present author could check betrays a marked lack of sound and reliable information. Often, the authors hardly went beyond rather fussy statements of how bad things were before community development started and how bright the future would be after community development has been properly implemented. We hardly learn anything about the state of things during the period under discussion here. Even where exact quantitative data is provided, it often does not tell us much, because only very little data of a relevant order is available from periods prior to the time when proper community development activities started. Therefore, it was impossible to evaluate the more recent data against the background of older information and thus give meaning to the former. Another reason for this author's abstention is that the authors writing on community development, rather than providing or preparing a critical appreciation, seem to unilaterally accept the government programmes and thus tend to neglect unfavourable aspects.[11] The last reason is that most of the writing on community development deals with conditions in single localities. However, what is needed with regard to community development in a study such as the one presented here is comparison and generalization. Yet, such comparison and generalization are inhibited by the fact that the working conditions of those various case-studies, such as the kinds and arrangement of items in questionnaires, do not appear to have been identical.

The author of this study is well aware of the fact that he himself did not live up to the requirement of generalization. Besides lacking studies comparable in nature to the one presented here, with the results of which he could have compared the findings and conclusions of his own and on the basis of which he could have made generalizations, he feels that it is the very nature of written rural sources which inhibits generalizations and will continue inhibiting them in

---

[10] The literature on community development in Korea which had been published up to the mid-sixties has been listed and annotated by Mrs. Alice Y. Chai.

Vid. Alice Y. Chai, *Community Development in Korea. A Bibliography of Works in the Korean Language,* comp., annotated . . ., Occasional Papers of Research Publications and Translations, Annotated Bibliography Series, ed. Institute of Advanced Projects, East-West Center, University of Hawaii, no. 5, Honolulu: 1968.

[11] Such criticism has already been pronounced by Professor Lee Hyo-chae in his review of one of the few books written on the subject in English. The present author readily confirms that such criticism applies to a much wider part of that literature.

Vid. Hyo-chae Lee, Review of Roh Chang Shub, *et al., A Study of Three Developing Rural Communities, Journal of Social Sciences and Humanities (Bulletin of the Korean Research Center),* no. 23, Seoul: 1965, pp. 45-48.

future studies of this kind for a long time to come. Written sources of rural
conditions either tend to convey ideals instead of facts, to tell how things should
be according to somebody's idea of them rather than what they actually are like.
As has repeatedly been stated, this is largely the case in Changjwa-ri. Or they
reflect the issues and tensions prevailing in a situation of abnormal friction and
dispute. The disputes having become disruptive to the extreme, and the
well-worn mechanisms of accomodation having become ineffective, the peasants
will resort to the unfamiliar way of settling disputes by writing things down or
have others write down regulations for them, in order to ensure a lasting new
appeasement. Since such documents have grown out of strife and dispute, they
will hardly contain anything related to the management of daily affairs, and
they thus tell us about the daily routine in an indirect manner only, if at all. Most
of the documents from rural Korea known to this author belong to the latter
category. A series of case-studies based on such written material may in the
future yield some insight into recurrent types of dispute and their solutions.
However, if by generalization one means summarizing statements concerning
not only recurrent abnormalities, but also statements concerning the nature and
extension, both in terms of space and time, of the daily rural routine, one will
have difficulty in drawing them from documents such as the ones discussed here.

APPENDIX 1: THE PLACE OF VILLAGES IN THE LEGAL LAY-OUT OF THE REPUBLIC OF KOREA

Art. 2 of the Law on Local Self-Government (*Chibang chach'i pŏp*) promulgated on July 4th, 1949, determined which local divisions were to be regarded as local self-government corporations. The villages did not appear in that article. They belonged to a separate kind of local division together with the counties, the urban districts (*ku* 區), and the *tong*, which were all mentioned in Art. 145 of that law. It was said in that article that counties were subdivisions of the provinces (*to* 道), urban districts were subdivisions of the capital as well as of cities (*si* 市) of 500.000 or more inhabitants, and *i* and *tong* were subdivisions of cities, townships, urban districts, and rural districts (*myŏn* 面).

The peculiar position of the counties and urban districts derived from the fact that the legislator had been compelled to acknowledge them as something close to corporations. On the other hand, however, the legislator denied them any legal importance and any capacity of representation. For the heads of those units were not regarded as representatives of their populace, but as agents of the heads of the local self-government corporations they belonged to. Moreover, the counties and districts were nowhere said to dispatch representatives to any of the organs of the superior self-government corporations.

The position of the villages differed only slightly from that of the counties and districts. The law was equally silent on the matter of representation. The village head was simply said to "help" the mayor of a city or a township or the heads of districts to "handle" those tasks of the nation or the self-government corporations which were to be executed within their jurisdictions, and to "direct and survey" his minor officials.[1] The significant difference between the villages on the one hand and the counties and districts on the other was that the village heads were elected by the people of their jurisdictions, and not appointed by the heads of the superior self-government corporations.[2]

This vestige of self-determination was only wiped out much later. In 1961, it was determined that the village heads be appointed to office by the heads of cities, townships, or districts.[3] Finally, in 1970, it was said that only those persons were eligible for the post who "have the power to guide the people of the village", and whose education was above the primary school level. Moreover, they were to be deeply imbued with anti-communist thought.[4] This meant,

---

[1] Vid. *Chibang chach'i pŏp,* Art. 147(3).
[2] Vid. *ibid.,* Art. 146(4).
[3] Vid. *Chibang chach'ie kwanhan imsi choch'i pŏp,* Art. 9(3.2).
[4] Vid. *Chibang chach'ie kwanhan imsi choch'i pŏp sihaengnyŏng* 施 行 令 , Art. 4.

among other things, that farmers were practically not eligible and that village administration was entirely taken out of the hands of the village population. Thus, the initial inconsistency of the law was entirely removed, and the village heads were made the agents of the government, to the exclusion of any other function.

Not having been acknowledged as local self-government corporations, the villages were also denied the right of legislation. In Art. 96 of the Constitution of the Republic of Korea (*Tae Han min'guk hŏnppŏp* 大 韓 民 國 憲 法), promulgated on July 17th, 1948, this right, together with other privileges, had been given to genuine local self-government corporations only. With the constitutional changes of October 27th, 1972, it has been planned to establish a new legal order of local self-government.[5] However, as far as the relevant provisions go, it is, according to the latest edition of South Korean laws available to this author, *i. e.* that of 1977, only Art. 4 of the Application Orders of the Law on Provisional Measures Concerning Local Self-Government (*Chibang chachie kwanhan imsi choch'i pŏp sihaengnyŏng*) that has been changed. The valid version, dated April 22nd, 1974 of that article lacks the requirement of education above primary school level and makes the appointment of village heads dependent on the regulations of the local self-government corporation concerned.

---

[5] Vid. *Hŏnbŏp kaejŏng an* 憲 法 개 정 案 , printed in *Tonga ilbo* 東 亞 日 報 , October 27th, 1972, p. 6.

APPENDIX 2: ELEMENTS OF KOREAN VILLAGE CULTURE

The Spread of Diverse Cultural Elements

Korean culture is usually described as being composed of "Confucian" and "Shaman" elements. The "Confucian" set of values and behavioural patterns is associated with the upper, literate class of the people, whereas the "Shaman" element is said to determine the views and behaviour of the simple folk. Such a flat statement is tantamount to saying that there are two different cultures for two different layers of the population. Supporters of this view fail to realize that concepts and practices commonly associated with one layer of the people have spread to the other as well. Such transfers started very early in Korean history. Much of the hierarchical morality, which is usually associated with Confucianism and the literate classes, is found among the common populace as well, almost totally determining the conceptual level of their ethics, whereas Shaman rituals were also practised at court and were frequented by the people of the literate classes who were connected with it. The documents from Changjwa-ri and other evidence allow some insight into this generally neglected coexistence of seemingly incompatible cultural elements within one and the same society.

An analysis of Korean village culture in terms of Confucianism and Shamanism may quickly divert us from the point that really matters. For it would be a cumbersome enterprise to find out whether any of the views on etiquette held among the villagers of Changjwa-ri and other places can really be traced back to any of the writings and sayings attributed to Confucius and his followers, or whether some religious practice in fact has its precedents in Central and North Asian Shamanism. Following such a path of investigation, we may quickly find ourselves involved in the discussion of the problems concerning the origins of Korean cultural concepts, and we may easily loose sight of the Korean culture itself, *viz.* the substance of cultural concepts and the phenomenon of the spread of diverging elements to several classes of society. As a matter of fact, division in village culture — and in Korean culture in general — cannot be denied even by the most perfunctory observer of Korea. Only, its nature appears to be insufficiently circumscribed by the terms "Confucianism" and "Shamanism". For reasons which cannot be discussed here, the present author is of the opinion that "Confucianism" and "Shamanism" should be replaced by "Sinicized culture" and "folk culture". The division in Korean culture thus appears to be rendered in a more adequate way, and at the same time, these terms allow for a meaningful investigation which can do without pedantic historical probing.

The dichotomy in village culture, of which the few examples to be discussed here may give an idea, is paralleled by the dichotomy in village ethic. It is obvious that the formal, hierarchical, and allegedly ideal ethic is closely associated with the Sinicized elements in village culture. In fact, most of the manifestations of the Sinicized culture are vestiges of ideals and rituals contained in the most prestigeous pieces of Chinese "Confucian" literature. Tentatively, we may venture the hypothesis that the egalitarian community ethic is similarly associated with folk religion and folk beliefs. Like the two sets of ethics, the various elements of village culture are neither opposed to each other in a really antagonistic way, nor have they been amalgamated into a continuous whole.

The Literacy of Korean Peasants

In Korea "Confucianism", above all, means familiarity with a certain set of canonical writings which have their origins in Chinese antiquity. Since the Chinese literary language is the vehicle by means of which the lore of the writings has been transmitted, the term "Confucianism" has easily come to include the mastery of the Chinese literary language and the familiarity with Chinese thought, history, and literature in general. How profound this kind of Sinicization has been in Korea is well illustrated by conditions of the remote village of Changjwa-ri. Although the villagers do not claim any *yangban* traditions, they have not been totally ignorant of the writings and lores of China.[1] In former times, the educational aspirations of the local populace were satisfied by a local school (*hyanggyo* 鄉 校)[2] in the vicinity of the village.

A faint echo of the achievements are the six scrolls ornating the shrine of General Song on General's Island.[2] They do not only testify to a familiarity with *topoi* from the *Rites of Chou (Chou li* 周 禮) and *Meng-tzu* 孟 子 , but they also bear witness to some skill in punning in Chinese, which educated people are so

[1] If one is willing to admit that the Ritual of Local Archery, to be discussed on p. 141 of this study, was ever practised in Changjwa-ri, this ritual could be taken as one more proof of the villagers' familiarity with the ritual and thought of ancient China.

[2] Until recently, such local schools could be met with in a great number of villages in the southern half of the peninsula, and even today, we occasionally come across them. They have been the main agents in the spread and maintenance of what is "Confucian" in Korean culture. Modern educational policies, it seems, have hitherto been unable to replace the ancient lore with something which is equally well adapted to the conditions of a Far Eastern rural society. In this sense, the gradual disappearance of the local schools is a heavy loss to Korea. The curriculum, the operation, and the merits of these local schools have been described with great sympathy by Bishop Rutt.
Vid. Richard Rutt, "The Chinese Learning and Pleasures of a Country Scholar. An Account of Traditional Chinese Studies in Rural Korea", *TKB,* vol. XXXVI, 1960, pp. 1-100.

[3] Vid. Document III.

fond of to demonstrate their mastery of Chinese literature and histories. In the fourth of the scrolls, we find an example particularly rich in connotations. There, the first reference to the Great Militant Lord is certainly to General Song, the tutelary spirit of the village. Having already observed that the reverence of the villagers does not only pertain to him, but also includes Chang Pogo, we may further take the title to include any of the war heroes associated with the area, such as Yi Sunsin 李 舜 臣 (1545—1598), the hero of the anti-Japanese struggle during the invasions of Toyotomi Hideyoshi 豊 臣 秀 吉 (1535—1598). Reference to Admiral Yi is already contained in the scroll preceding the one under discussion here. Finally, if one takes the Chinese characters as proper names, they also refer to either a "Lord Wu of the Han", in whom we may recognize Emperor Wu (140—87) of the Former Han (206-8 A. D.), or to the "Lords of Han and Wu", *i. e.* the rulers and generals of the kingdoms of Wu (222—280) and Shu 蜀 (221—263) who, after the fall of the Han dynasty in 220 A. D., fought among each other for supremacy in the empire and its restoration to its former grandeur.[4]

Besides displaying reverence for the powerful personality as such, that scroll testifies to a schoolbook knowledge which does not fall behind what we would expect from China. Examples like the one discussed here serve to refute the widespread, but entirely wrong idea of the illiteracy of the common Korean peasant.

The Dominance of Old Age

A Western reader of the *Regulations of Changjwa-ri* is surprised at the moralistic overtones of the text. Concern for morals and virtue in a record of law may appear strange to a Western student, but certainly not to somebody brought up in a tradition profoundly tempered by the preoccupation with the idea that correct behaviour should not be based on the observation of rules and laws but be dependent on a properly set mind, which takes its bearing from the exalted models of the past. This preoccupation is truly Confucian in the narrow sense of the term, and those elements in village culture which follow from such preoccupation are genuinely Confucian. We have had several opportunities pointing at the exhortations to observe frugality, to honour the past, to preserve the good customs of old, and to be loyal to the state. However, as has also been

---

[4] A relationship between the Han and the kingdom of Shu could be established, because the rulers of Shu were the descendants of the family which had ruled the Han empire. As such, the princes of Shu claimed legitimate succession to the throne of the empire.

Vid. Edwin O. Reischauer/John K. Fairbank, *East Asia: The Great Tradition,* A History of East Asian Civilizations, vol. 1, London: 1960, pp. 126-131.

said above, these exhortations rather conceal harsh and matter-of-fact duties and are not of a primarily educational order.

Truly moralistic in outlook are those provisions which demand respect for the elders, division according to age, and separation of the sexes. Men and women are to hold their village meetings separately.[5] A desire for decency is also behind the requirement that men and women should leave their homes only after having put on outer garments.[6] Since moral perfection is considered to be the base of all good behaviour, and since those who excel in acquiring merits of that kind should serve as examples to the others, "praise of those of good behaviour and of the meritorious and industrious" is made one of the tasks of the village committee.[7] Village society is divided into superiors and inferiors; age is the decisive criterion, and as the older persons are considered to be the wiser ones, people of greater age are always given preference. They are to be seated in places of honour. If during the elections for the posts of village head and village deputies, two or more candidates have won an equal number of votes, the oldest of them is considered to be elected.[8] The same preoccupation in favour of greater age made the authors of the *Regulations of Changjwa-ri* insert a provision demanding "praise of the fine achievements and good deeds of our forefathers".[9] Under such circumstances, it is not surprising to observe that it is not the task of the young people to improve and change their seniors' way of life, but to "succeed" them, and succession of this kind is ensured by "disciplining the youth".[10]

The Meeting in Respect of the Old

The most conspicuous demonstration of deference to greater age collectively required from the young people of the village is the Meeting in Respect of the Old.[11] The meeting used to be held twice a year, in spring and in autumn (and not once, as is said in the *Regulations*), for the benefit of those men and women of the village who had attained the age of 70 or more years. At the meetings, the oldest among them got a free meal and were given a souvenir of the event. The costs of the meeting were paid from the village fund. The Meeting in Respect of the Old was also an opportunity to make honourable mention of filial sons and daughters and of women who had dedicated themselves to their families and husbands to an extraordinary degree. However, the custom has meanwhile

[5] Vid. Art. 12.
[6] Vid. Arts. 9(4), 27(4).
[7] Vid. Art. 17(8).
[8] Vid. Arts. 9(5), 19.
[9] Vid. Art. 8(4).
[10] Vid. Arts. 6(3), 17(5), 26.
[11] Vid. Art. 9(3).

fallen victim to the trends in modern Korean society towards greater individual freedom and egalitarianism, and the readiness on the side of the younger villagers to prepare such meetings is weakening. Instead of holding such meetings in the villages, people of the region tend to organize them at the county level.

By its name, the meeting appears to have been a faint echo of an ancient Chinese custom which had already been recorded in the earliest Chinese works on ritual. There, the custom appears under the name of Entertaining the Aged (Chin. *yang lao*, Sin.-Kor. *yangno* 養老) and is traced back to the Golden Age of the Chou 周 (trad. dates 1122—221) and even to the times of the legendary cultural heroes and the "dynasties" preceding the Chou. One has to remember, however, that the manuals on ritual in which the Entertaining of the Aged is dated back to China's Golden Age themselves are more or less fabrications from the Han period. There is little evidence that the ceremony predates the times of Wang Mang 王莽 (reigned 9—23) and the Later Han (25—220), and as such was part of the government-fostered efforts to "confucianize" society.

On the one hand, Entertaining the Aged was one of the measures envisaged to alleviate the physical plight associated with old age. It stood on a level with grants of warm clothes, timely provisions of funeral dresses, and exemption from military duty and public appearance. On the other hand, it was a ritual conducted either as part of a ceremony celebrating the establishment of a school or after a royal visit to such a school. At such functions, the Chou king and the masters of the school would highlight the celebrations by a banquet given in honour of the older masters. The celebration was thus a reproduction, as it were, of the offerings made to the sages of former times. Learning the appropriate behaviour for such ceremonies was part of the curriculum of the crown princes and the noble youth of the country. The custom of Entertaining the Aged which, on the one hand, was a measure for soothing the hardships of old age, was, on the other, a display of filial piety which the living generation owed to the elder moral and spiritual leaders. The example set by the king was to be followed by the feudal lords and the local officials in their jurisdictions, and it was hoped that by means of this a similar mentality of filial piety and subjection could be awakened in the minds of even the simple peasants of the country. By some thinkers of Chinese antiquity, the custom of Entertaining the Aged was regarded as one of the fundamental conditions of establishing and securing peace and welfare.[12]

[12] In a recently published book on festivals in Classical China, Professor Dr. Derk Bodde devoted a whole chapter to the ceremony of Entertaining the Aged. Its conduct during the Han period differed from the one thought to have existed in antiquity. For the sake of conciseness, the present author has omitted any reference to the ceremony as it was observed under the Han, and the reader who wants to obtain a complete survey of that custom should consult Dr. Bodde's book on that matter.

Vid. *Shih-chi,* ch. 61 (= vol. 1, p. 0179b; Burton Watson, *Ssu-ma Ch'ien. Grand Historian of*

With regard to Korea, examples of a royal function of tending the old are amply supplied. They reach back as far as the early kings of Silla and Koguryŏ. Those from the Yi period in particular abound in number.[13] The custom was observed until the later days of the dynasty,[14] and even a photo of such a function is extant.[15] As could be expected from antiquarian scholars eager to make Korea follow the Chinese precedents as closely as possible, the custom of Entertaining the Aged as a royal function became a favourite topic in their writings. Several of these scholars expressed themselves at length on the subject, repeating and commenting upon the prescripts of the *Record of Ritual* (*Li chi* 禮 記) and even describing the procedures of dynasties later than Chou. In accordance with the *Record of Ritual*, the point they always wanted to carry home was how essential such a custom was in moulding submissive minds.[16]

China, New York/London: 1963[2], p. 188); *Chou li chu-shu*, ch. 10 (= vol. 1, p. 372.9ss; Biot, *Le Tcheou-li*, tome I, p. 209); *Li chi* (Séraphin Couvreur, *Li Ki. Mémoires sur les bienséances et les cérémonies*, tome I, Ho Kien Fou: 1913, repr. Paris: 1950, pp. 297s, 312-318, 468-471, 490-493); *Meng-tzu* (James Legge, *The Chinese Classics, With a Translation, Critical and Exegetical Notes, Prolegomena, and Copious Indexes*, by . . ., 2nd rev. ed., preface from December 1892, repr. Taipei: Wen-hsing shu-tien, 1966, vols. 1+2, pp. 460-462); *Kuan-tzu chiao-cheng*, ch. 7 (= vol. 5, pp. 109-111; W. Allyn Rickett, *Kuan-tzu. A Repertoire of Early Chinese Thought*, a Translation and Study of Twelve Chapters, by . . ., foreword by Derk Bodde, Hong Kong: 1965, vol. 1, pp. 67-71); Derk Bodde, *Festivals in Classical China. New Year and Other Annual Observances During the Han Dynasty, 206 B.C.—A.D. 220*, Princeton/N.J.: 1975, pp. 361-380.

[13] Vid. *Chŭngbo munhŏn pigo*, k. 83 (= vol. 2, pp. 52-59).

[14] A particularly valuable document of ceremonies of the kind of Entertaining the Aged pertains to a banquet given by king Sukchong 肅宗 (1675—1720) in honour of elder statesmen who had attained the regular second rank (*chŏng ip'um* 正 二 品) and were of 70 years of age or older. The ceremony took place on June 5th, 1719. Since the king himself had attained the age of sixty, he was admitted to the club of elder statesmen, and his presence at the function made it an extraordinary event worth documentation. King T'aejo 太 祖 (1392—1398), the founder of the dynasty, had established a Locale of Elder Statesmen (Kisa so 耆 士 所), where in the year 1394 a function was held which was similar in character to that of the year 1719. Since he and king Sukchong were the only sovereigns of the dynasty who lived longer than 60 years, only two such illustrious ceremonies were conducted during the whole of the Yi dynasty, of which only the latter is documented, by means of the *Album of the Club of Elder Statesmen (Kisa kyech'ŏp* 耆 士 契 帖).

The set of documents contains a preface, the king's address, his card of admission to the club, lists of attendants and assistants, paintings of the event, the portraits of the participants, and the poems written by them on that occasion. The whole set of documents, together with an introduction and explanatory texts in modern Korean and English, has been made accessible to a wider public by a reproduction published by the Museum of Ehwa Women's University in Seoul.

[15] Vid. Richard Rutt, *James Scarth Gale and His History of the Korean People. A New Edition of the History together with a Biography and Annotated Bibliographies*, by . . ., Seoul: 1972, illustration no. 7.

[16] The ideal and practice of Entertaining the Aged and related ceremonies during the deeply "Confucianized" Yi period still await a detailed study. The entries given below are

Pan'gye Yu Hyŏngwŏn 磻 溪 柳 馨 遠 (1622—1673) mentioned in passing that the ritual was also performed in the townships of the country, as an imitation of the court ritual.[17] This observation is confirmed by Tasan Chŏng Yagyong, who cited nine examples of local magistrates having invited and entertained old gentlemen of the region.[18] However, such a kind of entertainment should not be equated with popular rural customs like the meeting of Changjwa-ri. We have to take into consideration that normally a magistrate was a stranger to the region he was dispatched to and thus had to spend much of his time and energy in finding out about local conditions. Therefore, it is probably correct to assume that at least in part such entertainments as mentioned by Tasan were to serve the purposes of eliciting information from the local people and of securing their co-operation. This kind of entertainment was inspired by government interests and was basically a political affair.

Among Yi dynasty writings, the earliest mention of a celebration carrying the same name as the one in Changjwa-ri dates from the latter part of the 15th century.[19] The fact that such meetings were held was confirmed about a century later.[20] We further learn that in the township of Kangnŭng 江 陵 , Kangwŏn 江 原 Province, meetings in respect of the old people were organized in springtime for those of seventy years of age or more. A beautiful spot was selected for the occasion and even "despised people" (ch'ŏnin 賤 民)[21] were allowed to participate. The latter is a feature unheard of in the texts on ritual discussed so far. Sŏngho Yi Ik 星 湖 李 瀷 (1682—1764) mentioned a festivity called Meeting of Cleaning the Hoes (sesŏhoe 洗 鋤 會). It was

---

quite casual findings, and the list is far from complete. An examination of the township gazetteers in particular will yield insights into the spread and popularity of the custom.

Vid. *Iltu sŏnsaeng yujip,* k. 2. 9a.2-7; *Songja taejŏn,* k. 137.2b.6-4a.4 (= vol. 5, pp. 13s); *Pan'gye surok,* k. 26 (= vol. 2, pp. 457-472); *Sŏngho sasŏl,* "Insa mun" (= vol. 1, p. 358), "Kyŏng-sa mun" (= vol. 2, pp. 357s); *Tongguk sesi ki,* p. 245 (p. 25).

[17] As is often the case when a master's teachings have been transmitted to his disciples, the disciples tend to be stricter than their master was. Thus, Pan'gye criticized the peculiar Korean habit of admitting both the old gentlemen and their wives to such functions by saying that this was a severe deviation from the precedents of old, turning the solemn occasion into one of mere feasting.

[18] Vid. *Mongmin simsŏ,* k. 3, "Ae min yuk cho" (= vol. 1, pp. 575-578, 226-233).

[19] Vid. *Sinjŭng Tongguk yŏji sŭngnam,* k. 44.5a.2-4 (= p. 783).

[20] Vid. *Chibong yusŏl,* k. 2.43a.8-10 (= p. 41).

[21] The terms *ch'ŏnin* or *ch'ŏnmin* 民 signified the people from the lowest stratum of Yi dynasty society. It comprised the public and private slaves, artisans such as basket-makers and butchers, actors and singers, sorcerers and soothsayers. Normally, these people could neither pass any of the state examinations nor could they in any other way gain access to official posts.

Vid. *Han'guk sa,* vol. 3: Kŭnse chŏn'gi, comp. Yi Sangbaek, ed. Chindan hakhoe, Seoul: Ŭryu munhwasa, 1969[8], pp. 303-306, 316-324; Susan Shin, "The Social Structure of Kŭmhwa County in the Late Seventeenth Century", *Occasional Papers on Korea,* ed. James B. Palais, no. 1, March 1974, pp. 9-35.

celebrated after the harvest. Its main elements were banqueting and dancing, in both of which the rules of rank were strictly observed. Sŏngho recommended nationwide observance of this festivity because of its intrinsic moral value.[22] As far as can be told from those few documents, both kinds of festivities have not been initiated by any government authorities and have thus not been incorporated into the political pursuits of the government. Instead, they have to be regarded as genuine enterprises of the village community, although the hopes connected with them were not different from those which shine through the lofty court ritual of Entertaining the Aged.

There is one even more detailed account of a festivity in honour of village elders.[23] Both in spirit and organization, it is the one closest in character to the meeting in Changjwa-ri. The author of that text, although not giving any placename, seems to have collected his material by observation of some custom actually performed in his day. The old men of a township, whose names are recorded in a list attached to the regulations, had a house built and maintained "at a sport among the glittering streamlets and green stones". The third day of the third month and the ninth day of the ninth month were designated as the days for the banquets. Some time before those dates the intendant of the old men's club would clean the house and heat it, if necessary. It was the duty of the old men's sons to lend support to their fathers and accompany them to the meeting place, when the heat was excessive. Everybody was expected to carry a jar of wine with him and something to eat. Taking the infirmities of old age into consideration, everybody should see to it that frugality was observed, and nobody should have others eat and drink in excess, lest anyone should have to complain about physical indispositions. During the meal, the juniors would continuously fill the bowls and cups with what had been carried along and put them in front of the old gentlemen. Later, they would dance and sing for them and pay them their respects by kneeling down in front of them and wishing them a long life. The description of the meeting in respect of the old is followed by a record of contributions each member of the old men's club had to make when it came to jointly paying the expenses of a funeral for one of their members. Furthermore, there is a pattern to the parting address which was to be read in honour of the deceased, and a record of more procedures to be observed during the mourning functions. Thus, the meeting in respect of the old turns out to have been only one among several activities and duties, and in fact, this club of old

---

[22] The festivity known as *homisise* 鍬 洗 , which was observed in the forties of this century by Professor Suzuki Eitarō, seems to have been identical with the one described by Sŏngho.

Vid. *Sŏngho sasŏl*, "Insa mun" (= vol. 1, p. 358); *Han'guk nongch'on tapsagi*, comp. Suzuki Eitarō, pp. 112-115.

[23] Vid. *Hyangyak t'ongbyŏn*, "Kirodang yangnyŏng" 耆 老 堂 約 令 (= vol. 3, pp. 157-161).

gentlemen is to be regarded as a mutual benefit association established for the purpose of holding banquets and of organizing mourning ceremonies for its deceased members by means of contributions.

In his introductory remarks, the author of this text did not fail to remark that by conducting such meetings the nation's statutes of honouring the old could be said to be faithfully observed. Therefore, this text is a piece of evidence showing that the people concerned indeed viewed those joyous and simple banqueting parties as being closely associated with the elaborate and solemn ritual of Chinese antiquity imitated by the Korean court and officialdom. At the same time, this record is an example of how a ceremony invented and propagated by, and in the interest of, the rulers penetrated into the minds of the common people to such a degree that it became their genuine concern.

It is interesting to note that even during the period of Japanese occupation, such meetings were conducted in the Korean countryside. There is a list of places in South Ch'ungch'ŏng 忠 清 , South Kyŏngsang, and North P'yŏngan 平 安 Provinces where such meetings were held.[24] Here, the element *hoe* in the names of such meetings is to be taken as indicating a club, *i. e.* the meetings were prepared and conducted by an established organization, whereas the wording of Art. 9(3) of the *Regulations of Changjwa-ri* does not necessarily imply that the meetings were organized by such a firmly established club.

Chinese Elements in the Village Festival

Another interesting specimen among the Chinese elements in the village culture of Changjwa-ri is the village festival. The object of worship being a deified human being, the village festival of Changjwa-ri stands out from among the majority of similar festivals in Korea. Because of the worship of a deified human being, the Changjwa-ri festival is close in character to the ancestor worship of the type manifested in the ritual of Chinese antiquity and later periods. Just as the members of a clan pay respect to their — real or fictitious — creator-ancestor, the "village family" worships General Song as the creator-ancestor and symbol of village union.

The assumption that the village festival of Changjwa-ri is a ceremony somewhat "purified" and elevated above the common type of Korean village festival is further supported by the close connexion between worship and the semi-ritual village assembly. The procedure is strongly reminiscent of a kind of festivity which in 1401 and 1414 was envisaged to be conducted in so-called village communities (*isa* 里 社).[25] In each community, an altar was to be

---

[24] Vid. *CS*, vol. 2, p. 173.

[25] In a former article, the present author gave a more detailed account of the suggested ceremonies and explanations of the terms mentioned in that context. However, he then failed

established where people were to worship and pray for a good harvest. One person was to be elected as head of the meeting (*hoesu* 會 首) whose responsibility it was to care for the orderly state of the altar and the due preparation of food and utensils used in the ceremonies. When the worship was over, the people were to proceed to a so-called community drinking (*hoeŭm* 會 飮). On that occasion, a principal (*hyŏllyŏng* 先 令) would read a pledge (*sŏ* 誓), by which the participants in the meeting committed themselves to refrain from violence and to promote harmonious neighbourly relations. After having read the pledge, the people would sit down according to rank in age and eat and drink.

The parallels between this type of community festival and the village festival of Changjwa-ri are obvious and hardly need any comment. There are three points which matter here. Firstly, the suggested type of community ritual was consciously modelled upon precedents from China. Secondly, the professed aim of the allegedly new institution was to do away with the so-called illegal cults (*ŭmsa* 淫 祀)[26]. Thirdly, the suggestions were made by government officials.

We are unable to decide in what sense the village festival of Changjwa-ri, as we know it today, really owes its arrangement to policies such as those from the beginning of the 15th century. It could be that at an earlier stage in its history the worship of the villagers only pertained to nature deities as their tutelary spirits which were embodied by conspicuous natural objects. Such worship would have

---

to quote the writings by Edouard Chavannes (1865—1918) concerning the earliest connotations the term *isa* (Chin. *li she*) had in Chinese antiquity. *Li she* was the earth god, manifested by a heap of soil, possibly together with a tree and a tablet, of a settlement. It was the lowest of the deities called *she,* which presented the earthly energies of the administrative units. At a very early date, the term already came to mean the group of people who were considered to be attached to such a village earth god, and thus acquired the meaning it has in less ancient texts, *viz.* that of the human village society. It is important to remember that the establishment of such an earth altar and the designation of the people to be dependent on it were not left to the will of the local people, but required the initiative, or at least the consent, of government authorities. Earth altars erected without such government sanction were no proper *she.* Such interference of government authorities with religious life forestalled the policies from the beginning of the Yi period to be discussed here, and it suggests the degree of artificiality by which such policies are surrounded.

Vid. *CWS: Chŏngjong sillok,* k.6.10b.2-12 (= vol. 1, p. 188 — January 2nd, 1401); *T'aejong sillok,* k.27.4a.9-b.8 (= vol. 2, p. 2 — February 8th, 1414); Edouard Chavannes, *Le T'ai chan. Essai de monographie d'un culte chinois.* Appendice: Le dieu du sol dans la Chine antique, Annales du Musée Guimet, Bibliothèque d'Etudes, tome 21, Paris: 1910, pp. 437-525, esp. pp. 439-441; Dieter Eikemeier, "Villages and Quarters as Instruments of Local Control in Yi Dynasty Korea", pp. 75, 92-98.

[26] Some literature concerning the concept of illegal cults has been mentioned in note 67 of this author's article on villages and quarters. To it, we have to add a treatise by Oju Yi Kyugyŏng 五 洲 李 圭 景 , dating from the early 19th century.

Vid. *Oju yŏnmun changjŏn san'go,* k. 43, "Hwadong ŭmsa pyŏnjŭng sŏl" (= vol. 2, pp. 397-380b).

been of the same character as the worship of the Archery Arbour, the Plum Altar, and the well, which still today forms part of the village festival. In this case, the worship of a human being can be viewed as a later addition which can be ascribed to the more refined and generally anthropocentric Chinese — or Sinicized — concepts as described above. However, it could also be that the whole festival owes its very existence to such government policies. It would thus have begun to be conducted only about 200 years after General Song is said to have been active in the region. The present author is inclined to take the former possibility to be the real one. For considering the general inconsistency and inefficiency which tinted most of the local policies of the Yi period, it is hard to imagine that any local official could have been strong enough to initiate a festival and to make it popular among the simple folk. Therefore, we are probably correct if we assume that an original nature worship, which is characteristic of most Korean village festivals, was enriched, probably within the first century of the Yi dynasty, by those Chinese-inspired elements described above.

Echoes of "Shamanism" or "Confuciansm"?

Those features of the village festival and other elements of village culture which have their roots in folk belief need not be discussed here. Worship of conspicuous natural objects as deities, farmers' bands, colourful dresses, and farmers' standards can also be met with at other places in Korea and have been described and commented upon in the literature on Korean village festivals.[27] Observers of Korean folklore, however, sometimes tend to overlook its real complexity and thus fail to recognize those elements which have been imported from China. It is for this reason that the present author has emphasized the Sinicized elements in village culture; he has not done so, because he believes Changjwa-ri to be a mere copy of Chinese villages.

Among the objects used during the village festival of Changjwa-ri and connected with folk religion one calls for a word of explanation here. This object for once may be considered to be of real Shaman origin. When the present author attended the village festival in 1970, he saw three head-coverings called actor's crowns (ch'angbugwan 倡 夫 冠). They are not mentioned in any of the inventories of village property. An actor's crown consists of several slender, rod-shaped wooden sticks, all fixed to a ring which is put on the head. In one case, the sticks are linked to each other at their top ends by means of other sticks.

[27] The literature on Korean village festivals, as far as it was available to the present author, has been listed in note 68 of his article on villages and quarters as instruments of control. To this list, we have to add Han'guk minsokkwa munhak yŏn'gu, comp. Kim Yŏlgyu, pp. 264-275. For the farmers' standards, vid. Appendix 3, note 8 of this study.

The sticks are all wrapped in coloured paper. A lot of evidence suggests close relations between those actor's crowns on the one hand and genuine North and Central Asian Shamanism on the other.

Firstly, *ch'angbu* is the name of the eleventh of the twelve acts (*yŏltu kŏri* 十 二 巨 里, 十 二 祭 次) which are the basic repertoire of Shamans' performances in the Seoul region. The spirit which is at the centre of the *ch'angbu* act is considered to be that of dead males, particularly of deceased actors. It is thought to be identical with the spirit called *ch'ŏnggye* 청 계, a demon causing mental diseases. On Mount Tŏngmul (Tŏngmul-san 德 物 山), once the centre of a popular Shaman shrine festival in the vicinity of Kaesŏng 開 城, Kyŏnggi 京畿   Province, one of the minor shrines is exclusively consecrated to this spirit. It was therefore known by the name of Ch'ŏnggyedang or Ch'angbudang 堂. There the spirit — or spirits — are represented by two wooden masks called *mokkwangdae* 首 廣 大 .[28]

Secondly, *ch'angbu*, like *chaein* 才 人, *kwangdae* 廣 大, or *mubu* 巫 夫, is a name of the male Shamans who provide the musical accompaniment to the ritual performances of their femal consorts, the *mudang* 巫 堂, or in other ways satisfy their audience's desire for entertainment by means of dancing or acrobatics. These names, denoting male Shamans or male actors engaged in religious rituals, are particularly widespread in the Chŏlla provinces. Hence, *ch'angbu* came to mean actor.

Thirdly, because of their fragile structure and their airy appearance, these head-coverings are strongly reminiscent of crowns found in the tombs of Silla and Paekche 百済   (trad. dates 18 B.C.-663).[29] It has been a matter of dispute whether these crowns should be considered as having really been worn as headgear by the kings and aristocrats of those early kingdoms or not.[30] The question is of no great importance here; what really matters is the resemblance of those early Korean crowns to Shaman headgear of the northern and central parts of Asia. Both Silla crowns and the modest actor's crowns of Changjwa-ri may be regarded as vestiges of a culture which once extended from the central parts of Asia down to the Korean peninsula and to other parts of East Asia. Among the findings from the more recent excavations made in China, there is a bowl carrying the picture of headgear which is surprisingly reminiscent of the actor's crowns. That picture almost exactly depicts the crowns from Changjwa-

---

[28] Vid. *Chōsen fuzoku no kenkyū.* comp. Akamatsu Chijō/Akiba Takashi, Tōkyō: 1937/38, repr., re-ed. Kim Ikhwan, Seoul: Hangmun'gak, 1970, vol. 1, pp. 107-115 *et passim;* vol. 2, pp. 31, 33, 46s, 101-103, 108, 207-219 *et passim,* sankō toroku, plates nos. 29, 38, 39, 155; *Han'guk kamyŏn'gŭk,* comp. Yi Tuhyŏn, pp. 29, 147.

[29] Vid. Evelyn McCune, *The Arts of Korea. An Illustrated History,* Rutland, Vt./Tōkyō: 1962, pp. 124s; Chewon Kim/Won-yong Kim, *Korea. 2000 Jahre Kunstschaffen,* übers. aus dem Engl. v. I. Schaarschmidt-Richter, Fribourg/München: 1966, pp. 184-190.

[30] Vid. Carl Hentze, "Schamanenkronen zur Han-Zeit in Korea", *Ostasiatische Zeitschrift,* Bd. 19, Berlin/Leipzig: 1933, pp. 156-163.

ri.[31] Specimens like the one from North China bear witness to the extension in space and time and the vitality of that greater North-East Asian culture to which the Korean culture owes so much. If we consider the actor's crowns from Changjwa-ri as being related to the royal Silla crowns, we do not necessarily contradict this view, because it is a well-accepted theory among scholars that Silla kingship was closely associated with supreme priesthood in Silla religion, which is thought to have been akin to the Shamanism of Central Asia.[32]

However, neither the hats on pictures of the ch'angbu spirit nor those of the Shamans dressed for the ch'angbu act show any resemblance to the actor's crowns worn in Changjwa-ri. Besides, the crowns are not said to be worn during Shaman rituals at the village. Yet, such facts cannot serve to refute the idea of a relationship between North Asian Shamanism and the actor's crowns. Nor can they undo the idea of a relationship between them and Korean folk-religion, so-called "Shamanism". For the resemblance between the actor's crowns of Changjwa-ri and the crowns from the ancient kingdoms of Silla and Paekche, and hence between the latter and Shaman headgear from North Asia, is too striking to be neglected here.

It is also possible to regard the actors' crowns of Changjwa-ri as variants of headgear worn by actors in mask-dance dramas, in particular by those who mime literati-officials (yangban) of the Yi dynasty.[33] Those head-coverings, in turn, are clearly modelled upon various types of hats and caps, such as the Tongp'a kwan 東坡冠, Chŏng-ja kwan 程子冠, panggŏn 方巾, yugŏn 儒巾, changbogwan 章甫冠, ch'ŏnggŏn 青巾, and sangt'ugwan 상투관 which used to be worn as part of the attire of the literati-officials.[34] Being worn in mask-dance dramas, those head-coverings easily lent themselves to being worn in any other performing activity as well and thus also found their way into the farmers' band in Changjwa-ri.

The question is whether the actors' crowns of Changjwa-ri can be said to have sprung from "Confucian" customs for the simple reason that the objects they can be said to be modelled upon used to be worn by the powerful men in a "Confucian" state. Looking at Professor Sŏk Chusŏn's 石宙善 book on the history of Korean costumes, nobody can fail to realize the close similarity in contours between the head-coverings of the literati-official class and the crowns

[31] Vid. Vadime Eliséeff/M. T. Bobot, Catalogue de l'exposition *Trésors d'art chinois. Récentes découvertes archéologiques de la République Populaire de Chine*, rédigé par . . ., Paris: 1973, no. 23.

[32] Vid. *"Maripkan no gengi wo tazunete"*, comp. Mishina Akihide, *Chōsen gakuhō*, ed. Chōsen gakkai, vol. 13, Tenri: Tenri daigaku shuppan bu, 1958, pp. 1-25; *Kukhak yŏn'gu non'go,* comp. Yang Chudong, ed. Chŏng Chinsuk, Seoul: Ŭryu munhwasa, 1962, pp. 163s.

[33] Vid. *Han'guk kamyŏn'gŭk,* comp. Yi Tuhyŏn, pp. 193, 218 (plate 113), 286 (plates 195, 196), 296 (plate 223), 300 (plate 234), 369 (plate 332).

[34] Vid. *Han'guk poksik sa,* comp. Sŏk Chusŏn, ed. Pojinjae, Seoul: 1971, pp. 207-210, 220-223, 226s.

of Silla, the plates of which Professor Sŏk has so ingenuously placed in front of the *yangban* headgear.[35] In Korean headgear, we observe a continuity of shapes which people time and again returned to when they wanted to create conspicuous and festive head-coverings by means of which the bearers could be distinguished. In other words, there is a distinct type of Korean headgear, and it always seems to have been the festive occasion as such which had people manufacture specimens of that type, and not any religious or political commitment of the creator or bearer.

Therefore, the analysis of that headgear defies classification along the lines of religious and political commitment. It also defies classification in terms of social class. For the very existence of the actors' crowns of Changjwa-ri shows that a certain repertoire of shapes has not been the property of a certain — upper — class only. The rather inconspicuous actors' crowns of Changjwa-ri teach us a lesson about the unity of Korean artistic culture. Beyond the distinctions of social class, period of history, and religious commitment there exists a partially common repertoire of artistic means and shapes, which, of course, allows for variations, elaborations, and varying degrees of refinement, but nevertheless remains discernable as such. From among the objects and concepts of Changjwa-ri village culture, nothing can better illustrate the inappropriateness of analyzing Korean culture in terms of religious commitment, as the concept of "Shaman" and "Confucian" patterns suggests, or in terms of class distinctions. Those intellectual devices are the easily handled tools of the learned outsider, but they fail to grasp the concepts as they are rooted in the minds of the people in question.

The Names of the Archery Arbour and the Plum Altar

The present author was told that the northern and southern entrances to the village were once sites of fairly large and dense stretches of woodland. The trees had been planted to form protective shields against the winds, and the two sites were considered to be sacred places which the villagers hesitated to go into. The Plum Altar is the remnant of the northern stretch of the former woodland. The origin of its name appears to be unknown to the local people. The site of the Archery Arbour is a plot of land which has been reclaimed from the sea, and the tree is said to have been planted there in commemoration of that reclamation work. According to this author's informant, there stood, in the middle of the Yi period, a target about 300 m to the west of it, where the villagers used to practise shooting (Sin.-Kor. *sa* 射), and the tree is believed to have gotten its name from that former target.

[35] Vid. *ibid.,* p. 119.

The habit of practising shooting reminds us of an ancient Chinese ceremony known as the Ritual of Local Archery (Chin. *hsiang-she-li*, Sin.-Kor. *hyangsarye* 鄉 射 禮). It is described as having been organized by the magistrate and the notables of a locality, in order to manifest and secure mutual respect.[36] The very name of the Archery Arbour and the reference to a former shooting target could thus be taken as proof that this ancient ceremony so deeply penetrated into Korea that it reached even to the remote village of Changjwa-ri and thus made even that place a part of the world of ancient Chinese culture.

The element of "arbour" in the name of the tree suggests some connection between it and a type of pavilion which is particularly widespread in the southern provinces of Korea, where it is known as reed arbour (*mojŏng* 茅 亭), poetry arbour (*sijŏng* 詩), or umbrella pavilion (*usan'gak* 雨 傘 閣). These arbours are open edifices consisting of a set of pillars on which rests a straw roof. The edifices serve as meeting places where the villagers gather to hold their village assemblies and poetry contests, or where they simply meet to chat and drink with each other.[37] In former times, there may have been such a reed arbour in the vicinity of the tree called Archery Arbour today, or the tree itself may have long been regarded as such an arbour because of its projecting crown. Both evidence from the village documents and from oral information prove that the Archery Arbour does indeed not only figure as a religious object, but also as a

---

[36] Vid. *I li chu-shu* (Séraphin Couvreur, *Cérémonial*, [trad. par . . .], Les Humanités d'Extrême Orient, Paris: 1951, pp. 101-176); *Chou li chu-shu*, ch. 12 (= vol. 2, p. 427.10ss; Edouard Biot, *Le Tcheou-li ou Rites des Tcheou*, trad. par . . ., tome I, Paris: 1851, repr. 1939, pp. 243s); *Shih-chi*, ch. 130 (= vol. 1, p. 279b; Edouard Chavannes, *Les mémoires historiques de Se-ma Ts'ien*, traduits et annotés par . . ., Paris: 1895—1905, repr. Collection UNESCO d'oeuvres représentatives, série chinoise, Leiden: 1967, tome I, p. XXVI); *CWS: Sejong sillok*, k. 62.9b.14-16 (= vol. 3, p. 532 — December 9th, 1433); *Sŏngjong sillok*, k. 100.10a.2-6 (= vol. 9, p. 690 — February 1st, 1479); *ibid.*, k. 157.16b.8-17a.1 (= vol. 10, p. 500 — September 17th, 1483); *ibid.*, k. 174.5b.6-6a.2 (= vol. 10, pp. 663s — January 22nd, 1485); *ibid.*, k. 174.8a.11-b.3 (= vol. 10, p. 665 — January 24th, 1485); *ibid.*, k. 174.9b.11-13a.6 (= vol. 10, pp. 665-667 — January 25th, 1485); *ibid.*, k. 245.5a.1-6 (= vol. 11, p. 648 — September 18th, 1490); *ibid.*, k. 285.11b.2-4 (= vol. 12, p. 453 — January 26th, 1494); *ibid.*, k. 285.13a.3-7 (= vol. 12, p. 454 — January 27th, 1494); *Chungjong sillok*, k. 17.18b.5-7 (= vol. 14, p. 624 — December 30th, 1512); *ibid.*, k. 23.66a.8s (= vol. 15, p. 542 — July 4th, 1519); *Sinjŭng Tongguk yŏji sŭngnam*, k. 39.2a.8-b.1 (= p. 675); *CWS: Chungjong sillok*, k. 97.59b.4-11 (= vol. 18, p. 560 — March 30th, 1542); *ibid.*, k. 101.35b.5-7 (= vol. 19, p. 18 — November 21st, 1543); *ibid.*, k. 101.40a.5-11 (= vol. 19, p. 20 — November 26th, 1543); *Hyangyak t'ongbyŏn*, vol. 2, pp. 168-174; *Sunam ch'ongsŏ*, k. 17.28a.2-35b (= vol. 1, pp. 385-389); *Hyangnye happ'yŏn*, k. 2.1a-29b.7; *CWS: Chŏngjo sillok*, k. 35.36a.12-39a.11 (= vol. 47, pp. 245s — March 17th, 1800); *Oju yŏnmun changjŏn san'go*, k. 6 (= vol. 1, pp. 185b-191a); *Tongguk sesi ki*, pp. 258, 259 (pp. 79, 80); *Hyangnye samsŏn*, pp. 12a-18b.

[37] Vid. "Mojŏngi nongch'on sahoe kyŏngjee mich'inŭn yŏnghyang", comp. Ch'oe Chaeryul, *HMY*, vol. 4, 1966, pp. 1-67; "Mojŏngŭi sahoe-gyŏngjejŏk kinŭngŭi ch'ujŏn kwajŏng. Kŭ palchŏn hyŏngt'aerŭl chungsimŭro", comp. Pak Kwangsun, *loc. cit.*, pp. 69-109; *Han'guk minsok chonghap chosa pogosŏ*, vol. 1: Chŏlla namdo, pp. 239s; *Han'guk kamyŏn'gŭk*, comp. Yi Tuhyŏn, p. 54 (photo of the Plum Altar); Document XIII.13.

meeting place in secular affairs. Such arbours are quite a common sight even today in the southwestern provinces of Korea. Likewise, the morphophoneme *chŏng* frequently occurs in place-names of North Chŏlla Province (Chŏlla pukto 全 羅 北 道).[38] In township gazetteers of the two Chŏlla provinces from the end of the last century, Halls of Local Archery (*hyangsa tang* 堂) and the like are mentioned so often that it is impossible to list the relevant entries here.

Ethnographical evidence from several parts of South Chŏlla Province, however, suggests an explanation for the names of both the Archery Arbour and the Plum Altar which is quite different from that offered in Changjwa-ri. In several parts of that area there are huge trees called *sajang* trees (*sajang namu* 사 장 나 무). They serve as places where the land labourers hold a sacrifice at the time of the village festival, where the rope for the local tug-of-war uses to be plaited, where the elders of the village convene to pass judgments on misbehaviour, where the elder women use to hold meetings during which they prepare and eat flower-shaped rice cakes, or where the general village festival is held. Moreover, the *sajang* trees are places where small sacrifices are offered when the corpse of a dead person is carried to the graveyard or where, on the same occasion, things are burnt which have become unclean during the period of mourning. In particular with regard to the latter usage of the trees, their names are rendered as *sajang* 謝葬 "to thank and bury [somebody]" or *sajŏng* 謝 亭 "arbour of the dead" or "arbour of thanksgiving [to the dead]".[39] The *sa* 射 in the name of the Archery Arbour in Changjwa-ri may thus be taken as just another way of rendering a Sino-Korean word which elsewhere in South Chŏlla Province is rendered by the homonymic — and more adequate — 謝 . In other words, the so-called Archery Arbour may have gotten its name not from any connection with archery, but from its association with burial rituals of the kind described above.

Such conditions lead us to consider the *mae* 梅 in the name of the Plum Altar, too, to be a rendering of a near-homonymic word, *viz. mo* 茅 . If this assumption is correct, the so-called Plum Altar would have nothing to do with plums, but would just be another of the reed arbours which so often figure prominently in village festivals in the Chŏlla Provinces. In a conversation with the present author, Professor Chi Ch'unsang 池 春 相 , from South Chŏlla University (Chŏllam taehakkyo 全 南 大 學 校) and director of its museum, offered an even more likely explanation. According to him, in South Chŏlla Province *maedan* is the name of places where part of the offerings will be buried at the end of village festivals, so as to make sure that the deity will have it at its disposal even after the festive days. *Maedan* should therefore not be written in such a way that its rendering comes to mean Plum Altar, but by means of the homonymic 埋 壇 , meaning "altar of burying [offerings]".

[38] Vid. "Chŏnbuk chibang chŏllae chimyŏngŭi yŏn'gu", comp. Yu Chaeyŏng, pp. 209s.
[39] Vid. *Han'guk minsok chonghap chosa pogosŏ*, vol. 1: Chŏlla namdo, pp. 233s.

In the light of such considerations the local informants' explanations of the names of the two trees appear as etymologies which have been fabricated to accord with the *prima facie* meanings, *i. e.* the ideographical meanings, of the Chinese characters used in the documents to render the names, rather than with the actual role the trees play in rituals in Changjwa-ri and other places in the area. Rather than demonstrating early and deep "Confucian" influences in Changjwa-ri, the informants' etymologies bear witness to their obsession with relating something dear to their hearts to China and Chinese culture. Viewing the two big trees in Changjwa-ri and their names within the framework of the whole of Chŏlla folk religion, we easily recognize them not as manifestations of Chinese influences, but of indigenous local folk-culture. The worship of the two big trees clearly proves the survival of an element of folk religion which is independent of the Chinese influences which have so strongly tinted the cult of General Song. However, although these two strata of village religion are independent of each other in terms of origin, they manifest themselves within one and the same festival. Both the ideational opposition and the factual amalgamation of the two kinds of worship are examples which may further serve to illustrate the peculiarly Korean dichotomy of village culture.

APPENDIX 3: DOCUMENTS FROM CHANGJWA-RI

TRANSLATION

DOCUMENT I

Since the year *imsin* [February 6th, 1932 — January 25th, 1933]
Inventory of all the gongs and drums as well as of other donated cash and
valuables, list of the assets and liabilities of the Society as well as of the
uncollected contract violation fines.
Society for the Promotion of Folk Customs of Changjwa-ri

DOCUMENT II

Pledge

[We] take an oath that when [somebody] has with or without intention
damaged gongs or drums which are part of the village property, the evil-doer or
the household head of the evil-doer will without protest cover the expenses
needed for the repair of the things damaged, if requested by the ward head or the
keeper [of the instruments].

In the first month of the year 4279 after Tan'gun's accession to the throne
[January 1946].

the covenanters of Changjwa-ri: Hwang Pohyŏn (seal) and the seals of 140
other persons

DOCUMENT III

Scrolls [Celebrating] the Beginning of Spring

On the first day of spring good luck and safety for the village;
In [the era] *kŏnyang*[1] many blessings and peace for the country;
In the waters in front of us the tactics and the soldiers of Korea;

[1] *Kŏnyang* literally means "establishing the solar [calendar]". It is the name of the period
which started on January 1st, 1897 and ended in August 1898, when *kŏnyang* was replaced by
kwangmu 光武 as the name of the subsequent era. The name *kŏnyang* is due to the fact that
the Korean government, under Japanese influence, at that time decided to abolish the lunar
calendar and use the solar calendar instead. The selection of a Korean era name of its own was
meant by the Japanese to be a token of Korea's indepencence from China.

The camellia bushes as a wall wind around the altar of the Great Militant
Lord;
Prosperous harvest of the Five Grains;[2]
Abundance of the Six Animals[3]

DOCUMENT IV

Pattern of the Address Declaimed when Performing the Sacrifice at the Shrine

On the day (Heavenly Stems and Earthly Branches) of the month (Heavenly
Stems and Earthly Branches) of the year (Heavenly Stems and Earthly
Branches), the representatives of the people of Changjwa-ri (the names) call
upon General Song. Thy authority excelled in Thy Time and Thy spirit outlived
a hundred generations. We now raise our eyes to Thee and respectfully present
delicacies and reverently offer wine. May these offerings be acceptable to Thee!

DOCUMENT V

The Order of Roofing the House

[This document records the order by which the inhabitants of various parts
of the village have to renew the roof of General Song's shrine on General's
Island. The list is incomplete, because it contains the turns from six to eight
only.

For the purpose of roofing the shrine one makes use of a natural subdivision
of the village into three wards (ku 區), of which the inhabitants alternately
perform the task. In the third line from above, the names of the three wards are
given as village of the upper area, village of the central interior, and village of the

---

[2] The Five Grains is a stereotype taken from ancient Chinese literature. Four different
series are known, and among them the one appearing both in the *Rites of Chou* and in the first
part of the chapter "Duke Wen of T'eng" (T'eng Wen kung 滕 文 公) in *Meng-tzu* seems to
be the best known. There, the Five Grains are glutinous millet (Chin. *shu*, Sin.-Kor. *sǒ* 黍),
paddy (*tao, to* 稻), panicled millet (*chi, chik* 稷), wheat (*mo, maek* 麥), and pulse (*shu, suk*
菽).
Vid. *Meng-tzu* (Legge, *The Chinese Classics,* vols. 1+2, pp. 250s); *Chou li chu-shu,* ch. 5 (=
vol. 1, p. 169.7; Biot, *Le Tcheou-li,* tome I, pp. 95s).
[3] This is another stereotype borrowed from ancient Chinese literature. It is defined in the
Erh-ya 爾 雅, according to which it comprises horse (*ma* 馬), ox (*niu, u* 牛), sheep (*yang*
羊), pig (*shih, si* 豕), dog (*ch'üan, kyǒn* 犬), and chicken (*chi, kye* 鷄).
Vid. *Erh-ya chu-shu,* ch. 10 (= vol. 38, p. 462.2).

lower interior.[4] As the cyclical combinations in the last line show, each ward bears the responsibility for one year.]

DOCUMENT VI

Precedent of the Address Read on the Occasion of the Construction of the Shrine

On the twenty-first day of the twelfth month of the lunar calendar in the year 4298 after Tan'gun's accession to the throne [January 12th, 1966], Hwang Kŭnju as representative of the people of Changjwa-ri calls upon the Spirits of Heaven and Earth [and tells them that] now we are building a shrine-house. Although [we, who have been blessed by the] good luck which results from the good deeds of our forefathers, have not resigned ourselves to the admonitions of our ancestors, we [still dare to] fearfully await [new] favours and with respect offer Thee wine and fruit. With reverence I inform Thee about this, and humbly I bow to Thy Honourable Spirit, so that Thou mayest protect our everlasting welfare.

DOCUMENT VII

Village Articles of Changjwa-ri on Wan Island

§ 1 General Rules

Art. 1

As to these village articles, all the villagers will observe the laws of the country and, by means of humanism and fraternal love, will firmly establish unity among themselves; they will do away with the bad habits in society and plan for economic stability; everyone will completely meet his responsibilities and duties and will preserve the fine customs and beautiful manners and [thus] aim at the prosperity of the village and the loyal service to the country.

---

[4] Two brooklets running through the village are regarded as the border-lines separating the three parts from each other. The divisions are still acknowledged today, although the cluster of houses has become so dense that almost no space is left between the three parts, and the village appears as a single unit. In daily speech, the villagers will call the three parts not by their Sino-Korean names which appear in this document, but by their Korean names, *viz.* *utch'um* 웃춤 (upper edge), *kaunde maŭl* 가운데 마을 ("in-between-village"), and *araech'um* 아래춤 (lower edge).

Pledge

In order to promote fine customs and refine our native place in unanimous co-operation, we take an oath on the items recorded below, and at the same time, we decide that from those who fall under one of the articles we shall collect a fine for violation of articles.

Record

1) We decide that from those who, without [being hindered by any particular] incident, did not take part in the usual meetings or came late, we once collect one *toe* of washed grain of the season.

2) We decide that from those who, without [being hindered by any particular] incident, did not take part in the common compulsory labour or did not apply their vigour in the families, we collect an indemnity worth the pay of one day of hired labour.

Yet, those who have to avoid [public appearance] because of family affairs and the like, or who are seriously ill, are exempted from this regulation.

3) We decide that from those who in the sacred forests around the shrine of General Song on General's Island, the Plum Altar, and the Archery Arbour have illegally felled trees, broken of branches, pealed off bark, tied up cattle and sheep, stored beams used in seaweed culture, or piled up garbage and [thereby] disturbed the beauty of our native place, we confiscate the goods and collect a fine for violation of the articles of at least five thousand *hwan*[5].

4) We decide that from those who have illegally felled trees in village-owned forests, privately owned forests as well as in woodlands which are jointly taken charge of, used, and exploited by the village, we confiscate the goods and collect a fine for violation of the articles of at least five thousand *hwan*.

5) We decide that from those who have without permission encroached upon forestry products from the province-owned forests within the territory of our village, we confiscate the goods and charge against them a file with the authorities concerned.

6) As to those who have stolen other peoples' farm produce, we decide that it goes without saying that we shall indemnify the person concerned and banish [the evil-doer] from the village.

7) We decide that when [somebody] has let cattle graze freely, we once collect [from him] one *toe* of washed grain of the season.

8) We decide that from those who have let filthy water penetrate into the common well or wrung their laundry [there], or who by its side washed things

[5] From February 15th, 1953, until June 9th, 1962, the name of the South Korean currency was *hwan* 圜 , abbreviated as Hw. From June 10th, 1962, onwards it was called *wŏn* 圓 , abbreviated as W.

like clothes, seaweed, and fresh vegetables, we once collect one *toe* of washed grain of the season.

9) We decide that from those who on their own have collected seaweed or camellia fruit[6] growing within the territory of our village, before the announcement of joint collecting was issued, we confiscate the goods and collect a fine for violation of the articles of at least five thousand *hwan*.

10) As to the behaviour of employees and family members, we decide that we will not hold responsible the old and the young, but that all the covenanters will bear the responsibility [for their behaviour].

11) As to the disobedient behaviour of those living in the attached rooms, we decide that the landlord bears all the responsibility.

In order to authenticate this pledge we seal the items.

In the fifth month of the year 4285 after Tan'gun's accession to the throne [May 1952].

The covenanters from Changjwa-ri

DOCUMENT VIII

Regulations of Changjwa-ri

§ 1 General Rules

Art. 1

As to our village, we expect to rule it by means of self-government of the inhabitants under the guidance and superintendence by the government and [other] public offices of our country; we have the aim jointly to establish firm measures prodiving for the economic stability of the inhabitants, to do away with all the former bad habits in society, and to preserve the fine customs and beautiful manners characteristic [of our native place, thus] contributing to the loyal service to the country and the prosperity of the village.

Art. 2

The term "our village" designates Changjwa-ri, and by the term "inhabitants" we mean people who have their residences within the boundaries of our village.

---

[6] The fruits of the camellia bush yield an oil which is widely used for dressing the hair and thus much cherished among the local people.

Art. 3

The inhabitants enjoy the freedom of religious belief and of conscience and they have the right to, and the duty of, labour.

Art. 4

The inhabitants look for an improvement of the position of the village and submit entirely to the guidance by the government and [other] public offices.

Yet, in case of guidance which runs counter to democratic development, they are not bound by this provision.

§ 2 The Rights and Duties of the Inhabitants

Art. 5

The inhabitants have the right to elect the officers recorded below, and they have the duty to take charge of their posts during the period for which they are elected to the offices.

[There are?] the offices and the elections of the village head, of the heads of the corporations, and of other representatives.

Art. 6

The inhabitants hope to loyally serve the country by means of democratic development, and they have the duties recorded below.

1) Utmost faithfulness and strong effort for the sake of the unity and defense of the national territory,

2) Co-operation in the foundation and operation of democratic institutions,

3) Utmost effort in educating the children and co-operation in disciplining the youth,

4) Making [the idea of] the national holidays a concern of the family,

5) Raising the spirit of a democratic nation as well as thorough understanding of the idea of a nation,

6) Payment of all kinds of taxes as well as of miscellaneous fees raised by the government and [other] public offices, according to everybody's individual assignment.

7) Co-operation in the maintenance of peace and order and in police matters,

8) Co-operation in the performance of the rites in memory of soldiers who have died at the front, and the consolation of bereaved families,

9) Extending help to those in military service and to other draftees,

10) Co-operation in the fulfilment of the responsibilities and duties towards the country.

Art. 7

In order to care for the economic stability of the inhabitants, we devise improvements of the social ceremonies and we care for the further increase in productivity, as recorded below.

1) As to the participants in congratulatory banquets, [the participation of those] not belonging to the family is restricted to invited people.

2) As to wedding ceremonies, we make them solemn and frugal in accordance with the original meaning of marriage, and we avoid all expenses which are out of proportion,

3) At funerals we entirely abandon feasting with wine and food and offer gruel [instead],

4) As to mourning houses, we forbid the entrance of all except those busy with the preparation of the funeral ceremonies as well as condolers,

5) As to participants in the ceremony of announcing the parting, we abandon [the use of] mourning incense as well as [the habit of] conversation, thus expressing the idea of mourning,

6) To the bearers of the bier and the undertakers we provide extra wine and food,

7) As to family sacrifices, we perform them as seasonal sacrifices at the family shrines year by year,

8) Protection of woodlands and prevention of damage to agricultural products,

9) Joint efforts towards the increase of rice yields as well as of [other] agricultural products,

10) Joint efforts towards other kinds of utilization and towards the increase in vegetable yields,

11) Prevention of gambling as well as strong action towards frugality,

12) Joint efforts towards the increase in green manure as well as in high-quality compost.

13) We take strong action towards cattle rearing and swine feeding and prevent the breeding of rabbits and sheep as far as possible,

14) Prevention of the secret planting of seaweed and joint efforts towards the accumulation of all kinds of wealth,

Art. 8

In order to care for the refinement of our native place, we carry into effect the items recorded below.

1) Repair, enlargement, and preservation of the roads,

2) Preservation of naturally bizarre rocks at the seaside and in the mountains,

3) Protection of the sacred forests around the shrine of General Song on General's Island, of the Archery Arbour, as well as of the sacred forests of the Plum Altar,

4) Extolment of historical monuments as well as praise of the fine achievements and good deeds of our forefathers.

Art. 9

In order to preserve the fine customs and good manners and to change bad habits for the better, we practice the items recorded below.

1) We organize an association for help in wedding ceremonies and an association for contributions towards funeral expenses, and we have the necessary things provided for [mutual] help,

2) We organize an association for bier-bearers and an association for [other] burial ceremonies and place them at [the inhabitants'] disposal for the burial,

3) We have the youth conduct a meeting in respect of the old once a year,

4) We have men and women alike go out of the houses [only] after having them put on outer garments up and below,

5) We respect the superiors and care for the inferiors and, striving for affectionate relations among the people, we handle [the question of] seats, in accordance with the foregoing, in such a way that we seat the old persons in the places of honour,

6) Accumulation of common aid funds and mutual help in neighbourhood efforts.

Art. 10

In order to care for health and hygiene, we jointly urge [the inhabitants] that each private home be constantly kept clean and that the intrusion of filthy water into the common well be prevented.

Art. 11

The inhabitants have the duty to bear the village expenses, the school equipment expenses, and all other miscellaneous fees.

§ 3 Village Assemblies

Art. 12

Of village assemblies, we have two kinds, *viz.* the general assembly of the inhabitants and the village committee.

The ordinary general assembly of the inhabitants is held on the fifteenth day of the first month of each year of the lunar calendar; the extraordinary general assemblies are convened by the village head, when the village head and the heads of the corporations in our village think them to be necessary, or when there is a request from the side of the government and [other] public offices.

As to the number of participants, there is, under normal circumstances, one person from each household. In the meeting of the men, the men take part, in the meeting of the women, the women take part.

The assemblies meet upon oral announcement.

Art. 13

The village committee is convened by the village head, when the heads of the corporations within the village think it to be necessary. Three days beforehand, the village head must enter the agenda and make them known by issuing a circular.

The general assembly of the inhabitants elects a chairman.

The chairman has the right to give a vote on the maintenance of order at the meeting place, on the permission to speak, on the suspension of the right to speak, on the order of exclusion, and on voting; and if it occurs that there is an equal number of ayes and noes, he has the right of casting a vote.

Art. 14

A decision in the general assembly of the inhabitants and in the village committee is taken by [the votes of] more than half of the participants.

Art. 15

The village head and the heads of the corporations present bills to the general assembly of the inhabitants upon the decision of the village committee. The inhabitants present petitions after having obtained the consent of five or more people.

When the general assembly of the inhabitants is convoked because of matters indicated by the government and [other] public offices or because of urgent matters, [the standing orders] are not subject to these provisions.

Art. 16

The village head and the heads of the corporations attend the village assemblies, set forth their opinions, and answer questions, and upon request of the village assemblies, they have to attend and render account for [their administration].

Art. 17

The village committee is composed of those publicly elected at the assembly of the neighbourhood heads as well as of the village head. When the financial burdens are laid upon the inhabitants, it has the right of consent and dissent and decides upon the following matters:

1) Estimate of revenue and expenditure and settlement of accounts of the

village head, estimate of revenue and expenditure as well as settlement of accounts concerning the expenses of the corporations withing the village,

2) Distribution of the miscellaneous fees raised by the government and [other] public offices from among the inhabitants as well as distribution of the expenses of the county forest co-operative,

3) Loss and gain of village property as well as ways of administration together with ways of disposal,

4) Creation as well as abolition of regulations,

5) Distribution of equipment costs of Ch'ŏnghae School and of costs in connection with disciplining the youth,

6) Establishment of plans as well as of association contracts entailing financial burdens for the inhabitants,

7) Estimated expenditure and disbursement beyond the estimate,

8) Praise of those of good behaviour and of the meritorious and industrious ones,

9) Treatment of violators of the regulations as well as reduction of the allowances to those negligent of their duties,

10) Other matters deemed to be necessary.

§ 4 The Board

Art. 18

In order to deal with the village affairs, our village installs the following board: one village head, six village deputies, several neighbourhood heads, one village clerk, and one forest ranger.

[In general] the above mentioned board holds honorary posts, but we pay a certain amount of annual remuneration to the village head, the village clerk, and the forest ranger.

Yet, this depends on the decisions of the village assemblies.

Art. 19

The village head is elected by the general assembly of the inhabitants, the village deputies are elected by the assembly of the neighbourhood heads. In general, the elections are carried out by anonymous suffrage. The person who gains the majority of the votes is elected. When there is an equality of votes the oldest person is elected.

The neighbourhood heads are commissioned by the village head on recommendation of the members of the neighbourhoods; the village clerk is commissioned by the village head on recommendation of the village committee; the forest ranger is commissioned by the head of the forest association on recommendation of the village committee.

Art. 20

Upon the instructions of the authorities the village head manages the village affairs and represents our village. Depending on the decisions of the village committee, he attends to the village expenditure and raises the miscellancous fees.

The village deputies constitute the village committee and decide on all matters of Art. 18[7].

The neighbourhood heads represent the members of the neighbourhoods and assist the village head.

Upon instruction of the village head the village clerk handles the village affairs.

Upon instruction of the head of the forest association the forest ranger guards the forests.

Art. 21

The village head's term of office is two years.

The term of office of a village head who has taken office under a by-election is limited by the remaining term of office of the previous office holder.

Yet, re-election is possible.

§ 5 Finances

Art. 22

The financial calculations are based on [the estimates for] successive years. To the village committee the village head submits the estimate of revenue and expenditure of the village as well as the balance sheets, and the heads of the corporations submit their estimates of revenue and expenditure, the yearly ones and those of the running costs, as well as the balance sheets, and [both] have to await the village committee's decision.

Art. 23

As to the disbursement of reserve funds meant to be appropriated for the expenditure beyond the estimate or exceeding the estimate, the village head and the heads of the corporations have to obtain the approval of the village committee beforehand.

Without the decision of the village committee, the village head cannot lay financial burdens upon the inhabitants.

[7]This is a mistake in the text. The article in question is not no. 18, but no. 17.

§ 6 The Corporations Within the Village

Art. 24

The corporations within the village establish the regulations of their corporations, and they have to handle their affairs and to account for their expenditures along the lines of their estimates.

Yet, when they establish regulations and rules without [observing] the usual standards, they have to obtain the approval of the village committee.

Art. 25

The elections to office of the corporation deputies are dependent on the regulations of the corporations.

Art. 26

Upon request of the village head and the village committee, the youth of the village and the neighbourhood heads have, at any time, to fulfil their responsibilities and duties as an advance-guard and, striving for an improvement of the position of the village, [the neighbourhood heads] have to educate the personalities who are to succeed the old ones.

§7 The Handling of Violators of the Regulations and of Those Negligent of their Duties

Art. 27

As to those who as inhabitants fall under one of the items recorded below, the neighbourhood heads and the village deputies in joint deliberation discuss [their faults] and reprimand [the violators].

For those who reject the summons or do not respond to discussions and reprimands, we suspend the supply quotas.

1) Those who have defiled the name of the village by undecent behaviour,

2) Those who have been careless about humanism and righteousness and are intoxicated by their immediate private profits and private desires,

3) Those who have disregarded human rights and disturbed human relations,

4) Those who by neglect of propriety have gone out of the house without having put on outer garments,

5) Those who have raised rabbits and sheep, although being devoid of feed and cultivating grounds of which [the right to raise rabbits and sheep] has been confirmed by the inhabitants,

6) Those who without any function went into houses where there was a wedding or houses where people were in mourning, and obtained wine and food,

7) Those who without invitation have joined, or stayed close to, banqueting parties,

8) Those who without any particular reason have been remiss in the payment of the various kinds of taxes and miscellaneous fees and have [thereby] defiled the name of the village and enlarged its expenses,

9) Those who have impeded the execution of these regulations and have not protected our native place.

Art. 28

Those who come under one of the items recorded below, we regard as violators of the regulations, and from them we collect agricultural products of the season worth the pay of one day.

Yet, when the designated day has gone by, we shall collect them by force.

1) Those who without [having been hindered by any particular] incident did not take part in the usual meetings or came late,

2) Those who without [having been hindered by any particular] incident did not take part in the commune labour or did not apply their vigour in the families,

3) Those who let cattle and sheep graze freely near the Archery Arbour or the Plum Altar, or who tied them up at [those places],

4) Those who let filthy water penetrate into the common well or who wrung their laundry [there] or washed things like clothes, seaweed, and fresh vegetables [at that place],

5) Those who by having let cattle graze caused damage to the crops.

Art. 29

From those who come under one of the items below, we confiscate their commodities without compensation, and as regulation violation fine we once collect grain worth twice the sum of a one day pay.

Yet, when they do not pay at the designated date, we collect [it] by force.

1) Those who have gathered seaweed in the waters of the village territory, before the announcement of joint gathering was issued,

2) Those who in the sacred forests around the shrine of General Song on General's Island, the Plum Altar, or the Archery Arbour have illegally felled trees, broken off branches, pealed off bark, set fire, stored beams used in seaweed culture, and piled up fertilizers or [other] things,

3) Those who illegally felled trees in village-owned forests, privately owned forests, and jointly owned forests, or those who before announcement arbitrarily collected camellia fruit.

Art. 30

From those who in the province-owned forests within the territory of our village without permission felled young trees which they used for [purposes] other than [making] agricultural tools, we confiscate the goods without compensation.

Yet, when [somebody] does not respond [to our quest] in time, we file a charge against him with the authorities concerned.

Art. 31

As to those who have stolen other people's farm produce, domestic animals, clothes, raw cloth, seaweed, bamboo, and other things, it goes without saying that we indemnify the owner for the loss incurred, and we cut close relations [with those people], suspend the assignment of all kinds of supplied goods, suspend the assignment of lots to grow seaweed, refuse [them the right] to collect forest products, and banish them from the village.

Art. 32

As to the family conduct of the employees and the old and young ones, we altogether regard it as the conduct of the household heads and deal with [them accordingly].

Yet, when [somebody] does not respond [to our quest], we suspend the assignment of all kinds of supplies.

Art. 33

As to the conduct of lessees of houses or rooms, we regard it as the conduct of the lessors of houses or rooms and we have [the lessors] forthwith perform their duties.

Yet, when [somebody] does not respond [to our quest], we suspend the assignment of all kinds of supplies, and from the landlord or the lessor of a room, we by force collect grains or other things worth the amount of money which has been imposed [on the violator] and which he failed to pay.

Art. 34

To those who as officials of our village have not been diligent in the fulfilment of their duties, we only grant an allowance reduced by ten to fifty percent.

Yet, the percentage of the reduction in allowance will be decided upon by the village committee.

Amendment

Art. 35

As to the initial officials who have carried these regulations into effect, we confirm them as officials elected according to these regulations.

We take an oath to forthwith carry these regulations into effect, and jointly seal them. Convenanters are the household heads.

On the thirtieth day of the seventh month of the lunar calendar, in the year 4285 after Tan'gun's accession to the throne [September 18th, 1952]

Covenanters:

Village head:

Kim Chonggŭn

Village deputies:

Hwang Tongsŏp   Mun Ch'ŏlchu

Mun Ch'angju   Kim Namch'ŏl

Hwang Chonghŭi   Kim Sŭngp'yo

[and the names of 127 other persons]

DOCUMENT IX

Inventory of Gongs, Drums, and [Other] Things

The twentieth day of the first month of the year *pyŏngsul* [February 21st, 1946]

One pair of banners,[8]
one large gong,[9]

---

[8] These banners together with farmers' standards (*nonggi* 農旗) are at the centre of a ritual called salute to the banners (*kisebae* 旗歲拜), which is performed in various parts of the Chŏlla provinces either on the fifteenth day of the first month of the lunar calendar or in the middle of the seventh month. This ritual seems to be particularly popular in Iksan 益山 county, North Chŏlla Province. Farmers from several villages, about 25 men from each, normally gather at some place, from where they will start a procession to collect the flags of each village in succession. They will pay their respects to the banners at a convention, and afterwards they will have the flags salute each other. There are always two banners and two farmer's standards from each village. Sometimes, the rites will be followed by games in the course of which one party of banner-carrying farmers will try to snatch away the banners of another party. These games are called *kissaum* 旗싸움 or *nonggi ppaekki* 農旗 뺏기.

In Changjwa-ri, the banners are not used in any such ritual, but instead are simply carried in the procession leading to General's Island and are later shown in the village.

Vid. *Yŏnggi,* comp. Ch'oe Kilsŏng, Chungyo minsok charyo chosa pogosŏ, no. 23, [Seoul: Munhwa kongbo pu,] Munhwajae kwalliguk, 1970, esp. pp. 43-62, 69-71 (with a drawing).

[9] The instrument is normally known by the name of *ching* 鉦. The character 鉦 found in this inventory should therefore be regarded as a simple misspelling.

Following the systematization of Professor Chang Sahun 張師勛, we would have to take *ching* to be a generic name for gongs, of which there are two kinds, *viz.* large gongs (*taegŭm* 大金) and small gongs (*sogŭm* 小). The *ching* of this inventory, however, only refers to what Professor Chang calls *taegŭm.*

Vid. *Han'guk akki taegwan (Korean Musical Instruments),* comp. Chang Sahun, written

four small gongs,[10]
nine middle-size drums (made of neat's leather),
three small drums (two made of neat's leather, one made of cloth and wood),[11]
four tied hats,[12]
four coloured dresses (newly made objects),

under the sponsorship of the Ministry of Cultural Affairs and Public Information (Munhwa kongbo pu), Bureau for Cultural Properties (Munhwajae kwalliguk), Seoul: Han'guk akki hakhoe, 1969, pp. 121-123.

[10] These instruments are usually known by the names of *kkoengmaegi* 꾕 매 기 or *kkaengmaegi* 꺵. The rendering in the inventory of the names by means of Chinese characters betrays a curious popular etymology. For the character 廣, pronounced *kwang* in standard Korean, with a tendency to omit the labial, is used to represent the syllable 꺵. The change from *kwang* or *kang* to *k(k)aeng* is the result of a regressive vowel assimilation induced by the *mae*. Since this kind of assimilation is a common feature in the Korean language, the use of a character pronounced *kwang* or *kang* was sure to appear as a satisfactory device to represent the *k(k)aeng*. *Maegi*, in turn, seems to have been taken as the nominal form of the verb *maeda* "to weed", "to cut", for 釗, among others, has that very meaning. Thus, 釗 would be the translation of a Korean word erroneouly supposed to be behind the *maegi*. The "Chinese" rendering of *kkoengmaegi* must be thought to consist of one character used for its phonographic value and one used for its ideographic value.

Instead of *kkoengmaegi* or *kkaengmaegi*, this instrument is sometimes called *soe* 쇠. If we assume that it was this name which the villagers had in mind, the character 釗 *so* could be taken to represent the *soe*. In this case, the character 廣 should be regarded as a shortening of *kwangdae* 廣 大, which is one of the most common terms meaning "mask" or "actor" of the Korean mask-dance drama. Thus, 廣 釗 should be translated as "actor's gong". Indeed, the gongs in question here are used by the farmers' music band during the village festival. With their colourful dresses and hats its members have an actor-like appearance, although they do not perform in a formal mask-dance drama. In the light of such an interpretation, the "Chinese" rendering of the name of the gongs must be taken as consisting of two characters used for their phonographic value.

Vid. *ibid.*, pp. 122s; *Han'guk kamyŏn'gŭk*, comp. Yi Tuhyŏn, pp. 39-44, 124s, 134, 326-330; pp. 87s, 148-151; Documents IX—XII.

[11] These so-called middle-sized drums have nothing in common with the instrument of the same name described by Professor Chang Sahun. Instead, the middle-sized drums of Changjwa-ri resemble the so-called big drums (*t'aego* 太 鼓) used by the Korean Shaman sorceresses. The small drums used in Changjwa-ri, however, fit the description given under that entry by Professor Chang. Apart from the middle-sized drums the villagers use drums of the *changgo* 杖 鼓 and *kalgo* 羯 types. They are not mentioned in this inventory.

Vid. *Han'guk akki taegwan*, comp. Chang Sahun, pp. 128-131, 135s, 142s (with photographs); *Chōsen fuzoku no kenkyū*, comp. Akamatsu Chijō/Akiba Takashi, vol. 2, sankō toroku, p. 89, plate 175.

[12] The name is likely to have been derived from the fact that these hats are fastened to the chin by two straps. Sometimes, the first part of the name is found rendered by the character 戰, pronounced *chŏn* in Sino-Korean. Originally, these hats were worn by military officials, which equally well accounts for the use of the war-character in the Sino-Korean rendering of the name. Later they came to be used by dancing and singing girls. When performing in farmers' bands, the peasants will fix tassels to the top of these hats in such a manner that they can keep them moving in a rotating manner by jerking their heads.

Vid. *Han'guk poksik sa*, comp. Sŏk Chusŏn, pp. 53, 64, 217s, 249.

fifteen priest's hats (made of paper),[13]
one hunter's crown (made of neat's leather) [14]

When [somebody] has with or without intention damaged the objects mentioned above, it goes without saying that [he] will give compensation without objections. Likewise, the keeper [of the objects] in times of loss will give compensation according to the foregoing. The ward head will be made keeper [of the objects].

The twentieth day of the first month of the year *pyŏngsul* [February 21st, 1946]

Representatives of the villagers:

Hwang Pohyŏn   Hwang Chonghŭi
Kim Ch'aeho   Hwang Tongsŏp (present ward head)
Mun Ch'angju   Mun Ch'ŏlchu
Cho Pongnyŏn   Kim Namch'ŏl
Kim Nakchu

DOCUMENT X

Inventory of Gongs, Drums, and [Other] Things

The first day of the second month of the year *imjin* [February 25th, 1952]

One pair of banners,
one large gong,
five small gongs,
nine middle-size drums (made of neat's leather).
two small drums (made of neat's leather),
four tied hats,
four coloured dresses (old objects),
fifteen priest's hats (made of paper)

---

[13] Although *nap* usually means the whole of a priest's cassock, it is used here to signify the three-pointed hat of the Buddhist priests only. A more widespread name for this type of hat is *kokkal* 고 깔, under which it appears in the subsequent documents.

Somewhat similar in kind to it is a multi-coloured hat to which tassels are fixed. This kind of hat is generally known as *taeroyŏgŭm* 대 로 역 음. In Changjwa-ri, it is called by a local name *chorijong* 조 리 종. It is worn by the villagers during the village festival, but it does not appear in any of the inventories.

Vid. *ibid.*, pp. 46, 53, 108; *Kugŏ tae sajŏn,* comp. Yi Hŭisŭng, p. 193b.

[14] The hunter's crown consists of a tube-like bottom to which a wooden frame ornamented by tassels is fixed.

When [somebody] has with or without deliberation . . . [The text which follows is identical with the corresponding one in the preceding document.]

The first day of the second month (old calendar) in the year 4285 after Tan'gun's accession to the throne [February 25th, 1952]

Former village head:
Hwang Sambong

Village head:
Kim Chonggŭn

Representatives of the villagers:

Kim Yŏnhŭi	Kim Namch'ŏl
Hwang Kilchu	Cho Pongnyŏn
Kim Nakchu	Hwang Yŏngju
Mun Ch'ŏlchu	Hwang Tongsŏp
Mun Ch'angju	Kim Chŏngsu

An Additional Detailed List of Fixtures

One national flag,
two congratulatory flags,
one case for documents,
one writing-table,
one suspended lamp,
one standard lamp,
two padlocks,
twenty-six leaves of land registers (new leaves),
one book of land registers (old leaves),
one bell,
two *mal* measures of five *toe* (one kept at the house of Kim Nakchu for public use),
one *toe* measure of one *toe*,[15]
one pair of scales (for 510 *kŭn*),[16]
three sets of sportwear for the youth (three vests, three pairs of pants),
three straw-mats (old objects),
three linen awnings (made of cotton, old objects),
twenty pieces of brassware (new objects),[17]
two bamboo-mats (now given out for use in rooms),
one blackboard (now given out for [private] use)

[15] "One *mal* of five *toe*" means a *mal* type measure of 9.2l, and "one *toe* measure of one *toe*" means a *toe* type measure of 1.804l.
[16] One *kŭn* is equivalent to 600g.
[17] At present, the quantity of brassware amounts to 100 pieces.

[We] hand the above mentioned nineteen items over to the new village head.
The first day of the second month of the year 4285 (*imjin*) after Tan'gun's
accession to the throne [February 25th, 1952]

Former village head:
Hwang Sambong

New village head:
Kim Chonggŭn

Representatives of the villagers:

Mun Ch'angju	Cho Pongnyŏn
Kim Nakchu	Kim Chŏngsu
Kim Yŏnhŭi	Kim Namsun
Kim Namch'ŏl	Hwang Chongsik
Hwang Kilchu	

DOCUMENT XI

The twenty-first day of the third month (solar calendar) of the year 4289
after Tan'gun's accession to the throne [March 21st, 1956]

Inventory of Gongs, Drums, and [Other] Things

One pair of banners,
one large gong,
five small gongs,
one trumpet,[18]
one hour-glass drum,[19]
eight middle-size drums,
two small drums,
four tied hats,
four coloured dresses,
thirteen priest's hats,
one hunter's crown

---

[18] Vid. *Han'guk akki taegwan*, comp. Chang Sahun, p. 56.
[19] The instrument meant here is correctly written as 杖 鼓.
Vid. note 11 of this appendix; *Han'guk akki taegwan*, comp. Chang Sahun, pp. 128-130.

Detailed List of Fixtures
One national flag,
one farewell banner,[20]
one clock,
one case for documents,
one writing-table,
one standard lamp,
two candlesticks,
three sets of land registers,
one bell,
one pair of scales,
two straw-mats,
one tent,
three linen awnings,
one blackboard,
seventy-five pieces of brassware (ten sets of big ones, twenty middle-size
    ones, twenty-five small ones),
three measures for grain (two *mal* measures of five *toe*, one *toe* measure),
one volume [of documents] relating to woodlands,
one volume [of documents] relating to coastal affairs,[21]
two memorandum books of decisions,
two account books of particulars concerning the income, expenditure, and
    liquidation,
one cadastre of arable land,
one volume of household registers,
one volume of important documents,
a set of other documents

Without difference [we] hand over and [we] take over each of the above
mentioned items.

The twenty-first day of the third month (solar calendar) of the year 4289
after Tan'gun's accession to the throne [March 21st, 1956]

As the one who hands over:
Hwang Kilchu

As the one who takes over:
Kim Pangsin

Representatives of the villagers:

Mun Ch'angju	Kim Namch'ŏl
Hwang Chonghŭi	Mun Ch'ŏlchu
Hwang Tongsŏp	Hwang Chungsŏp

[20] This banner is set up on the occasion of farewell ceremonies held for those leaving the village for military service.

[21] This is the volume correctly called *Collection of Papers Concerning Affairs on the Coast.*

DOCUMENT XII

The twenty-sixth day of the second month (old calendar) of the year 4290 after Tan'gun's accession to the throne [March 27th, 1957]

One sample [of documents] relating to woodlands,
one sample [of documents] concerning events on the coast,
one sample of important documents,
one volume of agreements concerning musical instruments,
one volume of survey records concerning the actual conditions of summer grain [harvests],
the first volume of account books of particulars concerning income, expenditure, and liquidation,
one volume of protocols of decisions concerning the financial charges at any time within the village,
one sample of papers of decisions,
the second volume of account books of particulars concerning income, expenditure, and liquidation,
one cadastre of arable land,
one table of a population survey,
a set of other documents

Detailed List of Fixtures

One national flag,
one farewell banner,
one clock,
one case for documents,
one writing-table,
one standard-lamp,
four candlesticks,
three sets of land registers (one set old, ten leaves concerning present conditions),
one bell,
one pair of scales,
two straw-mats (wasted),[22]
one tent,
three awnings,
one blackboard,

----

[22] The term as it stands makes no sense in this connection. It is likely to mean that the mats had been damaged by long use and thus were in a bad state.

seventy-five pieces of brassware (ten sets of big ones, twenty middle-size
  ones, twenty-five small ones),
three measures for common use (one measure of one *mal*, one of five *toe*, one of
  one *toe*),

Inventory of Gongs, Drums, and [Other] Things

One pair of banners,
one large gong,
six small gongs (one is not used [?]),
one trumpet,
one hour-glass drum,
ten drums,
two small drums,
four tied hats,
seventeen coloured dresses,
twenty paper-flower hats,
one hunter's crown,
eight drum belts,[23]
one belt for the hour-glass drum,
one throat-band to hold the hat

[We] sign and seal in order to prove that each of the above mentioned items
have altogether been handed over and taken over without difference.

As the one who hands over:
Kim Pangsin

As the one who takes over:
Hwang Chungok

The men present:
Kim Chŏngsu   Ham P'irhyŏn
Mun Ch'ŏlchu   Kim Suman
Kwak Chuyŏng   Hwang Chungsŏp

---

[23] These are the belts by means of which the drums are hung around the neck so as to
enable the men to carry them.

DOCUMENT XIII

Collection of Decisions

1) March 3rd of the year 4288 after Tan'gun's accession to the throne [1955]
The amount of purchased village fixtures and tableware
Tableware: 10 big pieces
                    20 pieces of middle size
                    20 small pieces
10 soup bowls of the same kind
10 covers [for the soup bowls] of the same kind

Keeper:

The present village head

2) "Paper of Decisions"
a) As to the yearly salary of farm labourers, we decided [to pay] not more than Hw 25.000 in advance and Hw 4.000 upon retirement.
b) As to the salary of daily hired farm labourers, we decided [to give them] two *toe* of washed grain as a salary for the farming in the summer and autumn seasons, and in addition [we pay] Hw 200 in cash.
To itinerant farm labourers, we effect [payment] on the same day [the work is done]; as cash salary we pay Hw 300, and as payment in kind [we give] two *toe* of rice.
c) As to forest protection, we decided to settle matters in accordance with the village articles hitherto observed.
d) With regard to new revenues, we took a resolution that the administration committee and the neighbourhood heads will decide upon [them] in a joint meeting.
e) The question of repairing agricultural paths will be decided upon later.
f) As to the time of selling ducks, we determined the end of June of next year.
g) As guarantee fund [to be paid] at the bidding during the sale of coastal waters, we [determined] 20 % of the bidding sum. We [determined] that the total amount of the bid [be paid] within ten days from the day [of purchase].

We decided as recorded above.
In the second month (old calendar) of the year 4289 after Tan'gun's accession to the throne [February 12th — March 11th, 1956]

Village head:
Hwang Kilchu

Hwang Chonghŭi	Kim Namch'ŏl
Kim Ch'aeho	Kim Chŏngsu
Mun Ch'ŏlchu	Kwak Naeyun

3) "Protocol"

On April 7th of the year 4289 after Tan'gun's accession to the throne [1956], villagers interested [in the matters to be discussed], the administration committee, and the neighbourhood heads held a joint meeting and decided on matters as recorded below.

Matters decided upon:

a) As to the separate sheet listing the ranks of the village households, we regulated[24] [the matter] as per enclosure.

b) As to the successive ranks in apportionment in the enclosure which lists the ranks of the households, we decided to determine the apportionment by a difference of 10 % between two ranks from the fifth rank up to the first rank, and that from the sixth rank to the eleventh rank we shall arrange for an unequal difference of 20 %.

c) We decided to separately arrange for, and collect, the total amount of Hw 42.770 of the regular village administration expenses for the present year by means of a rank sheet.

In the month of April of the year 4289 after Tan'gun's accession to the throne [1956]

The participants in the meeting:

Kim Ch'aeho	Yi Chongbae
Hwang Chungsŏp	Mun Ch'ŏlchu
Hwang Chonghŭi	Kim Kwiju
Hwang Taebong	Kim Chŏngsu
Kim Kich'ae	Mun Kwiho
Kim Yŏngbong	Kim Namch'ŏl
Kim Namju	Kim Chonggŭn

Present village head:
Kim Pangsin

[Enclosure:] "A List of Inquiry into, and Stipulation of, the Rank of Each Household"

[24] 調定 chojŏng is a misspelling for the homonym 調整 "to regulate", "to adjust".

Rank	Name	Amount		
1	Hwang Chungsŏp	Hw 430		
	Kim Chŏngsu	430		
	Kim Tonggyu	430		
	3 people		Hw	1.290
2	Hwang Unok	Hw 410		
	Hwang Ungi	410		
	Hwang Haguk	410		
	Kim Namch'ŏl	410		
	Hwang Tongsŏp	410		
	Mun Ch'ŏlchu	410		
	6 people		Hw	2.460
3	Mun Ch'angju	Hw 390		
	Kim Ch'angguk	390		
	Mun Yun'gi	390		
	Mun Pyŏngju	390		
	Kim Chonggŭn	390		
	5 people		Hw	1.950
4	Kwak Hyŏn'gu	Hw 370		
	Hwang Yŏngju	370		
	Kim Kiru	370		
	Kim Namju	370		
	Mun Killam	370		
	Kim Sŏkchae	370		
	Ch'u Kwansŏk	370		
	Kim Kyebae	370		
	Hwang Kilsun	370		
	Kim Pyŏngju	370		
	Kim Namwŏn	370		
	Hong Hŭibaek	370		
4	Chŏng Taewŏn	Hw 370		
	Mun Yunch'un	370		
	Kim Pyŏnggi	370		
	Kim Mongp'il	370		
	Kim Yongt'oe	370		
	17 people		Hw	6.290

Rank	Name	Amount			
5	Kim Namsŏn	Hw	350		
	Hwang Chonghŭi		350		
	Mun Namsu		350		
	Hwang Kŭnju		350		
	Hwang Mongju		350		
	Hwang Kyuhwan		350		
	Hwang Mongsu		350		
	Hwang Sŏngt'aek		350		
	Hwang Yangmin		350		
	Kim Namgon		350		
	Chŏng Yŏngsun		350		
	Hwang Chungbon		350		
	12 people			Hw	4.200
6	Ch'u Ŭryŏp	Hw	320		
	Chong Yŏngyong		320		
	Kim Kibong		320		
	Kim Ponggi		320		
	Hwang Sŏngju		320		
	Mun Hanmyŏng		320		
	Mun Hyobong		320		
	Ch'u Irok		320		
	Kwak Kwinam		320		
	Kwak Kwanggwang		320		
	Kim Kwidong		320		
	Hwang Ŭihyŏng		320		
	Kim Kibyŏn		320		
	Kim Kwisŏn		320		
	Kwak Kwisŏk		320		
	O Changju		320		
	16 people			Hw	5.120
7	Kwak Han'gil	Hw	290		
	Hwang Sambong		290		
	Chŏng Sodong		290		
	Kwak Chuyŏng		290		
	Hwang Taebong		290		
	Kim Insŏng		290		
	Mung Sanghŭi		290		
	Kim Namsun		290		

Rank	Name	Amount	
	Yi Sangnyŏl	290	
	Kang Sangnam	290	
	Kim Chŏngnam	290	
	Kim Myŏngbyŏn	290	
	Kwak Naeyun	290	
	Hwang Ŭngu	290	
	Kim Paekkyu	290	
	Mun Panggyu	290	
	Kang Sangjun	290	
	Kim Yŏngbong	290	
	Mun Chŏngil	290	
	Kang Kwangwŏn	290	
	Hwang Kilchu	290	
	Ham P'irhyŏn	290	
	22 people		Hw 6.380
8	Hwang Chŏnggil	Hw 260	
	Kim Ch'ŏnsu	260	
	Kwak Sŏyun	260	
	Chŏng Ŭnsun	260	
	Mun Mandong	260	
	Hwang Sŏkchin	260	
	Kim Kwiju	260	
	Kim Mansu	260	
	Hwang Sŏkchu	260	
	Sŏ Sangsu	260	
	Hwang Chŏngbong	260	
	Kang Sangsun	260	
	12 people		Hw 3.120
9	Kim Hyongt'ae	Hw 230	
	Cho Tŏksu	230	
	Kim Inju	230	
	Kim Chong	230	
	Hwang Yonggil	230	
	Hwang Namsu	230	
	Hwang Sanggon	230	
	Kim Sŭngp'yo	230	
	Kim Munp'il	230	
	Kim Hyŏngt'aek	230	
	Hwang Ŭngdu	230	

Rank	Name		Amount
	Kim Mansun		230
	Kim Pongdo		230
	Kwak Toyun		230
	Kim Namdo		230
	Cho Samjŏng		230
	Ch'u Chŏngnae		230
	Hwang Chongch'ŏl		230
	Hwang Chungok		230
	Kim Chongp'il		230
	20 people		Hw 4.600
10	Hwang Hŭngju	Hw	200
	Kim Okkwang		200
	Pak Mŏngsik		200
	Kim Ch'anghyŏn		200
	Kim Namok		200
	Kim Chŏngbae		200
	Kim Namsŏk		200
	Kim Chio		200
	Kim P'yŏngok		200
	Kim Myŏngdo		200
	Kim Chŏngho		200
	Kang Pongch'un		200
	Kim Ch'anggi		200
	Kim Poktol		200
	Kim Hangnae		200
	Chŏng Pyŏnu		200
	Mun Hyosŏp		200
	Kim Chongjun		200
	Wi Yangi		200
	Mun Hongnyŏl		200
	Kwak Ch'unho		200
	Kim Wangnyŏn		200
	Kim Yongjae		200
	Kim Uni		200
	Ch'oe Sinhyu		200
	Kim Ch'anghyŏn		200
	Kim Kwisŏp		200
	Mun Chŏnggil		200
	Mun Sangsu		200
	Kwak Namjun		200
	30 people		Hw 6.000

Rank	Name	Amount
11	Wi Yangok	Hw 170
	Ch'u Pangguk	170
	Chŏng Taeu	170
	Kim Pangsik	170
	Kim Chongo	170
	Yi Sŏksun	170
	Mun Ŏkchu	170
	Kim Myŏngyun	170
	8 people	Hw 1.360

Total Hw 42.770

4) "Protocol"

On the second day of the sixth month (old calendar) of the year 4289 after Tan'gun's accession to the throne [July 9th, 1956], the village administration committee, people interested [in the matters to be discussed], and the neighbourhood heads held a joint meeting at the village office and decided on the matters recorded below.

Record

a) The allowances for the village head, the forest ranger, and the beadle [payable] in summer crops[25]

Village head: three *sŏk* (six *kamasu*, five *mal* according to the old measure)[26]

Forest ranger: three *sŏk* (six *kamasu*, five *mal* according to the old measure)

Beadle: three *sŏk* (six *kamasu*, five *mal* according to the old measure)

b) The wages for [village] service [payable] in summer crops

Exemption of Hwang Namhŭi, Kwak Tongyun, and Mun Kwŏnsu from [payment of] wages for [village] service in summer crops. (We decided that in future times [they] will altogether bear their shares in expenses.)

As to the wages for [village] service [payable] in summer crops, we decided upon a levy of six *toe* according to the old measure upon each household generation.

c) Extraordinary village expenses

As to the usual expenses for the three months' period from the first day of the sixth month until the 30th day of the eighth month, we decided to let the village head spend Hw 5.000 for each month [in addition] to the ordinary expenses, [thus] a total of Hw 15.000.

---

[25] Summer crops are wheat and barley.

[26] *Kamasu* is identical with the *kamani* mentioned before in this study. One *sŏk* is equal to 180.17l.

d) Extraordinary expenses
— Sundry expenses for the time of the public village meeting;
— Expenditures for the repair of the village office;
— Payments to those entering the army;
— Allotments in election times;
— Subscription fees for the newspaper;
— Reimbursement for lamp oil [purchased] for public use in the village;
— Costs of repair of the paths and roads;
— Expenditure for receptions in connection with administrative affairs;
— Expenditure for village representatives travelling to town in response to summons [from the side of the authorities];
— Expenditure for receptions in connection with cleaning works.
— [Costs] in connection with smallpox vaccination
As to the expenses coming under the items recorded above, we decided to apportion them within the village.

On the second day of the sixth month (old calendar) of the year 4289 after Tan'gun's accession to the throne [July 9th, 1956]

In order to confirm the above, each of us signs and seals [the protocol].
Participants:

Mun Ch'angju   Hwang Chongmun
Mun Ch'ŏlchu   Kim Namch'ŏl
Hwang Chonghŭi   Kim Yŏngbong
Kim Namju   Ham P'irhyŏn
Kim Ch'aeho   Hwang Chungsŏp

5) The first day of the second month (old calendar) of the year 4290 after Tan'gun's accession to the throne [March 2nd, 1957]

"Protocol of the General Assembly at the Beginning of the Year"
a) Selection of the members of the village administration committee
We have ten members in the village administration committee, and we nominated them upon public oral recommendation:
Kim Ch'aeho, Mun Ch'angju, Hwang Chonghŭi, Kim Namch'ŏl, Kim Chŏngsu, Mun Ch'ŏlchu, Kwak Kwangyun, Hwang Chungsŏp, Kim Suman, Ham P'irhyŏn

b) Allotment of the committee expenses to the action committee for the removal and construction of the 90 years old Ch'ŏnghae School
With regard to the allotment of committee expenditure, we decided to draft a paper [listing] the unequal ranks [of households] of the village and, at the same time, to issue allotments. The paper [listing] the unequal ranks [of households]

of the village will be decided upon by the village administration committee as well as the neighbourhood heads.

c) Election of the village head

In the election of the village head we follow the above directions.

d) Selection of the forest ranger

As to the forest ranger, we decided that he will be selected later upon mutual agreement among the village administration committee as well as the neighbourhood heads.

As to the village forests (ten sheets of paper), we decided not to buy or to sell in future times.

e) Report on the items carried into effect by the Fine Customs Society

We decided upon repair of the common village well [to be executed] under the auspices of the Fine Customs Society.

f) Settlement of accounts of the water storage reservoir

6) March 2nd of the year 4290 after Tan'gun's accession to the throne [1957]

"Protocol"

Concerning the question of the forest ranger

As to the topic, we decided [to nominate] Kim Hyangho, and with regard to the remuneration, we decided to provide six *kamasu* (*toe* in former times) for the first half of his term and six *kamasu* (*toe* in former times) of unhulled rice[27] for the second half, and at the same time, we sign and seal [the protocol so as to confirm] the decisions of the village administration committee.

Administration committee:
Kim Ch'aeho   Kim Chŏngsu
Kwak Chuyŏng   Ham P'irhyŏn
Kim Suman

Village head:
Kim Pangsin

7) "Protocol"

On April 1st of the year 4290 after Tan'gun's accession to the throne [1957], the village administration committee, the neighbourhood heads, and people interested [in the matters to be discussed] held a joint meeting at the village office and decided upon matters as recorded below.

---

[27] 正 粗 *chŏngjo* obviously is a misspelling for the homonym 正租 meaning unhulled rice.

Record

a) As to the assessment [by means of a] rank paper of the village, we decided that after having determined a paper [listing] 13 ranks, the assessment list [according to] ranks will be drafted separately and will receive the consent of the village administration committee.

b) As to the course [to be followed] in the mobilization for all kinds of commune labour, we shall have [the work] carried out by the [physically] strongest of each family, and therefore the weak among the old and young ones will by no means be allowed [to take part in commune labour]. As to those who, without [being hindered by any particular] incident, do not appear for work at the places they were assigned to, we decided to collect Hw 500 from each of those persons. In order to promote a positive [attitude] towards these [matters], we establish a mobilization section.

c) As to the expenditures required for the administration of the village, we decided to spend [the amount of] the extraordinary expenses only.

d) We decided to apportion Hw 30.000 for the estimated expenditures required for the administration of the village.

In order to give testimony to the firmness of the above decisions, each of us signs and seals [the protocol].

Participants:

Hwang Chonghŭi	Kwak Chuyŏng
Mun Ch'ŏlchu	Kim Suman
Kim Chŏngsu	Ham P'irhyŏn
Hwang Ungi	Kim Yŏngbong

8) On May 14th of the year 4290 after Tan'gun's accession to the throne [1957], the village administration committee, people interested [in the matters to be discussed], and the neighbourhood heads held a joint meeting and decided upon the matters recorded below.

Record

a) As to those conscribed to enter military service, we decided to grant Hw 500 as fare to each man.

b) As to the report on the rank paper in connection with village administration taxes, we adapt ourselves to the standard rank paper ordered by the township [administraton] and report by three ranks, *viz.* the fifth, sixth, and tenth. In our village, we consider the remuneration of the village head, in accordance with former precedents, as a uniform imposition, [but] apportion and collect the accompanying administrative expenditure as well as expenditure for writing materials in different [amounts] as indicated in the paper concerning the assessment by ranks within the village.

As times of collection, we determined the seventh and eleventh months.

The administration committee:

Kim Yŏnhŭi	Kim Chŏngsu
Mun Ch'angjŭ	Kwak Chuyŏng
Hwang Chonghŭi	Hwang Chungsŏp
Kim Namch'ŏl	Ham P'irhyŏn
Mun Ch'ŏlchu	Kim Suman

9) "Paper of Decisions"

The village administration committee, people interested [in the matters to be discussed], and the neighbourhood heads held a joint meeting and decided on the matters recorded below.

Records

a) As to the wages for [village] service [payable] in summer crops for the earlier half of this year, we decided on five *toe* per household.

b) As to goat raising, since the damages inflicted upon the crops as well as upon the forests and fields are numerous, we have our people altogether dispose of [their animals], in order [to implement] the prohibition of goat raising. As to those who will not dispose [of their animals], we decided to suspend the [supply of] fertilizers and all other supplies for one year.

c) As to those who distil liquor, we decided to confiscate their tools and goods, divest them of their yearly rights to seaweed and fishing lots, and suspend all supplies for one year.

d) Application of the village articles of Changjwa-ri

Since the village articles are an agreement to continue the beautification of our native place and to preserve the beautiful customs and good manners, and since [they are] related to the economy of the villagers, we decided to carry the village articles into effect by all means from now on.

July 16th of the year 4290 after Tan'gun's accession to the trone [1957]

The men who have taken the decisions as representatives of the people of Changjwa-ri:

Mun Ch'ŏlchu	Mun Kwiho
Kim Chŏngsu	Hwang Chŏngsik
Kwak Chuyŏng	Hwang Sanggon
Hwang Chungsŏp	Kim Chongp'il
Kim Chonggwŏn	Mun Chech'il
Ham P'irhyŏn	Mun Chech'ŏl
Yi Chongbae	Hwang Taebong

10) "Protocol"

On the 14th day of the seventh month (old calendar) of the year 4290 after Tan'gun's accession to the throne [August 9th, 1957], the village administration committee, the neighbourhood heads, and people interested [in the matters to be discussed] held a joint meeting and decided on the matters recorded below.

Matters decided upon:

a) On the 14th day of the seventh month of the year 4290 after Tan'gun's accession to the throne, we selected Kim Ch'ŏnok as forest ranger of the village-owned woodlands.

b) The remuneration of the forest ranger will rely on former precedents.

On the 14th day of the seventh month (old calendar) of the year 4290 after Tan'gun's accession to the throne

Kim Yŏnhŭi	Kim Chŏngsu
Mun Ch'angju	Hwang Chungsŏp
Hwang Chonghŭi	Ham P'irhyŏn
Kim Namch'ŏl	Kim Suman
Mun Ch'ŏlchu	Kwak Naeyun
Kwak Chuyŏng	Hwang Taebong

Present village head:
Hwang Chungok

11) "Protocol"

On the 18th day of the seventh month (old calendar) of the year 4290 after Tan'gun's accession to the throne [August 13th, 1957], the village administration committee, the neighbourhood heads, and people interested [in the matters to be discussed] held a joint meeting and decided upon the matters recorded below.

Matters decided upon:

a) We decided to make Kim Ch'anyu the village beadle on the 18th day of the seventh month (old calendar) of the year 4290 after Tan'gun's accession to the throne.

b) As to the remuneration, we shall rely on former precedents.

The 18th day of the seventh month (old calendar) of the year 4290 after Tan'gun's accession to the throne

Kim Yŏnhŭi	Kwak Chuyŏng
Mun Ch'angju	Hwang Chungsŏp
Hwang Chonghŭi	Ham P'irhyŏn
Kim Namch'ŏl	Kim Suman
Mun Ch'ŏlchu	Kwak Naeyun
Kim Chŏngsu	Hwang Taebong

Present village head:
Hwang Chungok

12) "Protocol"

In the evening of the eighth day of the eighth month (old calendar) of the year 4290 after Tan'gun's accession to the throne [September 1st, 1957], the village administration committee, people interested [in the matters to be discussed], and neighbourhood heads held a joint meeting at the village office and decided on the matters recorded below.

Record

a) As to the day of drawing the lots for the seaweed and fishing grounds, we determined the twelfth day of the eighth month [September 5th].

b) We decided to collect Hw 200 [to cover] the expenses for [the maintenance] of the seaweed and fishing grounds as well as [to cover] the expenses of the village administration.

c) As to the fare we have [hitherto] paid to those summoned into military service, we decided that from now on we shall not pay it [any longer].

d) As to those who have been entrusted with the arrangement of the seaweed and fishing grounds, we decided that they will be responsible for the arrangement of the fishing grounds as well as the handling of the places of the fishing equipment not yet determined. We decided that if at times the duties have not been attended to, we shall not pay [the offenders their] handling money.

e) As to those who in the past year have offended against [regulations concerning] the seaweed and fishing grounds, we shall draw the lots only after having arranged for a violation fine.

In order to give testimony to the firmness of the decisions recorded above, each of us signs and seals [the protocol].

Participants:
Hwang Chŏnghŭi	Kwak Naeyun
Mun Ch'ŏlchu	Ham P'irhyŏn
Kim Namch'ŏl	Hwang Chungsŏp
Hwang Ungi	Hwang Chungok (present village head)
Kim Pangsin	Kim Suman

13) "Protocol"

As to the application of [the arrangement obtained by] drawing the lots of the seaweed and fishing grounds at the Archery Arbour on the twelfth day of the eighth month (old calendar) of the year 4290 [September 5th, 1957], we decided on the matters as recorded below.

Record

a) As to this year's new entrance into [the arrangement concerning] seaweed and the placement of fishing equipment, we decided that Ch'oe Sinhyu pays Hw 5.000 of the Hw 11.000 of the entrance fee [which is due] according to the village articles at the time of the drawing and that we shall receive the remaining Hw 6.000 before the last day of the twelfth month according to the old calender.

b) As to the right [to appear] as applicant for [a grant of lots to grow] seaweed and place fishing equipment, it is limited to those who [have lived separately] for not less than half a year after having established a branch family.

c) As to those who have established a branch family, we determined that they will respond to all apportionments and to all kinds of [summons to] commune labour from the day on which they established a separate family.

d) As to the fields at Kara-ri, we determined that the right of cultivation of the whole area is entrusted upon the present village head and that the farm rent will be one *sŏk* of wheat. (The right of cultivation starts with the time of seeding wheat.)

e) As to the fishing grounds of the ten sections at Hup'o, we decided to trade with [their products] and to receive in advance a bidding sum for a guarantee fund. However, unless at least 10 % of the bidding sum have been paid, the bidding remains ineffective. We decided that the liquidation of the sum of a successful bidder should be effected until the 15th day of the eighth month according to the old calendar.

Kim Ch'aeho   Ham P'irhyŏn
Mun Ch'angju   Hwang Chungsŏp
Kim Namch'ŏl   Kwak Chuyŏng
Kim Chŏngsu   Kim Suman

Present village head:
Hwang Chungok

14) "Record of the Meeting on May 24th of the Year 4291 after Tan'gun's Accession to the Throne [1958]"

a) Kinds of disbursement of the extraordinary expenses;
— In matters concerning the administration;
— At times when the welfare of the villagers [is to be promoted], as far as it is related to the forests;
— [In matters concerning] smallpox vaccination and cleaning;
— [In matters] related to the duties of taxpaying;
— At times of other extraordinary events, decision of at least three members of the administration committee is required.

b) Prevention of distilling liquor as well as profiteering by trade within the village, prohibition of tobacco.

As to those who distil liquor within the village as well as to those who sell cakes and bread within the village and to those who own tobacco or lend tobacco leaves, we cancel all supplies of the village as well as the right to fishing grounds.

May 24th of the year 4291 after Tan'gun's accession to the throne

Participants:

Mun Ch'ŏlchu	Kim Namch'ŏl (present village head)
Hwang Kŭnju	Kim Sŭngp'yo
Kim Namju	Kim Suman
Kim Pangsin	Mun Hanmyŏng
Hwang Pangsin	Hwang Chungok
Hwang Ungi	together with other villagers
Kwak Naeyun	

15) "Protocol of a Joint Meeting Held by the Administration Committee as well as the Neighbourhood Heads"

a) Time

9 p. m. on June 24th of the year 4291 after Tan'gun's accession to the throne [1958]

b) Locality

Village office

c) Matters settled

— Assessment of the paper [listing] the ranks [of the households] of the village

Mr. Mun Ch'ŏlchu, head of the administration committee, as chairman of the meeting promptly read the past [list], and the participants in the meeting revised it in unity.

— Wages for [village] service [payable] in summer crops

— As to the wages for [village] service [payable] in summer crops, we determined the tenth day of the fifth month according to the old calendar [June 26th] [as date for payment].

— Prohibition of distilling liquor

As to those who distil liquor, we decided in accordance with the decisions of May 24th to suspend their rights to fishing grounds as well as to all other supplies.

We sign and seal [the fact] that we have firmly decided upon the above matters and will carry them into effect.

Administration committee:
Mun Ch'ŏlchu
Kim Namju
Kim Chŏngsu
Kim Sŭngp'yo

Hwang Kŭnju
Hwang Ungi
Mun Hanmyŏng

Neighbourhood heads:
Kim Pangsin
Hwang Chungsŏp
Kim Suman
Kim Munp'il

Ch'u Kwangsŏk
Chŏng Tuman
Hwang Chŏngsik

Village head:
Kim Namch'ŏl

16) "Protocol of the Administration Committee"
On December 5th of the year 4291 after Tan'gun's accession to the throne
[1958], the administration committee of Changjwa-ri held a meeting at the
village office and decided upon the apportionments as recorded below.
December 5th of the year 4291 after Tan'gun's accession to the throne

The administration committee of Changjwa-ri:
Mun Ch'ŏlchu
Hwang Sawŏn
Kim Chŏngsu
Hwang Kŭnju

Kwak Kwangsŏn
Kwak Naeyun
Kim Pangsin
Kim Sŭngp'yo
Representative of the neighbourhood heads:
Kim Suman

Matters decided upon:

a) As to the apportionment of wages for [village] service [payable]
according to rank for the autumn of the year 4291 after Tan'gun's accession to
the throne, we apportion six *sŏk* of unhulled rice as allowances [to be given] to
the village head for [his services in] the second half of the year, three *sŏk* of
unhulled rice as share of the village beadle, three *sŏk* of unhulled rice as share of
the forest ranger, and as sacrifice to be used in the village festival, we apportion
the collection in *sŏk*, *mal,* and *toe* of the volume obtained by summing up the
estimated quantities, by [imposing] 9.2 *toe* on each household.
b) As to the grain to be hired out for rent [which is to be used for the
construction] of a health centre at Ch'ŏnghae Primary School, we decided to
collect the average five *toe* per household, which were decided upon at a meeting
of the action committee, by [using] a list [subdividing the households into] five
ranks.

The list of ranks is as follows (drafted by the action committee):
First rank (1 to 4 together)
                          2 households 8   *toe* from each
Second rank (5 to 7 together)
                          34 households 7   *toe* from each
Third rank (8 and 9 together)
                          24 households 5.5 *toe* from each
Fourth rank (10 to 12 together)
                          48 households 3.5 *toe* from each
Fifth rank (13 and 14 together)
                          26 households 2   *toe* from each
_____

Total   156 households 7 *sŏk*, 8 *mal*, 2 *toe*

17) "Paper of Decisions"
   a) Allowance for the forest ranger
   As to the allowance for the forest ranger, we decided at a village assembly to
pay four *sŏk* for each half of the year.
   b) Improvement of agricultural paths
   As to the improvement of agricultural paths, we decided to improve them
within the first month.

   The third day of the first month (old calendar) of the year 4292 after
Tan'gun's accession to the throne [February 10th, 1959]

   The village administration committee:
Mun Ch'ŏlchu   Kim Namju
Hwang Kŭnju   Hwang Ungi
Kim Chŏngsu   Kim Pangsin
Kwak Kwangsŏn   Kwak Naeyun
Kim Sŭngp'yo

   Present village head:
Kim Namch'ŏl

18) "Protocol"
   On March 9th (first day of the second month according to the old calendar)
of the year 4292 after Tan'gun's accession to the throne [1959], we held a public
meeting of the people of Changjwa-ri at the village office and decided on the
matters recorded below.

   Record
   a) With regard to an improvement of the village administration committee
we decided on [the election of] eleven men, *viz.* Hwang Ungi, Mun Ch'ŏlchu,

Kim Sŭngp'yo, Kim Namch'ŏl, Kim Chŏngsu, Mun Hanmyŏng, Kwak Kwangsŏn, Kim Namju, Kim Sŏnje, Kwak Hyŏn'gu and Hwang Chŏnghŭi.

b) As to offenses against the village regulations, we decided with regard to punishments that the fine should be Hw 3.000, and if [the offender] does not carry out his obligations, we shall nullify his rights to fishing grounds, and when [he] exercises [his rights] on his own, the village administration committee will remove [him from the village].

c) With regard to the forests, we decided that those who illegally fell trees in village-owned forests [will be punished] by a regulation violation fine of Hw 500, and when [the offender] does not carry out his obligations, we shall report to the persons in charge of the county forests.

Yet, when people from other villages enter [our] woodlands, we shall report to the persons in charge of county forests immediately.

d) With regard to assessment by a rank paper, we made [the assessment] a common task of the village administration committee and the neighbourhood heads.

We sign and seal the fact that we have without disagreement decided on the matters recorded above.

The village administration committee:

Mun Ch'ŏlchu   Kim Sŭngp'yo
Hwang Ungi   Kim Namch'ŏl
Kim Chŏngsu   Mun Hanmyŏng
Kwak Kwangsŏn

Neighbourhood heads:
Kim Pangsin   Ch'u Ŭngyŏp
Kim Suman   Kim Munp'il
Hwang Chungsŏp

19) April 14th of the year 4294 after Tan'gun's accession to the throne [1961] "Protocol"

The village administration committee and the ward heads held a meeting and took decisions as recorded below.

Record

a) The ward heads will elect one person from each ward as member of the village administration committee, [but] the present assembly [is considered to have been] constituted on its own and is made up of the individual persons.

b) As to expenditure associated with the military police protection society, we [impose] Hw 730 on the first rank and in accordance with the rank paper successively apportion Hw 50 [less on the next ranks].

c) As to the deficiency [caused by the maintenance] of the health centre, we decided not to make apportionments to individuals, but will pay it from [the amount reserved for] the regular village expenditure.

d) As to the education taxes, we decided to limit [the payment] on those placing fishing equipment and to uniformly apportion Hw 180 to each of them.

e) As to the repair of the village office, we decided to repair the rooms only.

f) As to the roads and paths within the village, we decided to have each ward take charge of a section and to have [each ward] repair [it] under the responsibility of the ward head.

g) As forest ranger, we determined Kim Hyŏngt'ae, and with regard to the remuneration we adapt ourselves to [the habits of] earlier years.

h) As to those who, having made bids for fishing grounds as well as having applied for [admission to the agreement on] fishing grounds and forests, have not paid the application fee, we decided to cancel [their rights of] bidding again or the exercise of their rights, when they do not deliver the whole sum until the tenth day of the third month according to the old calendar [April 24th].

Participating committee members:

Mun Ch'ŏlchu	Kim Chŏngsu
Hwang Ungi	Kim Sŭngp'yo
Ward heads:	
Hwang Chŏngsik	Kim Samju
Chŏng Ch'angsu	Kim Chŏngbae
Ch'u Ŭngyŏp	Kim Chonggwŏn
Hwang Chongmun	Kim Tŏngman
Kim Tongju	

20) "Protocol"

At 8 o'clock in the evening of May 22nd of the year 4294 after Tan'gun's accession to the throne [1961], in accordance with the proclamation of an order of the Military Government, the administration committee as well as the ward heads and persons interested [in the matters to be discussed] held a joint meeting at the village office and decided on the matters recorded below.

Record

a) With regard to those who illegally fell trees near the Plum Altar and the shrine, we collect a regulation violation fine within three days of not less than Hw 1.000 and not more than Hw 3.000 for each trunk.

When there is an accomplice, we collect the same regulation violation fine from the accomplice, and when [the offenders] do not respond to this [regulation] or when they let expire the term, we decided to settle the affair according to law, and the village head will bring a charge against [them] with the institutions concerned.

b) As to those who unintentionally encroach upon woodlands of individuals which are within our district and gather fresh or withered wood, they pay to the forest association a regulation violation fine for once of at least Hw 500 in case of minors and Hw 1.000 in case of grown-ups.

However, when [the offenders] do not respond to these regulations, we leave the matter to the owner of the forest.

c) Even if privately owned forests and fields [are concerned], one is not allowed to enter the woodlands outside of the period determined for entering the forests.

However, when the forest association gives its consent, one may gather withered wood.

As to the [matters recorded] above, we shall carry them into effect from May 23rd of the year 4294 after Tan'gun's accession to the throne onwards.

Participating committee members:

Mun Ch'angju	Hwang Chongmun
Hwang Chonghŭi	Chŏng Ch'angsu
Kwak Kwangsŏn	Ch'u Ŭngyŏp
Kim Pyŏnggi	Hwang Chŏngsik
Kim Kiru	Kim Chonggwŏn
Mun Yunch'un	Mun Chaesik
Ham P'irhyŏn	

Present village head:
Kim Suman

21) "Paper of Decision"

On January 7th, 1962, we held a provisional village assembly and decided upon the following matters.

The following [matters]:

a) In connection with the usual expenditure for the village administration, we decided to apportion a monthly Hw 50 per household, and with particular regard to enclosed families, we decided to make the apportionment to the original household.

b) In connection with extraordinary expenses we limit ourselves to the following events:

— Expenditures in connection with village representatives travelling to the county seat for some particular reason;

— Expenditures for giving receptions to the heads of [government] organs;

— Expenditures in connection with assemblies.

In order to confirm the above matters, we sign and seal [them].

Representatives participating in the assembly:

Kim Chonggŭn	Mun Chaech'ŏl
Mun Ch'ŏlchu	Hwang Chŏngsik
Hwang Ungi	Kim Chŏngbae
Kim Namch'ŏl	Ham P'irhyŏn
Kim Pyŏnggi	Ch'u Ŭngyŏp
Kwak Chuyŏng	Kim Tŏngman
Kim Chŏngsu	Chŏng Ch'angsu
Kim Chonggwŏn	Hwang Ch'angu

Present village head:
Kim Suman

22) "Protocol"

On April 29th, 1962, at 9h p.m., the administration committee, the neighbourhood heads, and people interested [in the matters to be discussed] held a joint meeting at the village office and took decisions as recorded below.

Record

a) As to the custody of the village forests, we decided to abolish the responsibility of custody as of April 30th, 1962, and we decided that it goes without saying that the youth corps of the 4-H-Club will supervise and keep control of irregularities in connection with individual guarding of the forests, which [will be the rule] from that time onwards.

b) With regard to the distribution of all kinds of fertilizers, we decided [as follows]: As to the sums not[yet] paid into the public fund of our village, it goes without saying that we shall allocate [the fertilizers] to those entitled to receive [them only] when they pay off the window and door costs stipulated by the action committee of Ch'ŏnghae Primary School as last year's share, the costs of the ceremony in celebration of the completion of the building, and other sums not yet paid.

April 29th, 1962
Participants in the meeting:

Village head:
Kwak Kwangyun

Neighbourhood heads:

Kim Yongch'u	Kim Ch'angsik
Mun Chaesik	Wi Yangok
Ham P'irhyŏn	Kim Tŏngman
Kim Kakchong	Chŏng Tuman
Kim Tongju	Kwak Chonggil

People interested:

Hwang Chonghŭi   Kim Chŏngsu
Kim Chonggŭn   Hwang Ungi
Mun Ch'ŏlchu   Kwak Kwangsŏn

23) July 30th, 1962

"Protocol of a Provisional Assembly of People Interested [in the Matters to be Discussed], the Administration Committee, and the Neighbourhood Heads"

Concerning the collection of the costs of the reconstruction of the village office

We decided to notify the villagers of [the costs], to collect [the payments] within 17 days at the village office, and to oversee and urge those who have not yet paid [by the people indicated in] the attached list of names.

People interested;

Hwang Chonghŭi   Mun Yunch'un
Kwak Sŏyun   Hwang Ungi
Ch'u Irok   Kim Pangsin

Action committee:

Kim Suman   Kwak Chunggu
Kim Namsun   Ham P'irhyŏn
Hwang Chŏngsik   Hwang Ch'angu

Neighbourhood heads:

Kwak Chonggil   Kim Ch'angsik
Mun Chaesik   Wi Yangok
Kim Yongch'u   Chŏng Tuman
Kang Okki   Kim Kakchong

Administration committee:

Mun Chech'ŏl   Mun Ch'ŏlchu
Kwak Kwangsŏn   Kim Chŏngsu
Kim Chonggŭn   Kim Namch'ŏl

First and second neighbourhoods: Mun Chech'ŏl, Kwak Chonggil, Mun Chaesik, Hwang Chŏngsik, Hwang Chonghŭi;

third and fourth neighbourhoods: Kwak Tonggu, Ham P'irhyŏn, Ch'u Ŭngyŏp, Kim Kakchong, Kwak Kwangsŏn;

fifth and sixth neighbourhoods: Kim Suman, Kim Yongch'u, Kang Okki, Kim Chonggŭn;

seventh and eighth neighbourhoods: Kim Ch'angsik, Wi Yangok, Kim Namsun, Mun Yunch'un;

ninth and tenth neighbourhoods: Chŏng Tuman, Kim Tŏngman, Kim Chŏngsu, Hwang Ungi

24) "Paper of Decisions"

Notwithstanding this period of reconstruction of the nation, to our infinite regret the village has greatly deteriorated, and therefore we decided that in the great village meeting on the first day of the second month according to the old calendar [March 14th] we have to raise the spirit of reconstruction of the nation for future's sake and still more to strengthen the village regulations which have been practised since the 30th day of the seventh month of the year 4285 after Tan'gun's accession to the throne [September 18th, 1952], and we [decided] to revise the articles recorded below and to carry them into effect thoroughly.

Record

a) We change [the passage in] Art. 17 of the village regulations saying that the village committee is composed of those publicly elected at the assembly of the neighbourhood heads as well as of the village head into saying that it is only composed of those publicly elected at the assemblies of the neighbourhood members.

b) We change the six village deputies of Art. 18 and put one person from each neighbourhood [at their places].

c) We change [the passage in] Art. 19 saying that the village deputies are elected at the assemblies of the neighbourhood heads into saying that they are elected at the assemblies of the neighbourhoods.

d) We change [the passage in] Art. 20 saying that the village deputies constitute the village committee and decide on all matters of Art. 18 into saying that the village deputies constitute the village committee, handle all kinds of village affairs, and put a committee head [at its top] and that [the committee head] represents the committee, assists the village head, and supervises him.

e) We change [the passage in] Art. 21 saying that the village head's term of office is two years into saying that it is one year.

f) We change [the passage in] Art. 26 mentioning the youth within the village and the neighbourhood heads [in such a way] that [they] enter the 4-H-Club.

g) As to those who [are mentioned] in Art. 28 [as] having let cattle graze freely and [thereby] having caused damage to the crops, it is understood that such a person [has to pay] an indemnification, and furthermore we decide to collect W 100 as regulation violation fine and give half of it to the one having discovered [the offense].

h) We change [the passage in] Art. 29 saying that as regulation violation fine we once collect grain worth twice the sum of a one day pay into saying that the regulation violation fine will be decided upon by the committee according to the circumstances of the violation of the regulations.

i) We pledge to carry these regulations into effect immediately, and since there have not yet been [suggested] modifications with regard to the other things we have [already] signed and sealed [before], we shall only enter modifications

coming from the side of the household heads and [alterations] pertaining to
things omitted [so far] and alter [the regulations] and sign them.

In the year 1964
Head of the village committee:
Kim Chonggŭn

Committee members:

Hwang Kŭnju

Kim Munp'il

Ham P'irhyŏn

Kwak Kwangsŏn

Kim Chonggwŏn

Mun Yunch'un

Kim Pyŏnggi

Mun Ch'ŏlchu

Hwang Sawŏn

TEXT

Document I

壬申以起

金鼓部及其他寄附金品芳名錄
會有財産未收入及違約金未收錄

長佐里民風振興會

Document II

誓約書

本里里有에係한金鼓物을故意又는不注意로因하야破傷한時에는其
破傷者又는其破傷者의戶主는異議업이區長又는保管者의請求에　依하
여其破傷物補充費을賠償하기로誓約함

檀紀四千貳百七拾九年正月　日

長佐里誓約人黃甫玄 ㊞
〔外一四○名 ㊞〕

Document III

立書書

立春大吉國泰平
建陽多慶洞無事
水澤在前韓兵船之陣法
栢樹繞城漢武候之祠堂
五穀豐登兮
六畜繁盛矣

Document IV

堂祭祝文式

維
歲次干支何月干支朔何日干支
長佐里民代表某敢昭告于
干支

未大將軍威冠一代靈存百世兹
值上望謹以淸酌庶羞恭伸奠獻尚饗

Document V

盖 屋 順 次

第六回	一區	上坪村	乙亥
	二區	中內村	丙子
	三區	下內村	丁丑
第七回	一區	上	戊寅
	二區	中	己卯
	三區	下	庚辰
第八回	一區	上	辛巳
	二區	中	壬午
	三區	下	癸未

Document VI

維

檀紀四二九八年陰十二月二十一日長佐里民代表黃謹周敢昭告于

天地神明今爲營建舍餘慶所及不隧先訓惶恐蒙恩謹以酒果用伸虔告伏惟

尊靈庫護永寧

Document VII

莞島長佐里洞約

第一章 總則

第一條　이 洞約은 全洞民이 國法을 遵守하고 人道와 同族愛로서 團結을 鞏
固히 하여 모든 社會的 弊習을 打破하고 經濟的 安定을 圖謀하며
各人의 責任과 義務를 完遂하고 美風良俗을 保存하여 興村報國을
目的으로 한다.

誓約者

本人等은 共同一致로서 本里 美風을 作興하고 鄉土를 美化하기 爲하야 左
記 各項을 誓約한 同時 各號의 一에 該當한 者는 違約金을 徵收키로 한다.

記

一、特別한 事故없이 集會에 不參 又는 遲刻한 者는 一回에 隨時 精穀 一升을 徵收기로 함

二、特別한 事故없이 共同賦役에 不出 又는 家族中의 壯力者를 不出한 者는 一日賃金의 倍額을 徵收기로 함

（但 親等의 忌中이나 重病者는 此限에 不在함）

三、將島末大將軍廟의 風致林이나 梅壇의 風致林 封亭의 風致林에서 盜伐 折枝 脫皮 牛羊繫留 海苔抗木藏置 腐敗物을 積置等 鄕土美化에 妨害한 者는 其物品을 沒收하고 五千圓以上의 違約金을 徵收기로 함

四、洞有林 又는 個人所有林 並 洞里에서 共同으로 管理 使用 收金한 林野에서 盜伐한 者는 現物을 沒收하고 違約金 五千圓以上을 徵收기로 함

五、本里區域內 道有林에서 許司없이 産物을 盜伐한 者는 現物을 沒收하고 該當 官署에 告發기로 함

六、他人의 農産物을 切取한 者는 該主에게 現物辨償은 勿論이요 洞里에서 追出기로 함

七、償牛를 放牧한 時는 一回에 隨時로 精穀 一升을 徵收기로 함

八、共同井戶에 汚穢水浸入 又는 洗衣搾置 側近에서 衣類 海苔類 生菜類를 洗濯한 者는 一回에 隨時로 精穀 一升을 徵收기로 함

九、本里區域內産의 菖蒲藁 及 榛實을 共同採取 警告 以前에 單獨行爲를 한 者는 現品을 沒收하고 違約金 五千圓以上을 徵收기로 함

一〇、雇傭人 又는 家族等의 行爲는 老少人을 不問하고 總誓約者가 責任을 負擔기로 함

一一、挾室內에 居住한 者의 違反行爲는 一切原主宅人이 責任을 履行기로 함

此誓約을 證하기 爲하여 各自 連名捺印함

檀紀四二八五年五月 日

長佐里 誓約者

Document VIII

長佐里規約

第一章 總則

第一條　本里는 本里를 本郡 官公署의 指導監督下에 住民이 自治로서 實行함을 期함과 共히 住民 經濟安定의 方策을 確立하여 從來의 社會的 모든 弊習을 打破하고 固有의 美風良俗을 保存하여 報國興村에 資함을 目的하다

第二條　本里라 함은 長佐里를 云함이요 住民이라 함은 本里區內에 住所가 있는 者를 云한다

第三條　住民은 信仰과 良心의 自由를 가지며 勤勞의 權利와 義務를 가진다。

第四條　住民은 里位 向上을 期하여 官公署의 指導에 順從한다 但 民主的 發展에 背馳되는 指導에는 此限에 不在한다

第二章 住民의 權利와 義務

第五條　住民은 左의 各任員을 選擧할 權利를 가지며 又는 各任員에 當選 時에는 擔任을 義務를 가진다
　　　里長 各團體長 及 其他 代表者의 選擧와 擔任

第六條　住民은 民主的 發展으로서 報國을 期하여 左의 義務를 가진다
一′ 國土의 統一과 防衛에 盡忠竭力
一′ 民主的 諸制度 樹立과 實施에 協助
一′ 子弟 敎育에 盡力하고 靑年 鍊成에 協助
一′ 國慶祝節日의 家庭化
一′ 民主國民 精神 作興 及 國家觀念의 徹底
一′ 各種 稅金 及 官公署의 雜賦金 個人割當額 持參 納付
一′ 治安 確保와 警防에 協助
一′ 戰病死 軍人 招魂祭 擧行과 遺族 慰安에 協助
一′ 現役軍人 及 應徵 援助
一′ 國債務 消化에 協助

第七條　住民의 經濟安定을 圖하기 爲하여 社交儀禮에 있어서 左와 如히 改

普又는 生產增强을 圖한다

一' 祝宴에 參加한 者는 親族威 以外는 招待人에 限한다

一' 婚儀는 結婚의 本義에 依하여 莊嚴鄭重히 하고 分外의 各費用은 全廢한다

一' 喪葬에는 酒食의 饗應을 全廢하고 粥을 供한다

一' 喪家에는 葬儀準備人 及 吊慰客 以外의 出入을 禁한다

一' 告別式에 參加한 者는 喫煙 及 談話를 廢하여 哀悼의 意를 表한다

一' 運輝者 又는 葬役者에게는 特히 酒食을 供한다

一' 家庭祭祀는 時祭로서 家廟에서 年一次 行한다

一' 山林의 保護와 農作物 侵害 防止

一' 米作增産 及 麥作增産 共勵

一' 空地利用과 蔬菜增産 共勵

一' 賭博防止 及 節酒勵行

一' 綠肥增産 及 優良堆肥增産 共勵

一' 畜牛養豚 勵行하고 兎羊飼育을 可及的 防止한다

一' 海苔密植 防止와 近海漁業 共勵

一' 牡蠣養殖 獎勵와 各種貯金 共勵

第八條 鄕土의 美化를 圖하기 爲하여 左의 各項을 施行한다

一' 各道路의 修繕 擴張과 保存

一' 海岸 及 山中의 天然的 靈石의 保存

一' 將島 未大將軍廟의 風致林 封亭 及 梅檀의 風致林 保護

一' 史蹟 記念物 顯彰 及 先人의 美事善行 顯揚

第九條 美風良俗을 保存하고 弊習을 改善기 爲하여 左의 各項을 行한다

一' 助婚契 又는 喪賻契를 組織하여 所要物品을 助給케 한다

一' 運輝契 又는 葬行契를 組織하여 運柩 及 理葬에 便宜케 한다

一' 青年들로서 敬老會를 年一回 行케 한다

一' 男女 共히 上下 外衣를 着用하고 戶外에 出케 한다

一' 敬上愛下하여 親睦을 圖하고 坐席은 前과 如히 年長者를 上位에 座

定케한다

一' 共濟資料蓄積과 隣保 勢力 相助

第十條 保健衛生을 圖키 爲하여 各自의 家庭을 常時 清潔히 하고 共同井戶
　　　에 汚穢水 侵入 防止에 共勵한다

第十一條 住民은 里費 又는 學校 設備費 其他 各雜賦金을 負擔할 義務를
　　　가진다

第三章　洞　會

第十二條 洞會는 住民總會 又는 里委員會의 二種으로 한다

　　　住民의 通常總會는 每年 陰正月十五日에 開하고 臨時總會는 里長
　　　又는 本里의 團體長이 必要로 認한 時' 官公署의 要請이 有할 時에
　　　里長이 招集한다

　　　但 出席員數는 特別한 事由가 없는 限 每戶에 一人으로 하되 男子
　　　會議에는 男子' 女子會議에는 女子가 出席한다

　　　集會는 聲告로써 한다

第十三條 里委員會는 里內의 團體長이 必要로 認한 時에 里長이 召集하되
　　　三日 前에 會議事項을 記入하여 回章으로써 發送하야 告知하야야 한
　　　다

　　　住民總會는 議長 一人을 選擧한다。議長은 議場의 秩序維持와 發言
　　　權의 許否와 言權의 停止와 退場命令과 議決에 있어서 表決權을 가
　　　지며 可否同數된 境遇에는 決定權을 가진다

第十四條 住民總會 又는 里委員會의 議決은 出席員數의 過半數로써 한다

第十五條 里長 又는 各團體長은 里委員會의 議決을 經하여 住民總會에 議
　　　案을 提出한다。住民은 五人 以上의 同意를 얻어서 建議案을 提出
　　　한다

　　　但 官公署의 指示事項 又는 緊急事項으로 住民總會를 開催한 時는
　　　此限에 不在한다

第十六條 里長 又는 各團體長은 洞會에 出席하여 意見을 陳述하고 質問에
　　　應答하며 洞會의 要求가 있는 時는 出席 答辯하여야 한다

第七條　里委員會는 班長會에 公選된 者 及 里長으로 組織하여 住民에게
　　　　財政的 負擔을 지우는 時에 同意權과 拒否權을 가지며 左의 各項을
　　　　議決한다

一´里費 收支 豫算과 決算과 里內의 各團體 經費 收支 豫算 及 決算
一´官公署의 雜賦金을 住民에게 分配 及 郡 山林組合費 分配
一´里有財産의 得喪 及 管理 並 處分方法
一´諸規程의 設定 及 廢止
一´淸海學校 施設費 及 靑年 鍊成費 分配
一´住民 負擔이 될 計劃 樹立 及 契約
一´豫算費와 豫算外의 支出
一´善行者 功勞者 勤勞者 表彰
一´違約者 處分 及 職務 怠慢者 手當 減下
一´其他 必要로 認한 事項

第四章　任　員

第十八條　本里는 里事務를 處理하기 爲하여 左의 任員을 둔다
　　　　里長 一人´里委員 六人´班長 若干人´里書記 一人´山監 一人
　　　　前記 任員은 名譽職으로 하되 里長 里書記 山監은 若干의 年手當金
　　　　을 支給한다
　　　　但 洞會의 決議에 依한다

第十九條　里長은 住民總會에서 選擧하고 里委員은 班長會에서 選擧한다
　　　　選擧는 總히 無記名 投票로 하되 多票者가 當選하고 同票의 時는
　　　　年長者가 當選한다
　　　　班長은 班員의 推薦에 依하여 里長이 委囑하고 里書記는 里委員會
　　　　의 推薦에 依하여 里長이 委囑하며 山監은 里委員會의 推薦에 依하
　　　　여 山林契長이 委囑한다

第二十條　里長은 上司의 指揮를 承하여 里事務를 處理하고 本里를 代表하며
　　　　里委員會의 決議에 依하여 里費 及 各雜賦金을 賦課하며 處理한다
　　　　里委員은 里委員會를 構成하여 第十七條의 各項을 議決한다

班長은 班員을 代表하고 里長을 補佐한다

里書記는 里長의 指揮를 承하여 里事務를 執行한다

山監은 山林契長의 指揮를 承하여 山林을 監守한다

第二十一條 里長의 任期는 二年으로 한다

補缺選擧에 依하여 就任한 里長의 任期는 前任者의 殘任期限으로 한다

但 再選도 한다

第五章 會 計

第二十二條 會計年度는 歷年에 依한다。里長은 里費收支豫算 及 決算書

各團體은 每年度 經費收支豫算 及 決算書를 里委員會에 提出하여 議決을 얻어야 한다

第二十三條 里長 又는 各團體長은 豫算外의 支出 又는 豫算超過支出에 充當하기 爲한 豫備費支出은 豫히 里委員會의 承認을 얻어야 한다

里長은 里委員會의 決議없이는 住民에게 財政的 負擔을 하지 못한다

第六章 里內의 各團體

第二十四條 里內의 各團體는 그 團體의 規約을 制定하며 事務를 處理하고 經費를 豫算에 依하여 經理하여야 한다

但 準則 없이 規約 及 規程을 制定한 時는 里委員會의 承認을 얻어야 한다

第二十五條 各團體 任員의 選任은 그 團體 規約에 依한다

第二十六條 里內의 靑年 及 班長은 里長 又는 里委員會의 要請에 依하여 언제든지 前衛部隊의 責任과 義務를 履行하여 里位向上을 期하고 老年은 後繼人物을 養成하여야 한다

第七章 違約者 及 職務怠慢者 處分

第二十七條 住民으로서 左의 各號의 一에 該當한 者에게는 班長 及 里委員 合席下에 說諭 又는 譴責한다

但 呼出에 拒絶 又는 說諭와 譴責에 不應한 者에게는 配給品 割當

　　　　을 中正하다

一′ 不正한 行爲로서 里名을 汚損한 者

一′ 人道와 正義에 無誠하여 眼前의 私利私慾에 醉한 者

一′ 人權을 無視하여 親睦을 妨害한 者

一′ 禮儀를 輕視하여 外衣를 着服치 않고 戶外에 出한 者

一′ 住民이 確認한 飼料栽培場 없이 兎 又는 羊을 飼育한 者

一′ 何等의 規責 없이 婚姻家 又는 喪家에 出入하여 酒飯을 取食한 者

一′ 招待 없이 宴席에 參加 又는 側近한 者

一′ 特別한 事由 없이 各種 稅金 又는 各種 雜賦金을 滯納하여 里名을 汚損하며 洞費를 多케 한 者

一′ 本規約 實施를 妨害하여 鄕土를 愛護치 않은 者

第二十八條　左의 各號의 一에 該當한 者에게는 違約者로 하여 一回에 一日 賃金에 當한 時産穀物을 徵한다

　　但 指定日字를 經過한 時는 强制로 徵한다

一′ 特別한 事故 없이 集會에 不參 又는 遲刻한 者

一′ 特別한 事故 없이 賦役에 不參한 者 又는 家族中에 壯力者를 不出한 者

一′ 射亭 又는 梅壇에서 牛羊을 放牧 又는 繫留한 者

一′ 犢牛를 放牧하여 農作物에 侵害한 者

一′ 共同井戶에 汚穢水를 侵入케 한 者 又는 濯衣를 擢置한 者′ 衣類海苔類生菜類를 洗濯한 者

第二十九條　左의 各號의 一에 該當한 者에 對하여는 그 物品은 無償沒收하고 違約金으로 一回에 一日 賃金의 倍額에 當한 穀物을 徵한다

　　但 指定日字에 納入치 않는 時는 强制로 徵한다

一′ 本里區內의 水面에서 菖蒲藻를 共同採取 警告前에 採取한 者

一′ 將局末大將軍廟의 風致林梅壇의 風致林射亭의 風致林에서 流伐折枝脫皮放火海苔抗木留置肥料 又는 物品을 積置한 者

一′ 里有林個人所有林共有林에 流伐한 者 又는 警告前에 梅實을 任意

　　　　　로 採取한 者

第三十條　本里區內의 道有林에서 許可없이 農具 以外에 使用할 生木을 盜

　　　　　伐한 者에 對하여는 現物을 無價 沒收한다

　　　　　但 不應한 時는 該當署에 告發한다

第三十一條　他人의 農產物 家畜物 衣類 服地 生海苔 生青苔 其他 物品을

　　　　　竊取한 者에 對하여는 原主에게 現品 賠償은 勿論이오 親善 拒絕

　　　　　各種 配給品 割當 中止 海苔 養殖場 分配 中止 林產物 採取 拒絕을

　　　　　實施하고 里外로 放逐한다

第三十二條　雇備人 又는 老幼한 家族 行為는 總히 戶主의 行為로 看做하여

　　　　　處分한다

　　　　　但 不應할 時는 各種 配給品 割當을 中止한다

第三十三條　借家人 又는 借房人의 行為는 貸家人 又는 貸房人의 行為로 看

　　　　　做하여 其義務를 即時 履行케 한다

　　　　　但 不應히 時는 各種 配給品 割當을 中止하고 分配金 滯納額에 當

　　　　　한 穀物 又는 其他 物品을 家主 又는 貸房主에게서 强制로 徵收한다

第三十四條　本里의 任員으로서 職務에 勤勉치 않은 者에게는 手當金에서

　　　　　一割 乃至 五割을 減下 支給한다

　　　　　但 減額率은 里委員會에서 決定한다

　　　　　　　　附　　　則

第三十五條　이 規約을 實施한 當初의 任員은 이 規約에 依하여 選任한 任

　　　　員으로 確認한다

　　　　이 規約을 即日 實施하기로 誓約하고 連署捺印한다。誓約人은 戶主

　　　로 한다

　　　檀紀四二八五年 陰七月三十日

　　　　　　　誓約者　　　里長　　　金　鍾　根

　　　　　　　　〃　　　　里委員　　黃　東　燮　周

　　　　　　　　〃　　　　　〃　　　黃　文　昌　周

　　　　　　　　〃　　　　　〃　　　黃　鍾　熙　熙

鐵文柱　〃　〃

金南喆品　〃　〃

金升杓約　〃　〃

外　二七名

金鼓物目錄

丙戌 正月二十日 現在

一、令旗　　　　　　　　壹雙

一、錚　　　　　　　　　壹個

一、廣釗　　　　　　　　四個

一、中鼓　　　　　　　　九個　牛皮製

一、小鼓　　　　　　　　參個　牛皮製貳、布木製壹

一、鑼笠　　　　　　　　四個

一、色服　　　　　　　　拾四個　新造品

一、栍笠　　　　　　　　拾五個（紙製）

一、鉤手冠　　　　　　　壹個（牛皮製）

以上

右物品을 故意又는 不注意로 因하여 破傷의 時는 異議없이 臨價할을 勿論이오 保管者가 紛失의 時에도 前項計如히 倍償함。但 保管者는 區長으로 呈計。

丙戌 正月二十日

里民代表　黃甫玄

金採昊

趙文昌

周連柱

黃金熙

黃鍾福

時區長　黃東燮

文 鐵 柱

金 南 喆

金鼓物目錄 丙戌正月二十日現在

一、令旗　　　　　　　　　壹雙

一、錚　　　　　　　　　　壹個

一、廣釗　　　　　　　　　四個

一、中鼓　　　　　　　　　九個　牛皮製

一、小鼓　　　　　　　　　參個　牛皮製貳、布木製壹

一、纏笠　　　　　　　　　四個

一、色服　　　　　　　　　拾四組　新造品

一、柶　　　　　　　　　　拾五個（紙製）

一、鉤手冠　　　　　　　　壹個（牛皮製）

以上

右物品을 故意又는 不注意로 因하야 破傷이 時는 異議업이 賠償함을 勿論이오 保管者가 紛失이 時에도 前項과 如히 賠償함 但保管은 區長으로 함

丙戌正月二十日

里民代表　黃甫玄

金採昊

趙文昌　周連周

黃金樂　周鍾熙

時區長　黃東燮

金文鐵柱

金南喆

Document X

金鼓物目錄 壬辰年二月一日現在

一、令旗   壹雙
一、鎗劍   壹個
一、廣劍   五個
一、中鼓   九個 牛皮製
一、小鼓   二個 牛皮製
一、纏笠   四個
一、色服   十四組 古品
一、立笠   十五枚 紙製

以上

一、前記物品을 故意又는 不注意로 因하여 破傷이時는 異議업이 賠償
함을 勿論이오 保管者가 紛失의 時에도 前項과 如히 賠償함
但 保管은 里長으로 함

檀紀四二八五年二月一日

前里長 黃三峰
里長 金鍾根
里民代表 金淵禧 金樂周 周文 黃吉周
趙福連 金永南 黃正守 金文昌 周喆柱
黃東變

外에 備品明細記

一、國旗   一枚
一、祝旗   二枚
一、書籍   一個
一、冊床   一個
一、掛燈   一個(計五品)

一、坐燈　　　　　　　　一個(已至三)

一、門　　　　　　　　　二個

一、地籍圖　　　　　　　二十六枚(新圖)

一、地籍圖　　　　　　　一册(古圖)

一、素　　　　　　　　　一個

一、五升斗　　　　　　　二個(一個은 金樂周宅置 公用함)

一、一升升　　　　　　　一個

一、大層衡　　　　　　　一本(百五十斤지지足)

一、青年運動服　　　　　三組(上下三枚 벨트三枚)

一、草席　　　　　　　　二枚(古物)

一、布帳　　　　　　　　三枚(唐木製古物)

一、鐵器　　　　　　　　二十個新品

一、竹席　　　　　　　　二枚(現在房使用分)

一、墨板　　　　　　　　一枚(現在使用分)

以上十九種目의 物品을 新里長에게 引繼함

檀紀四二八五年(壬辰年)二月一日

前里長　黃三峰

新里長　金鐘根

里民代表　金文昌周　金樂周

　　　　　金淵禧　　金南喆

　　　　　黃吉周　　趙福連

　　　　　金正守　　金南順

　　　　　黃鐘植

Document XI　　金鼓物目錄　檀紀四二八九年陽三月二十一日現在

一、令旗　　　　　　　　壹雙

一、鏴　　　　　　　　　壹個

一、廣劍　　　　　　　　五個

一、計믹　　　　　　　　　　壹個

一、長鼓　　　　　　　　　　壹個

一、中鼓　　　　　　　　　　八個

一、小鼓　　　　　　　　　　貳個

一、갈笠　　　　　　　　　　四個

一、色服　　　　　　　　　　四組

一、袱　　　　　　　　　　　拾參個

一、銅手冠　　　　　　　　　壹個

備品目錄

一、國旗　　　　　　　　　　壹枚

一、入營旗　　　　　　　　　壹枚

一、時計　　　　　　　　　　壹個

一、書箱　　　　　　　　　　壹個

一、冊床　　　　　　　　　　壹個

一、座燈　　　　　　　　　　壹個

一、錠　　　　　　　　　　　貳個

一、地籍圖　　　　　　　　　參組

一、鍾衡　　　　　　　　　　壹個

一、大層衡　　　　　　　　　壹個

一、草席　　　　　　　　　　貳枚

一、天幕　　　　　　　　　　壹個

一、布張　　　　　　　　　　參枚

一、墨板　　　　　　　　　　壹個

一、鑄器　　　　　七拾五個(六一〇組´中二〇個´小二五個)

一、穀用升　　　　　參個(五升斗二個´一升用一個)

一、山林關係册　　　　　　　壹卷

一、海岸關係　　　　　　　　壹卷

一、決議簿　貳巻

一、收支決算內譯簿　貳巻

一、農地臺帳　壹巻

一、戶籍簿　壹巻

一、重要書類冊　壹巻

一、其他書類一切

右 各項에相違없이引繼引受함

단기四二八九年陽三月二十一日

引繼者　黃　吉　周

引受者　金　芳　信

里民代表　黃　文　昌　周　信

　　　　　黃　東　鍾　熙

　　　　　黃　東　變

　　　　　金　南　喆　柱

　　　　　黃　重　鐵　變

Document XII

檀紀四二九〇年舊三月二十六日

一、山林關係綴　　　　壹巻

一、海岸事件書類綴　　壹巻

一、重要書類綴　　　　壹巻

一、樂具穀册　　　　　壹巻

一、夏穀實態調查記　　壹巻

一、收支決算內譯簿第一號　壹巻

一、洞中糧當金每回分配決議錄　壹巻

一、決議書綴　　　　　壹巻

一、收支決算內譯簿第二號　壹巻

一、耕地臺帳　　　　　壹巻

一、人口調査表　　　　　壹卷

一、其他書類一切

備品目錄

一、國　　旗　　　　　壹枚

一、入　營　旗　　　　壹枚

一、時　　計　　　　　壹個

一、書　　箱　　　　　壹個

一、册　　床　　　　　壹個

一、座　　燈　　　　　壹個

一、錠　　　　　　　　四個

一、地　籍　圖　　　參組(壹組은舊분이으로 拾枚)

一、鍾　　　　　　　　壹個

一、大　層　衡　　　　壹個

一、草　　席　　　　貳枚(消耗)

一、天　　幕　　　　　壹個

一、帳　　幃　　　　　參枚

一、墨　　板　　　　　壹個

一、鑰　　器　　　七拾五個(大拾組、中貳拾個、小貳拾五個)

一、共用斗升　　　參個(壹斗壹個、五升壹個、壹升壹個)

金鼓物目錄

一、令　　旗　　　　　壹雙

一、錚　　　　　　　　壹個

一、銑　　劍　　　　六個(壹個使用不)

一、斗　　빌　　　　　壹個

一、長　　鼓　　　　　壹個

一、鼓　　　　　　　　拾壹個

一、小　　鼓　　　　　貳個

一、괄　　笠　　　　　四個

一' 色服 .... 拾七枚
一' 紙花笠 .... 貳拾個
一' 鉤手冠 .... 壹個
一' 皷帶 .... 八個
一' 長皷帶 .... 壹個
一' 纓帶 .... 壹個

右各項에 相違없이 一切를 引繼引受함을 證하기 爲하여 各 署名捺印함

引繼者 金芳信
引受者 黃中王
參席人 金正守
　　　 文鐵柱
　　　 郭成永
　　　 金守萬
　　　 黃重燮

1　Document XIII

決議書綴

長　佐　里

檀紀四二八八年三月三日
部落備品食器購入量

食器 ｛ 大品 .... 一〇〇個
　　　　 中品 .... 一二〇個
　　　　 小品 .... 一二〇個
대적 一種品 .... 一〇個
일계 一種品 .... 一〇個

保管者 時里長

2 決議書

一、雇傭人年賃은 最高先賃金 貳萬五阡圓 又는 退賃金四萬圓으로 함

一、日傭人賃金은 夏秋期農役賃金은 精穀貳升으로 함。其外는 現金貳百圓으로 함

移種은 當日로 實施하되 賃金은 參百圓現物은 米貳升으로 함

一、山林保護는 從前洞約에 依하여 處斷키로 함

一、新入金은 運營委員班長 合席會合時 決議키로 함

一、農路修繕問題는 次後로 決議함

一、鴨陳賣却의 期間은 翌年六月末로 함

一、海岸賣却入札保證金은 入札金額의 二割로 함

入札全額金은 當日부터 十日間으로 함

右와 如히 決議함

檀紀四二八九年舊二月　日

里長　黃吉周
　　　黃連熙
　　　金采吳
　　　金文鐵杜
　　　金南喆
　　　郭乃正尤
　　　　　守

3 決議錄

檀紀四二八九年四月七日里有志運營委員 班長合同會議를 開하여 事項을 右記와 如히 決議함

決議事項

一、里民別等級은 別紙와 如히 調定함

一、戶別等級의 分配次等은 五等以上至一等은 壹割大額으로 分配할 것

이요 自六等으로 至十一等은 貳割式 減額이 不均等配定기로 함

一、本年度 里行政經常費 一部 四萬貳阡七百七拾圓을 等級別로 配定 收入키로 함

檀紀四二八九年四月 日

會議參席者

黃重變	金采昊	
黃大峯	黃鍾熙	
李永奉	金采琪	
金鍾貴	金南鐵	
文貴根	金南正	

時里長 金芳信

Enclosure to Document XIII. 3

里別等級調定表

等級	姓名	金額
一等	黃重變	四三○圓
	金正守	四三○〃
	金東圭	四三○〃
二等	黃云玉	四一○〃
	黃夏喆	四一○〃
	黃東變	四一○〃
三等 六名	文周局	四六○〃
	金昌周	三九○〃
	金秉奇	三九○〃
	文尚周	三九○〃
	金鍾根	三九○〃

等級	姓名	金額
四等 五名	郭文求	三七○圓
	黃永玄	三七○〃
	金吉周	三七○〃
	文吉南	三七○〃
	金石才	三七○〃
	黃秀培	三七○〃
	金吉石	三七○〃
	黃順石	三七○〃
	洪周源	三七○〃
	鄭大元	三七○〃
	金炳菲	三七○〃
	文炳奇	三七○〃

右 側 (金額・姓名・等級)

等級	姓名	金額
	鄭國東	三九〇〃
	黃大峰	三九〇〃
	金仁相	三九〇〃
	金南順	三九〇〃
	郭乃應	三九〇〃
	文伯芳	三九〇〃
	姜永俊	三九〇〃
	金正奉	三九〇〃
	咸吉遠	三九〇〃
六、		三、一三〇〃
八等 十二名	黃正吉	三八〇〃
	文天玥	三六〇〃
	鄭瑞銀	三六〇〃
	文錫萬	三六〇〃
	金貴萬	三六〇〃
	徐相石	三六〇〃
	黃正峰	三六〇〃
三、		三、二三〇〃
九等 十二名	金字大	三二〇〃

左 側 (金額・姓名・等級)

等級	姓名	金額
五等 十七名	金用明	三七〇〃
	黃南善	三五〇〃
	黃鍾熙	三五〇〃
	黃謹周	三五〇〃
	黃夢圭	三五〇〃
	黃夢守	三五〇〃
	黃成澤	三五〇〃
	金南珉	三五〇〃
	鄭永峰	三五〇〃
四、		三、一〇〇〃
六等 十六名	金秋乙	三三〇〃
	金鳳奉	三三〇〃
	黃成明	三三〇〃
	文孝明	三三〇〃
	郭日玉	三三〇〃
	郭貴男	三三〇〃
	黃義享	三三〇〃
	金琪采	三三〇〃
	吳柱石	三三〇〃
	郭壯先	三三〇〃
五、		二、一二〇〃
七等	黃漢吉	二九〇〃
	三峰	二九〇〃

左側 表

等級	姓名	金額
九等	趙德守	二三〇圓
	金仁珠	二三〇〃
	金龍吉	二三〇〃
	黃南鐘	二三〇〃
	黃相守	二三〇〃
	金升表	二三〇〃
	金文弼	二三〇〃
	黃形澤	二三〇〃
	黃應斗	二三〇〃
	金萬道	二三〇〃
	郭奉允	二三〇〃
	金南道	二三〇〃
	趙三來	二三〇〃
	黃政喆	二三〇〃
	黃正王	二三〇〃
	金鍾弼	二三〇〃
	金仲玉	二三〇〃
二〇名		四、六〇〇〇
一〇等	黃興周	二〇〇〃
	金王先	二〇〇〃
	朴明植	二〇〇〃
	金昌玉	二〇〇〃
	金南培	二〇〇〃
	郭正石	二〇〇〃
	金智吾	二〇〇〃
	金平玉	二〇〇〃
	金明道	二〇〇〃
	丁浩王	二〇〇〃

右側 表

等級	姓名	金額
一〇等	姜奉吉	二〇〇圓
	金昌奇	二〇〇〃
	金福突	二〇〇〃
	鄭采雨	二〇〇〃
	金宗變	二〇〇〃
	郭烈鐍	二〇〇〃
	金旺連	二〇〇〃
	金云才	二〇〇〃
	金信休	二〇〇〃
	文貫燮	二〇〇〃
	郭俊株	二〇〇〃
十一等	魏良玉	一七〇圓
	秋芳菊	一七〇〃
	鄭大雨	一七〇〃
	金萬植	一七〇〃
	李鍾吾	一七〇〃
	文石順	一七〇〃
	金億允	一七〇〃
	文明住	一七〇〃
八名		一、三六〇〃

計 四萬貳千七百七拾圓整

議事錄　決議

四二八九年舊六月二日本里事務所에서里運營委員、有志、班長合同會議

4

을 開하여 左記 各項을 決議함

記

1. 夏穀 里長 山監 小使手當에 關한 件

    1. 里長 三石(六 以 舊五斗入)

    1. 山監 三石(〃)

    1. 小使 三石(〃)

1. 夏穀 役價에 關한 件

    1. 黃南熙 郭東九 文權等 夏穀役價 除外(읖으로 一般負擔金은 負擔키로 함)

    1. 夏穀役價는 每戶 世當 舊六升 徵收키로 함

1. 里特別經費에 關한 件

    1. 自六月 一日 至八月 三十日 三個月間의 普通經費는 每月 五阡圜 計 壹萬五阡圜을 里長에게 支撥키로 함

1. 特別經費 1. 里公會時의 雜費 2. 里事務所修理費 3. 入營者接費 4. 選擧時配當額 5. 新聞購讀料 6. 里公用燈油代 7. 農路改繕費 8. 治道關係接費 9. 召集에 依하여 里代表入邑費 10. 淸潔에 關한 接費 11. 種痘의 關係

右記 各項에 該當한 費用은 里中分配키로 함

右記 檀紀四二八九年 舊六月 二日

右을 確認하기 爲하여 各者 署名捺印함

       參席者 文昌周 文鐵柱

             黃鍾熙 金南周

             金宋昊 黃鍾文

             金南喆 黃永奉

             成丙現 黃鍾燮

5

檀紀四二九○年 舊三月 一日

年始總會決議錄

1′ 里政運營委員選定의件

里政運營委員은 十名으로 하되 口頭公薦으로 함

金彩吳' 文昌周' 黃鍾熙' 金南品' 金正守' 文鐵柱' 郭廣允' 黃重燮' 金守萬' 成弼現

1′ 九○年度淸海校移築期成會會員割當의件。會費割當에 있어서는 洞里 不均等級을 調定함과 同時에 割當하기로 함。但 里政運營委員 및 班長의 決議로서 不均等級을 決議함

1′ 里長選擧의件

里長選擧는 上部의 指示에 準함

1′ 山監選定의件

山監은 後日에 里政運營委員 및 班長의 合意下에 選定기로 함

里林(멀치앙)은 앞으로 賣員치 않기로 함

1′ 美風會實施事項報告의件

美風會主催로서 里共用井戶 修繕기로 함

1′ 貯水池決算의件

6

檀紀四二九○年二月一日

決 議 錄

1′ 山監問題에關한件

首題의件에關하여는 金亨鎬로 決定하고 報酬는 上半期 六○(舊升) 下半期正租六○(舊升)을 支給기로 하되 同時 里政運營委員이 決議하여 署名捺印함

運營委員 金永吳

郭周萬

金守現

金正守

成弼現

里長 金芳信

7 決議錄

檀紀四二九〇年四月一日里事務所에서里政運營委員·班長·有志合席會議를開하여左記各項을決議함

記

一、里等級査定은十三等級으로定하다等級査定表는別途로作成하여里政運營委員의承認을受할것으로함

一、諸般出役動員方針은各家의最高實力者로履行케하다老弱과孩弱은切對不許하고所定에無故하고出役치옿은者는돈전으로金五百圓씩을徵收기로決定함。此에對한積極推進을爲하여動員部를配置함

一、里政運營所要經費는特別經費만을支拂기로定함

一、里政運營所要經費豫算金參萬圓을分配기로定함

右決議事項이確實함을證하기爲하여各署名捺印함

參席人　黃鍾熙　文鐵柱
金正守　黃熊伊
郭成弼　周永現　金守萬　奉

8 決議錄

檀紀四二九〇年五月十四日里運營委員·有志·班長合席會議를開催하여左記事項을決議함

記

一、壯丁入營者에對하여는一人當五百圓의車資를贈與기로함

一、里政稅等級報告書는邑의指示한票準等級에準하여五等六等十等의三等級으로報告하되本里에서는前例에依하여里長이報告함은均一賦課로하고隨伴된經費및文具費는里査定等級에有差別로分配徵收함 但徵收時期는夏七月秋十一月의二期로定함

運營委員　金淵禧　文昌周　黃鍾熙

文　鐵　柱　　成　丙　現
金　南　喆

郭　周　永

金　正　守

黃　重　燮

金　守　萬

9

決　議　書

里運營委員 有志 班長 合席會議를 開催하여 左記各項을 決議함

記

一, 今年度 上半期 夏穀役價는 白當 五升으로 함

一, 염소養育에 있어서는 모든 農作物 및 林野에 被害가 많으므로 염소養育을 禁止하기 爲하여 今月末까지 本人으로 하여 一濟히 處分키로 하되 萬若 處分치 않은 者에 對하여는 肥料 및 其他 配給物 一切를 一年間 中止키로 함

一, 燒酒製造者에 있어서는 其器具 및 現物을 押收하고 一年間의 海苔漁場權을 박탈하고 配給物 一切를 中止키로 함

一, 長佐里 洞約實施의 件

洞約은 鄕土美化 及 美風良俗을 保存, 里民 經濟에 關한 約束이니 自今 以後로는 이 洞約을 必히 實施하기로 함

檀紀 四二九〇年 七月 十六日

長佐里民 代表決議人

文鐵柱, 金正守, 郭周永, 黃重燮, 金宗權, 成丙現, 李鍾培, 文貴鉶, 黃正植, 黃相坤, 金鍾弼, 文濟七, 文濟喆, 黃大峰

10

決　議　錄

檀紀 四二九〇年 舊七月 十四日 里運營委員, 班長 有志 合同會議를 開催하여 左記事項을 決議함

決議事項

一, 洞有林 山藍을 金干玉에게 檀紀 四二九〇年 七月 十四日 付 選定함

一、山監報酬는 前例에 依함

檀紀四二九〇年 舊七月十四日

金淵禧　文昌周
黃鍾熙　金南卨
文鐵正　郭周永
金乃現　黃重燮
郭時里長　金大王
　　　　黃中峰

11 決議錄

檀紀四二九〇年 舊七月十八日 里運營委員 班長 有志 合同會議를 開催하여 左記事項을 決議함

決議事項

一、洞小使를 金賛有에게 檀紀四二九〇年 舊七月十八日付로 決定함

一、報酬는 前例에 依함

檀紀四二九〇年 舊七月十八日

金淵禧　文昌周
黃鍾熙　金南卨
文鐵正　郭周永
金乃現　黃重燮
郭時里長　金大王

　　　　黃　大　峰
時里長　黃　中　玉

12　決議錄

檀紀四二九〇年舊八月八日夜 里事務室에서 里政運營委員, 有志, 各班長 合同會議를 開催하여 左記各項을 決議함

記

一, 今年度海苔漁場추키日은 八月十一日로 定함
一, 海苔漁場費 及 里運營經費로 貳百圜을 徵收키로 定함
一, 兵務召集者에 支拂하였는 車費는 今後부터 支拂치 않기로 함
一, 今年度海苔漁場整理를 責任진 者는 漁場整理 及 不定建築處理를 責任지기로 하되 萬若 其責任을 不履行時는 整理費를 支拂치 않기로 함
一, 過年度에 海苔漁場違反者는 違約金을 整理한 後 추키로 함

右記決議事項이 確實함을 認하기 爲하여 各署名捺印함

參席人　黃　鍾　熙　　文　　鐵
　　　　金　南　喆　　黃　熊　伊　柱
　　　　金　芳　信　　郭　　乃
　　　　金　成　弼　現　黃　重　燮
時里長　黃　中　玉　　金　守　萬

13　決議錄

檀紀四二九〇年舊八月十一日 海苔漁場추키을 射亭에서 施行함에 對하여 左記各項을 決議함

記

一, 今年度海苔建濱新加入者 崔信休는 洞約에依한 新加入金壹萬壹阡圜인中 추키當時에 一部金五阡圜을 納入하고 殘金六阡圜은 舊十二月末日까지에 受入키로 함
一, 海苔建濱申込者의 權利는 分家한 日부터 半年以上이 된 者에 限함

一´ 分家한 者는 分家日부터 一般分配金諸般부역에 應하기로 定함

一´ 渴鷗洞里田地 全面積의 耕作權은 時里長에게 責任하고 小作料는 麥壹石으로 定함(但 耕作은 今年度麥播種時로부터)

一´ 後浦十區漁場은 賣買를하되 保證金은 札金額을 先納기로 함 但 保證金이 臺割未滿時는 入札을 無效로 함 落札된 者의 金額請算은 舊八月十五日까지 納入기로 함

金 宋 吳   文 昌 周

金 南 喆   金 正 守

成 弼 現   黃 重 燮

郭 周 永   金 守 萬

時里長 黃 中 玉

14   檀紀四二九一年五月二十四日 會議錄

一´ 特別經費支出種類

1´ 治道에 關한 事 2´ 山林關係里民의 福利가 有할 時´ 3´ 種痘´ 清潔´ 4´ 人口調查´ 5´ 稅務關係´ 6´ 其他特別한 經過時運營委員三人以上의 決議를 要.

一´ 燒酒製造 및 洞內商利防止´ 토막禁止

里內에서 燒酒製造 및 洞里內에서 果子 及 빵을 賣한 者. 토막한 者 및 토막장을 貸與한 者는 洞里配給一切 및 漁場權을 取消함.

檀紀四二九一年五月二十四日

參席人 文 鐵 柱

黃 謹 周

金 南 信 周

郭 芳 伊

金 熊 允

黃 乃

時里長 金 南 喆

金升表
金守萬
文漢明
黃中王
外 里民一同

15

運營委員 및 班長 合同會議 決議錄

一、日時 檀紀四二九一年 六月二十四日 下午九時
一、場所 洞事務所
一、打合事項
　1、里等級査定의件、運營委員長 文鐵柱氏 司會로 過去를 朗讀하여 會合員이 一致로 査定하였음
　2、夏穀役價의件、夏穀役價는 舊五月十日로 決定하였음
　3、燒酒製造禁止의件、燒酒를 製造한 者는 五月二十四日字 一般의 決議한바와 如히 漁場權 및 其他一切의 配給品을 中止키로 함
右各項을 確實히 決議하고 施行할것을 署名捺印함

運營委員 文鐵柱　金南周
　　　　 金正守　黃升表
　　　　 黃謹周　金熊伊
　　　　 文漢明　黃重燮
班　　長 金芳信　鄭斗萬
　　　　 金守萬　金文兩
　　　　 黃秋植
里　　長 金南昌

16

運營委員 決議錄

檀紀四二九一年十二月五日 里長佐 里運營委員會議를 里事務所에서 開催

하고 左記와 如히 分配를 決議함

　　　　檀紀四二九一年十二月五日

運營委員長佐里　　文　鐵　柱

　　　　　　　　黃　四　元　守

　　　　　　　　金　正　周

　　　　　　　　黃　謹　先

　　　　　　　　郭　廣　九

　　　　　　　　金　乃　信

　　　　　　　　金　芳　表

各班長代表　　　　金　守　萬

決議事項

一、檀紀四二九一年度 秋等役價를 分配함에 對하여 里長下半期手當 正租 六石, 里小使分 正租 參石, 山監分 正租 參石, 堂祭享米로 確定量을 統計數量 石斗升 收集을 每戶當 九升貳으로 分配하였음

二、淸海國民學校 保健場에 對한 賃貸料穀을 期成會會議에 決定된 每戶當 平均 五升을 等級 五等級으로 하여 收集하기로 議決함

等級如左(期成會分)

壹等(一、二、三、四、合)　　貳四戶　　戶當 八升

貳等(五、六、七、合)　　　　參四戶　　　　七升

參等(八、九、合)　　　　　　貳四戶　　　　五升五合

四等(一〇、一一、一二合)　　四八戶　　　　參升五合

五等(一三、一四合)　　　　　貳六戶　　　　貳升五合

　　　　計 壹五六戶　　　　　　七石八斗貳升

17　決議書

一、山監手當의 件

山監手當은 上、下半期로 各各 四石式 支拂키로 洞會議席上에서 決議함

一′ 農路 改繕의 件

農路 改繕에 있어서는 一月內로 改繕키로 함

檀紀 四二九二年 舊正月 三日

里運營委員　文　鐵　柱

黃　謹　周

金　正　守

郭　廣　先

金　南　周

金　升　表

黃　熊　伊

金　芳　信

郭　乃　允

時里長　金　南　喆

18　決　議　錄

檀紀 四二九二年 三月 九日(舊 二月 一日) 長佐里民公會를 里事務所에서 開催하고 左記 各項을 決議함

記

一′ 里運營委員 改編에 對하여 黃熊伊′ 文鐵柱′ 金升表′ 金南喆′ 金正守′ 文護明′ 郭廣先′ 金南周′ 金善濟′ 郭文求′ 黃鍾熙′ 十一人으로 決議함

一′ 洞規約 違反者 處罰者에 對하여 處罰金을 參阡圜으로 하고 萬一 不履行時는 漁場權을 無效로 하고 自由로 行使할때는 里運營委員이 撤去키로 함

一′ 山林에 對하여 洞部落林에서 盜伐한 者는 違約金 五百圜으로 하고 不履行時는 郡山林係로 報告기로 함

但 他部落者가 入山할時는 即時 郡山林係로 報告키로 함

一′ 等級査定에 對하여 里運營委員과 班長에게 一任기로 함

右記 各項 相違없이 決議함을 署名捺印함

里運營委員　文　鐵　柱

黃熊伊

金正守

郭廣先

金升表

文漢明

班長　金芳喆

金守萬

黃重變

金應兩

文煒弼

決議錄　檀紀四二九四年四月十四日

里運營委員坊長會議를 開催하고 左記와 如히 決議함

記

一' 里運營委員은 坊長이 各坊에서 一名式 選出하고 時議員은 自動的으로 되어 一一名으로 構成함

一' 軍警援護會費는 一等을 七三〇圜으로 하고 等級次는 五〇圜次로 分配기로 함

一' 保健場 不足額은 個人分配치 않고 里經常費 內에서 支拂기로 함

一' 教育稅는 建築者에 限하여 一八〇圜式 均分配기로 함

一' 事務所修理는 房만 修理기로 함

一' 洞里內에 길을 各坊別로 區間을 分擔하고 坊長責任下에 修理기로 함

一' 山監은 金亨泰로 定하고 보수는 例年에 準함

一' 各種漁場入札者 및 漁場 및 山林申込者中 申込金을 未納한 者는 舊三月十日까지 全額納付치 않을 時는 再入札 又는 權利行使를 取消함

參席委員　文　鐵　柱

黃　熊　伊

金正守
金升正
表植洙
文圭

坊長
黃秋金
鄭昌應
金應鍾
金東培
金三周
金正三
金鍾權
金德萬

20

決議錄

檀紀四二九四年五月二十一日 夜間八時 洞事務所에서 軍政令布告에 依
하여 運營委員 및 坊長有志連席會議를 開催하고 左記各項을 決議함

　記

一、梅丹立木 又는 神堂立木을 盜伐하는 者에 對하여는 每株에 金壹阡圜以上
　　參阡圜以下의 違約金을 三日以內에 徵收함
　　但連累者가 有할 時는 連累者도 同一違約金을 徵收하고 萬一 此에 不應
　　又는 期限을 經過한 時는 依法조치하기로 하여 里長이 기관에 告發함
二、本區內에 所在한 個人山林에 意無로 侵入하여 生木 又는 枯死木을 採取
　　한 者에 對하여는 兒童은 一回에 金五百圜以上 大人은 一回에 壹阡圜
　　以上의 違約金을 山林契에 納付함
　　但 此에 不應 時는 山主에 一任함
三、自己의 所有林野라도 所定入山期間以外에는 入山을 하지 못함
　　但 山林契의 承認이 있는 때에는 枯死木을 採取할 수 있다
右는 檀紀四二九四年五月二十二日부터 施行하기로 함
　　參席委員 文昌周

黃鍾熙

郭廣先

金炳奇

文吉佑

成允春

黃丙現

鄭鍾文

昌應植

洙烽

黃正植

秋鍾權

金在萬

文守

時里長　金文植

21　　決議書

西紀一九六二年一月七日 部落臨時會議를 開催하고 다음 各項을 決議함

다음

一' 里運營普通經費에 關하여는 戶當月五拾園式을 配定키로 하고 십가에 限하여는 元戶에 分配키로 함

二' 特別經費에 關하여는 다음의 經由에 限함

　1' 特別事由로 部落代表 入邑費

　2' 各機關長 接費

　3' 會議費

右各項을 確約하기 爲하여 署名捺印함

　會議參席代表　金鍾根　文鐵柱

　　　　　　　　黃炳熊　金周南

　　　　　　　　金正守　郭鍾權　永

植 現 宇 萬
正 弱 德 昌
黃 成 黃
嘖 培 燁
在 正 湅
文 金 鄭 昌
秋

時里長 金守萬

22 決議錄

西紀一九六二年四月二十九日午後九時里事務所에서運營委員班長有
志合同會議를開催하고左記와如히決議함

記

一、里山林監守는西紀一九六二年四月三十日限으로其監守責을 廢止기로
하고 玆以以後는 山林의 保護를 各自守護는 勿論 本里「4H青年團으
로 不正取締團束기로함

一、今般無償肥料의分布에對하여는受配者로서本里의諸公金의未納額은
勿論過年分淸海國民學校期成會慈戶費未納 맞務成戊費未收 其外의
未收全部를淸算함과同時受配토록決定함

西紀一九六二年四月二十九日

會議參席者

里長 郭廣允

班長 金用推,文在植,成弱現,金角宗,金秉圭,金昌植,魏良玉,
金德萬,鄭斗萬,郭宗吉,

運委長 金南順

有志 黃鍾熙,金鍾根,文鐵柱,金正守,黃熊伊,郭廣允

23 一九六二年七月十三日

有志運營委員班長臨時會議決議錄

一、里事務所新築工事費徵收에關한件

里民에게通告하여十七日로事務所에서徵收하고 未徵收者는別紙名

單只如히奮勵기로함

	有志	黃鍾熙	郭瑞允	秋一玉	文允著	黃照伊	金芳信
推進委員	金守萬	金南順	黃正植	郭重求	成弼現	黃昌宇
班長	郭宗吉	文在植	金用推	姜玉基	金昌植	魏良玉	鄭斗萬
	金贊鍾
運營委員	文濟品	郭廣先	金鍾根	文鐵柱	金正守	金南品
一'二班	文濟品	郭宗吉	文在植	黃正植	黃鍾熙
三'四班	郭東求	成弼現	秋應燁	金贊鍾	郭廣先
五'六班	金守萬	金用推	姜玉基	金鍾根
七'八班	金昌植	魏良玉	金南順	文允著
九'十班	鄭斗萬	金應萬	金正守	黃熊伊

24　　決議書

國家再建이 此際임으로도 不拘하고 里運營한 代表者等이 無能한 關係로 部
落이 特히 腐敗되믜이 遺憾千萬之事임으로 今年舊二月初一日 大洞公會時에 將
來를 爲해 國家再建精神을 作興하야 檀紀四二八五年陰七月三十日字로 實
施한 里規約을 一層强化하야 左記條項을 改定又는 設定하고 徹底히 實行키
로 決定함

記
一' 里規約「第十七條 里委員會는 班長會에서 公選한 者及 里長으로 組織
　　하여를」「但 班員會에서 公選한 者로 組織하여」로 改定함
一' 「第十八條 委員六人」을 改定 各班當 一人式으로 한다
一' 「第十九條 里委員은 班長會에서 選擧한다」를「班員會에서 選擧한다」로
　　改定함
一' 「第二十條 里委員은 里委員會를 構成하여 第十八條의 各項을 議決한다」
　　를「里委員은 里委員會를 構成하여 里諸般事를 處理하며 委員長 一人을
　　두고 委員會를 代表하여 里長을 補佐하며 監督한다」로 改正함
一' 「第二十一條 里長의 任期는 二年」을「一年」으로 改正함

一' 「第二十六條 里內의 靑年及班長은」을 4日까지를 加入함

一' 第二十八條 成牛（장인덕은 소）를 放牧하여 農作物에 侵害가 有한 時는
本人의 損害賠償은 勿論이요, 違約金으로 百원을 徵收하여 半分을 發見
者에게 支給기로 함

一' 「第二十九條 違約金으로 하여 一回에 一日賃金의 倍額에 當한 穀物을 徵
한다」를 「違約金은 違約된 事件에 依하여 委員會에서 決定한다」로 改定
함

一' 「이 規約을 卽日實施하기로 誓約하고 連署捺印한다」란 것은 아직 變更
이 없음으로 戶主의 變更과 누락된 것에 限하여 記入又는 修正捺印함

西紀 一九六四年 陰　月　日

里委員長　金　鍾　根
里委員　　黃　謹　周
　　　　　金　文　弼
　　　　　郭　廣　現
　　　　　金　鍾　先
　　　　　金　允　春
　　　　　黃　奇　柱
　　　　　文　四　元

Addenda

Recent Publications

Unfortunately, the publication of this manuscript, completed in the summer of the year 1974, has been delayed for an extraordinarily long period of time. Therefore, some of what has been presented as recent publications in this book has since then been outstripped by even more recent ones. The conclusions drawn from some of these more recent publications could be incorporated into the book, others could not, for their inclusion would have considerably disturbed the outer arrangement of text, notes, and bibliography. Incidentally, only a very few of the publications excluded from the main body of this study pertain to the main topics discussed here, and they do so in a way which does not entail fundamental changes of what has been said before. These few publications will be discussed shortly below. (Publications on topics of marginal importance here, such as the types of village festivals, for instance, are much more numerous. The reader will easily find them by simply reviewing relevant periodicals such as *MIH, Han'guk minsokhak* 韓 國 民 俗 學, and, above all, the recently completed series *Han'guk minsok chonghap chosa pogosŏ* 韓 國 民 俗 綜 合 調 查 報 告 書.)

The book to be first mentioned here is that by Mr. Alan Macfarlane on the reconstruction of historical communities, as in its initial chapters the author deals with problems of method. He then continues by demonstrating his research techniques by means of references to sources from Britain's rural past. The reader not primarily concerned with Britain expects the first part to be particularly helpful in his own efforts, but he may find it to be less so after having read it. The point in question is Mr. Macfarlane's distinction between "the myth of the community", which he dismisses as having no foundations in reality, and "the communication study as a method". The quotations adduced by him to dismiss the community as a myth certainly do serve this end, but this cannot mean that there are no more sophisticated concepts of community, which in turn correspond to distinct human societies deserving a name of their own. Mr. Macfarlane would have only had to look at Dr. Bader's carefully adapted concept of community. Besides, Mr. Macfarlane's insistence on community studies as a method only does not carry him very far. For in order to define his area of research, he time and again has to refer to community in another than simply a methodological sense, *i. e.* in a sense other than as an area which conveniently lends itself to the collection and organization of research data. In the eyes of a Koreanologist, the greatest merit of Mr. Macfarlane's book lies in its demonstration of what can be achieved if only the relevant sources are well arranged and made easily available. This availability is something the Koreanologist can only dream of for some more time to come.

Dr. Mun Pyŏngjip 文 炳 鏶, in his book on Korean villages, mainly deals with the history of rural property and modes of rural production, and he does so in quasi-Marxist terms. Somebody who tries to base his statements on a careful study of sources will find it difficult to comment on presentations flat as those of Dr. Mun's; the discrepancy between the kind of generalization Dr. Mun aims at and what may be considered sound knowledge is just too big. As far as phenomena are concerned which are at the focus of the present study, Dr. Mun does not present facts which have not already been known from other publications. His dissertations on *kongdongch'e* make a tedious reading, for that term has been presented in too many publications before without having been made plausible by any of the authors concerned.

Another publication to be mentioned here is an article by Dr. Ch'oe Chaesŏk, which is a detailed inquiry into village leadership structure, presented along the lines of *yangban* and non-*yangban* villages. As such, the object of this article lies somewhat beyond the confines of the present study.

In Dr. Ko Sŭngje's 高 承 濟 study on the history of Korean village society, the chapters dealing with early modern and contemporary conditions are of particular interest here. In these chapters Dr. Ko mainly discusses the rural policy during the period of Japanese rule over Korea, the credit cooperatives of that time, the structure of village leadership, class differentiations in village society, and imminent urbanization of villages. The book appears to be a genuine achievement in these respects. However, the book is of little use here, because almost nowhere Dr. Ko deals with phenomena figuring prominently in the present study, except for a passage where he mentions that positions of leadership in villages increasingly tend to be filled by educated and implicitly better qualified people. This development deals a heavy blow to the traditional privileges of the village elders. He further states that the conduct of village affairs has come to be put into the hands of the development committee (*kaebal wiwŏnhoe* 開 發 委 員 會) and that its head often acts as village head at the same time. These findings perfectly correspond to those from Changjwa-ri.

An article by Professor Gerard F. Kennedy is one of the few sound and meaningful descriptions in a Western language of the present-day Korean *kye*. Professor Kennedy has concentrated on what he calls urban-fiscal *kye*, and thus on a phenomenon which is not typical of the Korean countryside. Still, the article is of importance here, because the author accounts for the reasons of the *kye* system's vitality and thus helps to answer a question which has also been asked in this study. According to Professor Kennedy, *kye* type associations are favoured by the Koreans, because they are both based on, and reproduce, extra-economic social relations and trustworthiness among people, and in this respect differ markedly from modes of organization of the money market as offered by banks.

Vid. Alan Macfarlane, in collaboration with Sarah Harrison/Charles Jardine, *Reconstructing Historical Communities,* Cambridge/London/New York/Melbourne: 1977, pp. 10s, 28, 33s, 35s; *Han'gugŭi ch'ollak* 韓 國 의 村 落 , comp. Mun Pyŏngjip, ed. An Chongguk 安 鍾 國 , Seoul: Chinmyŏng munhwasa 進 明 文 化 社 , 1973, pp. 48 – 52, 181 – 190; "Han'guk ch'ollagŭi kwŏllyŏk kujo yŏn'gu" 韓 國 村 落 의 權 力 構 造 研 究, comp. Ch'oe Chaesŏk, *Asea yŏn'gu* 亞 細 亞 研 究, vol. XVIII, Nr. 1 (51), Seoul: 1974, pp. 165 – 194; *Han'guk ch'ollak sahoesa yŏn'gu* 韓 國 村 落 社 會 史 研 究 , comp. Ko Sŭngje, ed. Kim Sŏngjae 金 聖 哉 , Seoul: Ilchi sa 一 志 社 , 1977, pp. 376 – 380; Gerard F. Kennedy, "The Korean *Kye.* Maintaining Human Scale in a Modernizing Form", *Korean Studies,* publ. University Press of Hawaii for the Center for Korean Studies, vol. 1, Honolulu/Hawaii: 1977, pp. 197 – 222.

More Sources

In the fall of 1978, the present author had another opportunity to pay a short visit to Wan Island. When reviewing the set of documents from Changjwa-ri, he found two texts which had come to light, he learnt, after the year 1973. One of the texts is called *Draft of a Village Contract of Changjwa-ri (Changjwa-ri tongyak ch'oan* 長 佐 里 洞 約 草 案), dated April 15th, 1962. The other is called *Documents of the Age-Peers' Association of [Those Born in the Year] Imsul (Imsul saeng kapkye an* 壬 戌 生 甲 稧 案), the cover page of which is dated March, 1959.

From a quick reading of the documents the present author learnt that they did not seem to contain anything which would fundamentally change the conclusions arrived at in this study. However, for the sake of completeness he intends to translate, comment upon, and publish those two texts at a later date.

BIBLIOGRAPHY*

Sources

with the exception of the documents from Changjwa-ri

1 *Changhyŏn-dong chochiku-kyōsai-kai kiyaku* 長 絃 洞 貯 蓄 共 濟 稧 規 約, from Hwanghae-do 黃 海 道, Yŏmbaek-kun 延 白 郡, Hae-sŏng-myŏn 海 城 面, Ch'oyang-ni 草 陽 里, Changhyŏn-dong, no date, in *CS*, vol. 2, pp. 244s

2 *Changsu-gun Changsu-myŏn Wŏnsongch'ŏl-li chokokukumiai kiyaku* 長 水 郡 長 水 面 元 松 川 里 貯 穀 組 合 規 約, from Chŏlla pukto 全 羅 北 道, established after 1928, in *CS*, vol. 2, pp. 210s

3 *Chibong yusŏl* 芝 峰 類 說, comp. Chibong Yi Sugwang 李 睟 光 (1563—1628), 20 *kwŏn*, publ. in 1614, Han'gukhak kibon ch'ongsŏ 韓 國 學 基 本 叢 書, ed. Han Sangha 韓 相 夏, no. 2, Seoul: Kyŏngin munhwasa 景 仁 文 化 社, 1970

4 *Chosŏn wangjo sillok* 朝 鮮 王 朝 實 錄, publ. Kuksa p'yŏnch'an wiwŏnhoe 國 史 編 纂 委 員 會, 48 vols. + Index, Seoul: 1968—1970

5 *Chou li chu-shu* 周 禮 注 疏, comm. Cheng Hsüan 鄭 玄 / Lu Te-ming 陸 德 明, 12 *chüan*, Shih-san ching chu-shu 十 三 經 注 疏, no. 4, vols. 11—14, [Shang-hai 上 海 :] Chung-hua shu-chü ch'u-pan-she 中 華 書 局 出 版 社, no date

6 *Chŭngbo munhŏn pigo* 增 補 文 獻 備 考, comp. Mukhŏn Hong Ponghan 默 軒 洪 鳳 漢 (1713—1778) *et al.*, 1770, rev. Igikchae Yi Manun 翼 翼 齋 李 萬 運 (b. 1736) *et al.*, 1782, 2nd rev. 1908, 250 *kwŏn*, publ. Kojŏn kanhaenghoe 古 典 刊 行 會, 3 vols., Seoul: Tongguk munhwasa 東 國 文 化 社, 1959, repr. 1970

7 *Chuyŏng p'yŏn* 晝 永 編, comp. Hyŏndong Chŏng Tongyu 玄 同 鄭 東 愈 (1744—1808), 1805/6, 2 *kwŏn*, transl. Nam Mansŏng 南 晚 星, 2 vols., Ŭryu mun'go 乙 酉 文 庫, vols. 77s, Seoul: Ŭryu munhwasa 文 化 社, 1971

8 *Dantai kiyakusho* 團 體 規 約 書, from P'yŏngan pukto 平 安 北 道, Chŏngju-gun 定 州 郡, Iŏn-myŏn 伊 產 面, Ch'imhyang-dong 沈 香 洞, dated February 1916, in *CS*, vol. 2, pp. 121-123

---

* Bibliographies of German scholarly publications may not contain sources, books, and articles which have not actually been quoted in the book to which the bibliography belongs. Therefore, this bibliography cannot be considered to be a comprehensive bibliography or a study guide of any of the fields dealt with in this book.

9 *Erh-ya chu-shu* 爾 雅 注 疏 , comm. Kuo P'o 郭 璞 , sub-comm. Hsing Ping 邢 昺 , 10 *chüan*, Shih-san ching chu-shu (vid. no. 5), no. 12, vol. 38

10 *Gosōkei kiyaku* 護 喪 稧 規 約 , from Kangwŏn-do 江 原 道 , Kŭmhwa-gun 金 化 郡 , Kŭndong-myŏn 近 東 面 , Haso-ri 下 所 里 , established in April 1929 or later (?), in *CS*, vol. 2, pp. 268-271

11 *Haesŏng-myŏn Changhyŏn-dong kinrō-shōrei-kai kiyaku* 海 城 面 長 絃 洞 勤 勞 獎 勵 會 規 約 , vid. no. 1, established in 1928 or later (?), in *CS*, vol. 2, pp. 245-248

12 *Haewŏl sambeikairyōkumiai kiyaku* 海 月 產 米 改 良 組 合 規 約 , from Chŏlla namdo 全 羅 南 道 , Hamp'yŏng-gun 咸 平 郡 , Haebo-myŏn 海 保 面 , Munjang-ni 文 場 里 , no date, in *CS*, vol. 2, pp. 72-76

13 *Hinoeuma tap-kei kiyaku* 丙 午 畓 契 規 約 , from Hamgyŏng pukto 咸 鏡 北 道 , Myŏngch'ŏn-gun 明 川 郡 , Sŏmyŏn 西 面 , Myŏng-nam-dong 明 南 洞 , dated March 4th, 1923, in *CS*, vol. 2, pp. 281s

14 *Hongch'ŏn Sŏmyŏn Kuŏm-ni chŭk Yŏndong Yun pansŏ t'aek iban'gye ch'ŏ* 洪 川 西 面 九 業 里 郞 蓮 洞 尹 判 書 宅 立 案 稧 處 , Library of Seoul National University, no. *ko* 古 5129-31

15 *Hwajŏng-ni igu junzankei kiyaku* 花 井 里 二 區 巡 山 契 規 約 , from Kyŏnggi-do 京 畿 道 , Koyang-gun 高 陽 郡 , Chido-myŏn 知 道 面 , Naengjŏng-dong 冷 井 洞 , Hwajŏng-ni, enacted on April 20th, 1928, in *CS*, vol. 2, pp. 175s

16 *Hyangnye happ'yŏn* 鄕 禮 合 編 , comp. Chŏngsujae Yi Pyŏngmo 靜 水 齋 李 秉 模 (1742—1806) *et al.*, 1797, 3 *kwŏn*, 2 *ch'aek*

17 *Hyangnye samsŏn* 鄕 禮 三 選 , comp. Min Yŏngjun 閔 泳 駿 (fl. 2nd half 19th century), 1888, 1 *ch'aek*

18 *Hyangyak t'ongbyŏn* 鄕 約 通 變 , comp. Hong Chungsam 洪 重 三 , 1706, 6 *kwŏn*, rev., copied Ijae Chŏn Sŭnggil 怡 齋 全 承 吉 / Ch'widang Yi Kŭnhan 翠 堂 李 根 漢 , with a preface by Ijae Chŏn Sŭnggil, 3 vols., Seoul: 1970, property of the author of this study

19 *Ijūminkumiai kiyaku* 移 住 民 組 合 規 約 , from Kyŏngsang namdo 慶 尙 南 道 , Hadong-gun 河 東 郡 , Chin'go-myŏn 辰 橋 面 , Wŏnsong-burak 元 松 部 落 and Songŭl-li 松 隱 里 , dated September 1st, 1919, in *CS*, vol. 2, pp. 87-91

20 *I li* 儀 禮 , comm. Cheng Hsüan 鄭 玄 , 17 *chüan*, vid. no. 122

21 *Iltu sŏnsaeng yujip* 一 蠹 先 生 遺 集 , comp. Iltu Chŏng Yŏch'ang 鄭 汝 昌 (1450—1504), 2 *kwŏn*, 1 *ch'aek*

22 *Kangjin-hyŏn yŏji sŭngnam* 康 津 縣 輿 地 勝 覽 , Honam ŭpchi 湖 南 邑 誌 , 1899

23 *Kangjin-hyŏn yŏng-ŭp-chin chi* 康 津 縣 營 邑 鎭 誌 , (cover-title: *Ŭpchi pu sarye* 邑 誌 附 事 例), Honam ŭpchi 湖 南 邑 誌 , 1872

24 *Kisa kyech'ŏp* 耆 士 契 帖 , foreword by Such'on Im Pang 水 村 任 埅 (1640—1724), dated from between December 29th, 1720, and January 7th,

1721, photogr. reprod., with introduction and translations in modern Korean and English, Ihwa yŏja taehakkyo pangmulgwan torok 梨 花 女 子 大 學 校 博 物 館 圖 錄, ed. Ihwa yŏja taehakkyo pangmulgwan, no. 5, foreword by Chin Hongsŏp 진 홍 섭, Seoul: Ihwa taehakkyo ch'ulp'anbu 出 版 部, 1976

25 *Kuan-tzu chiao-cheng* 管 子 校 正, coll. Liu Hsiang 劉 向, comm. Yin Chih-chang 尹 知 章, rev. Tai Wang 戴望, 24 *chüan,* Chu-tzu chi-ch'eng 諸 子 集 成, vol. 5, [Shang-hai:] Chung-hua shu-chü ch'u-pan-she (vid. no. 5)

26 *Kwangsŏng-myŏn Isa-ri yōtonkumiai kiyaku* 光 石 面 梨 寺 里 養 豚 組 合 規 約, from Ch'ungch'ŏng namdo 忠 清 南 道, Nonsan-gun 論 山 郡, Kwangsŏng-myŏn, Isa-ri, established in 1924, in *CS,* vol. 2, pp. 35-38

27 *Kyōsaikumiai kiyaku junsoku* 共 濟 組 合 規 約 集 書, from Kyŏng-sang pukto 慶 尙 北 道, Yŏngch'ŏn-gun 永 川 郡, Yŏngch'ŏn-myŏn 面, Kŭmno-dong 金 老 洞, established 1922, in *CS* vol. 2, pp. 82-84

28 *Li chi* 禮 記, comm. Cheng Hsüan 鄭 玄, sub-comm. K'ung Ying-ta 孔穎 達, 63 *chüan,* vid. no. 121

29 *Meng-tzu* 孟 子, 14 *chüan,* vid. no. 155

30 *Mongmin simsŏ* 牧 民 心 書, comp. Tasan Chŏng Yagyong 茶 山 丁 若 鏞 (1762—1836), 14 *kwŏn,* Kugyŏk Mongmin simsŏ 국 역, publ. Minjok munhwa ch'ujin hoe 민 족 문 화 추 진 회, 3 vols., Kojŏn kugyŏk ch'ongsŏ 고 전 국 역 총 서, vols. 37-39, Seoul: 1969

31 *Namp'yŏng sangyōkumiai kiyaku* 南 平 蠶 業 組 合 規 約, from Chŏlla namdo 全 羅 南 道, Naju-gun 羅 州 郡, Namp'yŏng-myŏn 面, Namp'yŏng-ni 里, established in 1921, rev. February 5th, 1928, in *CS,* vol. 2, pp. 62-66

32 *Nonsan-gun Kwangsŏng-myŏn Kalsal-li buraku yōsankumiai kiyaku* 論 山 郡 光 石 面 葛 山 里 部 落 養 蠶 組 合 規 約, from Ch'ung-ch'ŏng namdo, Nonsan-gun, Kwangsŏng-myŏn (vid. no. 26), Kalsal-li, dated May 2nd. 1926, in *CS,* vol. 2, pp. 198s

33 *Obong-myŏn Sŏmmo-dong taneosu-ushi-kei kiyaku* 五 峰 面 仙 帽 洞 種 牡 牛 契 規 約, from P'yŏngan pukto 平 安 北 道, Kwisŏng-gun 龜 城 郡, Obong-myŏn, Sŏmmo-dong, established in April 1928 (?), in *CS,* vol. 2, pp. 253-256

34 *Oju yŏnmun changjŏn san'go* 五 洲 衍 文 長 箋 散 稿, comp. Oju Yi Kyugyŏng 李 圭 景, early 19th century, 60 *kwŏn,* publ. Kojŏn kanhaeng-hoe (vid. no. 6), 3 vols., Seoul: Tongguk munhwasa (vid. no. 6), 1969

35 *Ŏnju-myŏn einōkumiai kiyaku* 彦 州 面 營 農 組 合 規 約, from Kyŏnggi-do 京 畿 道, Kwangju-gun 廣 州 郡, Kwangju-myŏn 面, Yŏksam-ni 驛 三 里, dated February 1927, in *CS,* vol. 2, pp. 18-21

36 *Ŏranjin gakkōkumiai kiyaku* 於 蘭 鎭 學 校 組 合 規 約, from

Chŏlla namdo 全 羅 南 道, Haenam-gun 海 南 郡, Songji-myŏn 松 旨 面, Ŏran-jin, established in 1917, in *CS*, vol. 2, pp. 53-55

37 *Pan'gye surok* 磻 溪 隨 錄 comp. Pan'gye Yu Hyŏngwŏn 柳 馨 遠 (1622—1673), 26 *kwŏn* + supplements, comm., transl. Han Changgyŏng 韓 長 庚, Kojŏn yŏnyŏkhoe ch'ongsŏ 古 典 演 譯 會 叢 書, ed. Ch'ungnam taehakkyo 忠 南 大 學 校, no. 1, 4 vols. (text, translation, commentary), Taejŏn 大田 : 1962-1968

38 *Poŭn-gun Songni-myŏn Chungbal-li fujinkei kiyaku* 報 恩 郡 俗 離 面 中 板 里 婦 人 契 規 約, from Ch'ungch'ŏng namdo 忠 清 南 道, Poŭn-gun, Songni-myŏn, Chungbal-li, enacted on January 15th, 1925, in *CS*, vol. 2, pp. 189s

39 *Regulations of the Tai Tong Kei* [*taedonggye* 大 同 契] *in Kwang Choo* [Kwangju 廣州], in Philip L. Gillet (vid. no. 136), pp. 14-17

40 *Regulations Used in the Ye Choong Kei* [*ijunggye* 里 中 契 ?] *and By-Laws*, in Philipp L. Gillet (vid. no 136), pp. 17-25

41 *Sambeikairyōkumiai kiyaku* 產 米 改 良 組 合 規 約, from Kyŏngsang namdo, Hadong-gun, Chin'go-myŏn (vid. no. 19), dated May 28th, 1925, in *CS*, vol. 2, pp. 91-93

42 *Samguk yusa* 三 國 遺 事, comp. Iryŏn 一然 (1206-1289), 1285, publ. 1512, 5 *kwŏn*, *Sinjŏng Samguk yusa* 新 訂, rev., comm. Yuktang Ch'oe Namsŏn 六 堂 崔 南 善 (1890—1957), publ. Ōyama Hisashi 大 山 壽 Kēijo: Sanchūtō shoten 三 中 堂 書 店, 1943

43 *Shih chi* 史 記, comp. Ssu-ma Ch'ien 司 馬 遷 (154?—90?), 130 *chüan*, Erh-shih-wu shih 二 十 五 史, [Hong Kong:] Hsiang-kang wen-hsüeh yen-chiu-she 香 港 文 學 研 究 社, 1959, vol. 1, pp. 1-287

44 *Sinch'ŏl-li menzaku-kairyō-kei kiyaku* 新 泉 里 棉 作 改 良 契 規 約 from Kyŏngsang namdo 慶 尚 南 道, Hamyang-gun 咸 陽 郡, Hamyang-myŏn 面, Sinch'ŏl-li, established before 1933, in *CS*, vol. 2, pp. 240-242

45 *Sindang kinnō-kyōrai-kumiai kiyaku* 新 堂 勤 農 共 濟 組 合 規 約, from Kyŏngsang namdo 慶 尚 南 道, Ch'angnyŏng-gun 昌 寧 郡, Kyesŏng-myŏn 桂 城 面, Sindang-ni 里, established in 1928, in *CS*, vol. 2, pp. 233s

46 *Sinjŭng Tongguk yŏji sŭngnam* 新 增 東 國 輿 地 勝 覽, comp. Pojinjae No Sasin 葆 眞 齋 盧 思 愼 (1427—1498), 1481, rev., enlarged Yongjae Yi Haeng 容 齋 李 荇 (1478—1534) *et al.*, publ. 1530, 55 *kwŏn*, publ. Kojŏn kanhaenghoe, Seoul: Tongguk munhwasa (vid. no. 6), 1957, repr. 1964

47 *Sŏkkong-myŏn Tangwŏl-li shinkōkai kiyaku* 石 谷 面 堂 月 里 振 興 會 規 約, from Chŏlla namdo 全 羅 南 道, Koksŏng-gun 谷 城 郡, Sŏkkong-myŏn, Tangwŏl-li, enacted on January 1st, 1925, in *CS*, vol. 2, pp. 215-220

48 *Sŏngho sasŏl* 星 湖 僿 說 , comp. Sŏngho Yi Ik 李瀷 (1687—1763), ed.
Sunam An Chŏngbok 順 庵 安 鼎 福 (1712—1791), 10 *kwŏn*, publ.
Chŏng Chongo 鄭 鍾 午, 2 vols., Seoul: Kyŏnghŭi ch'ulp'ansa 慶 熙 出
版 社 , 1967

49 *Songja taejŏn* 宋 子 大 全, comp. Uam Song Siyŏl 尤 庵 宋 時 烈
(1607—1689), compiled Simjae Song Hwan'gi 心 齋 宋 煥 箕 (d. 1807)
et al., 1787, 215 *kwŏn* + *Song sŏ sŏbyu* 宋 書 拾 遺 (4 *ch'aek*) + *Song sŏ
sok sŏbyu* 續 (2 *ch'aek*), comp. Yŏngjae Song Pyŏnsŏn 淵齋 宋秉 璿
(1836-1905), publ. 1929, photolith. repr., ed. Samun hakhoe 斯 文 學 會,
7 vols., Seoul: 1971

50 *Songji shōgakkōkumiai kiyaku* 松 旨 小 學 校 組 合 規 約, from
Chŏlla namdo 全 羅 南 道, Haenam-gun 海 南 郡, Songji-myŏn 面,
no date, in *CS*, vol. 2, pp. 57s

51 *Sunam ch'ongsŏ* 順 庵 叢 書, comp. Sunam An Chŏngbok 安 鼎 福
(1712—1791), compiled, ed. Yi Usŏng 李 佑 成, 2 vols., Seoul:
Sŏnggyun'gwan taehakkyo Taedong munhwa yŏn'guwŏn 成 均 館 大
學 校 大 東 文 化 研 究院, 1970

52 "Tongguk kunwang kaeguk yŏndae pyŏng sŏ" 東 國 君 王 開 國 年
代 所 序, comp. Tongan kŏsa Yi Sŭnghyu 動 安 居 士 李 承 休
(1425—1301), *Chewang un'gi* 帝 王 韻 記, written 1295—1296, k. 2 (=
Samguk yusa [vid. no. 42], Sinjŭng Samguk yusa purok 附錄 , pp. 50-53)

53 *Tongguk sesi ki* 東 國 歲 時 記, comp. Toae Hong Sŏngmo 陶厓洪錫謨
(fl. 1st half 19th century), 1 *kwŏn*, 1849, publ. 1911, transl. Yi Sŏkho
李 錫 浩, Ŭryu mun'go (vid. no. 7), vol. 25, Seoul: Ŭryu munhwasa (vid.
no. 7), 1972[4]

54 *T'onggye yŏnbo* 통 계 연 보 (*Statistical Yearbook*), publ. Wando-gun 완
도 군, vol. 12, 1972

55 *Tonggyŏng nōzei-chokin-kumiai kiyaku* 東 井 納 稅 貯 金 組 合 規
約 , from Hamgyŏng namdo 咸 鏡 南 道, Hamju-gun 咸 州 郡,
Hagich'ŏn-myŏn 下 岐 川 面, Tonggyŏng-ni 里, established in 1926 or
later, in *CS*, vol. 2, pp. 271-273

56 *Tonghŏn choyak* 洞 憲 條 約, in Chosŏn kyŏngje mun'go 朝 鮮 經 済
文 庫 of the library of Seoul National University, no. *ko* 古 7752 D 717

57 "Tongmyŏng-wang p'yŏn" 東 明 王 篇, comp. Paegun sanin Yi Kyubo
白 雲 山 人 李 奎 報 (1168—1241), 1193 (?), *Tongguk Yi Sangguk
chip* 東 國 李 相 國 集, k.3 (= *Samguk yusa* [vid. no. 42], Sinjŭng
Samguk yusa purok [vid. no. 52], pp. 44-48)

58 *Tongmyŏn sambeikairyōkumiai kiyaku* 東 面 產 米 改 良 組 合 規 約,
from Kyŏnggi-do 京 畿 道, Kaep'ung-gun 開 豊 郡, Tongmyŏn,
Paekchŏl-li 白 田 里, Sinch'on-dong 新 村 洞, established in February 1927, in *CS*, vol. 2, pp. 27-30

59 *Yukchŏn chorye* 六 典 條 例, Hojŏn p'yŏn 戶 典 篇, publ. 1867,
republ. Pŏpche charyo 법 제 자 료 by Pŏpchech'ŏ 법 제 처, Seoul:
1973

Literature in the Korean and Japanese Languages

60 *Burakusai* 部 落 祭 , comp. Murayama Chijun 村 山 智 順 *et al.*,
   Chōsa shiryō 調 查 資 料, ed. Chōsen sōtokufu 朝 鮮 總 督 府, no. 44
   (Chōsen no kyōdo shinji 朝 鮮 の 鄉 土 神 祀, part 1), Keijō: 1937,
   photolithogr. repr. Min'gan sinang charyo ch'ongsŏ 民 間 信 仰 資 料
   叢 書 , no. 2, publ. Wǒn'gwang taehak minsokhak yǒn'guso 圓 光 大 學
   民 俗 學 研 究 所 , [Seoul:] 1971

61 "Chǒnbuk chibang chǒllae chimyǒngǔi yǒn'gu" 全 北 地 方 傳 來 地
   名의 研 究 , comp. Yu Chaeyóng 柳 在 泳, [Wǒn'gwang taehakkyo]
   Nonmun chip 圓 光 大 學 校 論 文 集, ed. Pak Kilchin 朴 吉 眞,
   vol. VI, [Iri 裡 里 :] 1972, pp. 137-268

62 *Ch'ǒnghae pisa* 清 海 秘 史, comp. Kim Sonam 金 小 南, Pusan 釜
   山 : Nongch'on kyemong munhwasa 農 村 啓 蒙 文 化 社, 1955

63 *Chōsen fuzoku no kenkyū* 朝 鮮 巫 俗 の 研 究, comp. Akamatsu
   Chijō 赤 松 智 城 / Akiba Takashi 秋 葉 隆, 2 vols., Tōkyō: 1937/
   38, repr., ed. Kim Ikhwan 金 益 桓, Seoul: Hangmun'gak 學 文 閣, 1970

64 *Chōsen no shuraku* 朝 鮮 の 聚 落, Chōsa shiryō 調 查 資 料, publ.
   Chōsen sōtokufu (vid. no. 60), nos. 38, 39, 41, Keijō: 1933-1935

65 *Chōsen shakai keizai shi* 朝 鮮 社 會 經 濟 史, comp. Paek Namun 白
   南 雲, Keizaigaku zenshū 經 濟 學 全 集, vol. 61, Tōkyō: Kaizōsha
   改 造 社, 1933

66 "Chosǒn ch'ogi hogu yǒn'gu" 朝 鮮 初 期 戶 口 研 究, comp. Yi
   Sugǒn 李 樹 健, [Yǒngnam taehakkyo] *Nonmun chip* 論 文 集 (Inmun
   kwahak p'yon 人 文 科 學 篇), ed. Yǒngnam taehakkyo nonmun chip
   p'yǒnch'an wiwǒnhoe 嶺 南 大 學 校 論 文 集 編 纂 委 員 會,
   vol. 5, [Taegu 大 邱 :] Yǒngnam taehakkyo ch'ulp'anbu 出 版 部, 1972,
   pp. 107-162

67 *Chosǒn wangjoǔi nodong pǒpche* 朝 鮮 王 朝의 勞 動 法 制 , comp.
   Yi Chongha 李 鍾 河, Seoul: Pagyǒngsa 博 英 社, 1969

68 *Chosǒn yǒn'gǔk sa* 朝 鮮 演 劇 史, comp. Kim Chaech'ǒl 金 在 喆
   (1907—1933), ed. Kim Chaesǒng 金 在 誠, Chosǒn mun'go 文 庫,
   vol. 5, part 2, Keijō: Hagyesa 學 藝 社, 1939²

69 *Han'gugǔi nonggigu* 한 국의 농 기 구, comp. Kim Kwangǒn 김 광
   언 , Minsok charyo chosa pogosǒ 민 속자료조 사 보 고 서, publ.
   Munhwa kongbo pu 문 화 공 보 부 / Munhwajae kwalliguk 문 화
   재 관 리 국, no. 20, Seoul: 1969

70 *Han'guk akki taegwan* 韓 國 樂 器 大 觀 (*Korean Musical Instruments*),
   comp. Chang Sahun 張 師 勛, written under the sponsorship of the Ministry of Cultural Affairs and Publìc Information (Munhwa kongbo pu 文
   化 公 報 部), Bureau for Cultural Properties (Munhwajae kwalliguk 文
   化 財 管 理 局), Seoul: Han'guk akki hakhoe 學 會, 1969

71 *Han'guk kamyŏn'gŭk* 韓 國 假 面 劇 (*Korean Mask-Dance Drama*), comp. Yi Tuhyŏn 李 杜 鉉, written under the sponsorship of the Ministry of Cultural Affairs and Public Information, Bureau for Cultural Properties (vid. no. 70), Seoul: Han'guk kamyŏn'gŭk yŏn'guhoe 研 究 會, 1969

72 *Han'guk kodae sahoewa kŭ munhwa* 韓 國 古 代 社 會와 그文 化, comp. Yi Pyŏngdo 李 丙 燾, Sŏmun mun'go 瑞 文 文 庫, no. 071, Seoul: Sŏmundang 瑞 文 堂, 1973

73 *Han'guk minsok chonghap chosa pogosŏ* 韓 國 民 俗 綜 合 調 査 報 告 書, comp. Han'guk munhwaillyuhakhoe 文 化 人 類 學 會, publ. Munhwa kongbo pu, Munhwajae kwalliguk (vid. no. 70), vol. 1: Chŏlla namdo 全 羅 南 道, Seoul: 1969

74 *Han'guk minsokkwa munhak yŏn'gu* 韓 國 民 俗과文 學 研 究, comp. Kim Yŏlgyu 金 烈 圭, Seoul: Ilchogak 一 潮 閣, 1972²

75 *Han'guk nongch'on sahoe tapsagi* 韓 國 農 村 社 會 踏 査 記, comp. Suzuki Eitarō 鈴 木 榮 太 郎, transl. Idae sahoehakkwa 梨 大 社 會 學 科, Seoul: Idae ch'ulp'anbu 出 版 部, 1961

76 *Han'guk nongch'on sahoe yŏn'gu* 韓 國 農 村 社 會 研 究, comp. Ch'oe Chaesŏk 崔 在 錫, Seoul: Ilchisa 一 志 社, 1975

77 *Han'guk nongch'on tanch'e sa* 韓 國 農 村 團 體 史, comp. Mun Chŏngch'ang 文 定 昌, Seoul: Ilchogak (vid. no. 74), 1961

78 "Han'guk nongch'one issŏsŏ nodongnyŏk tongwŏnŭi hyŏngt'ae punsŏk" 韓 國 農 村에 있어서 勞 動 力 動 員의 形 態 分 析, comp. Kim Kwangŏk 金 光 億, *MIH*, no. 6, 1973/74, pp. 168-174

79 *Han'guk nongch'onŭi ch'ollak kujo* 韓 國 農 村의 村 落 構 造, comp. Yang Hoesu 梁 會 水, Asea munje yŏn'guso 亞 細 亞 問 題 研 究 所, Han'guk sahoegwahak yŏn'gu ch'ongsŏ 韓 國 社 會 科 學 研 究 叢 書, no. 9, Seoul: Asea munje yŏn'guso, 1967

80 *Han'guk nongch'onŭi sahoe kujo. Kyŏnggi-do yukkae ch'ollagŭi sahoehak-chŏk yŏn'gu* 韓 國 農 村의 社 會 構 造. 京 畿 道 六 個 村 落의 社 會 學的 研 究, comp. Yi Man'gap 李 萬 甲, Han'guk yŏn'gu ch'ongsŏ 研 究 叢書, ed. Han'guk yŏn'gu tosŏgwan 圖 書 館, vol. 5, Seoul: 1960

81 "Han'guk ŏŏp kongdongch'eŭi sŏngnipkwa chollip yangt'aee kwanhan chosa yŏn'gu. Ŏch'on'gyerŭl chungsimŭro" 韓 國 漁 業 共 同 體의 成 立과 存 立 樣 態에 관한 調 査 研 究. 漁 村 契를 中 心으로, comp. Pak Kwangsun 朴 光 淳, *Kyŏngjehak yŏn'gu* 經 濟 學 研 究 (*The Korean Economic Review*), ed. Han'guk kyŏngjehakhoe 經 濟 學 會, no. 19, Seoul: 1971, pp. 118-139

82 *Han'guk poksik sa* 韓 國 服 飾 史, comp. Sŏk Chusŏn 石 宙 善, ed. Pojinjae 寶 晋 齋, Seoul: 1971

83 *Han'guk sa* 韓 國 史, vol. 3: Kŭnse chŏn'gi 近 世 前 期, comp. Yi Sangbaek 李 相 佰, ed. Chindan hakhoe 震 檀 學 會, Seoul: Ŭryu munhwasa (vid. no. 7), 1969⁸

84 *Han'guk sahoe kyŏngje sa yŏn'gu. Kyeŭi yŏn'gu* 韓 國 社 會 經 濟 史 庶 究. 契의 研 究, comp. Kim Samsu 金 三 守, rev. ed., Seoul: Pagyŏngsa (vid. no. 67), 1966³

85 *Jimmei jisho* 人 名 辭 書, ed. Chōsen sōtokufu (vid. no. 60), Keijō: 1937

86 "Kei" 契, comp. Hatada Takashi 旗 田 巍, *Seikai dai hyakka jiten* 世 界 大 百 科 事 典, ed. Shimonaka Kuniyoshi 下 中 邦 彦, vol. 7, Tōkyō: Heibonsha 平 凡 社, 1968, pp. 110s

87 "Kodaeŭi muyŏk hyŏngt'aewa Ramarŭi haesang palchŏne ch'wihaya. Ch'ŏnghae-jin taesa Chang Pogorŭl churo haya" 古 代의 貿 易 形 態와 羅 末의 海 上 發 展에 就하야. 清 海 鎮 大 使 張 保 皋를 主로 하야, comp. Kim Sanggi 金 庠 基, *Chindan hakpo* 震 檀 學 報 ed. Chindan hakhoe (vid. no. 83), vol. 1, Seoul: 1934, pp. 86-112; vol. 2, 1935, pp. 115-133, photolithogr. repr. Seoul: Kyŏngin munhwasa (vid. no. 3), 1973

88 *Kugŏ tae sajŏn* 국 어 대 사 전, comp. Yi Hŭisŭng 이 희 승, Seoul: Minjung sŏgwan 민 중 서 관, 1972¹⁹

89 *Kukhak yŏn'gu non'go* 國 學 研 究 論 考, comp. Yang Chudong 梁 柱 東, ed. Chŏng Chinsuk 鄭 鎮 肅, Seoul: Ŭryu munhwasa (vid. no. 7), 1962

90 *Kyega idong nongŏp hyŏptong chohabe mich'inŭn yŏnghyang. Ch'ungch'ŏng pukto ch'ilsibo idonge taehan chosa* 契가 里 洞 農 業 協 同 組 合에 미치는 影 響. 忠 清 北 道 75 里 洞에 對한 調 査, comp. Kang Ch'anggyu 姜 昌 圭, [Ch'ŏngju 清 州:] Sangdang inswaesa 上 黨 印 刷 社, 1969

91 "Kyejiptan yŏn'guŭi sŏnggwawa kwaje. Kŭ chiptanjŏk sŏnggyŏkkwa kinŭngŭl chungsimŭro" 契 集 團 研 究의 成 果와 課 題. 그 集 團的 性 格과 機 能을 中心으로, comp. Ch'oe Chaesŏk (vid. no. 76), *Kim Chaewŏn paksa hoegap kinyŏm nonch'ong* 金 載 元 博 士 回 甲 紀 念 論 叢, ed. Kungnip pangmulgwan 國 立 博 物 館, Seoul: Ŭryu munhwasa (vid. no. 7), 1969, pp. 581-599

92 *"Maripkan no gengi wo tazunete"* 麻 立 干의 原 義를 尋わて, comp. Mishina Akihide 三 品 彰 英, *Chōsen gakuhō* 朝 鮮 學 報, ed. Chōsen gakkai 學 會, vol. 13, 1958, pp. 1-25

93 "Mojŏngi nongch'on sahoe kyŏngjee mich'inŭn yŏnghyang" 茅 亭이 農 村 社 會 經 濟에 미치는 影 響, comp. Ch'oe Chaeryul 崔 在 律, *HMY*, vol. 4, 1966, pp. 1-67

94 "Mojŏngŭi sahoe-gyŏngjejŏk kinŭngŭi ch'ujŏn kwajŏng. Kŭ palchŏn hyŏngt'aerŭl chungsimŭro" 茅 亭의 社 會 經 濟的 機 能의 推 轉 過 程. 그 發 展 形 態를 中心으로, comp. Pak Kwangsun (vid. no. 81), *HMY*, vol. 4, 1966, pp. 69-109

95 "Nongch'on palchŏn'gwa chidojaŭi yŏkhal" 農 村 發 展과 指 導 者의 役 割, comp. Yi Kwanggyu 李 光 奎, *MIH*, no. 5 (Im Sŏkchae sŏnsaeng kohŭi kinyŏm nonch'ong 任 晳 宰 先 生 古 稀 紀 念 論 叢), 1972, pp. 151-194

96 *Nongch'on'gyee kwanhan yŏn'gu. Nonghyŏpkwaŭi pigyorŭl chungsimŭro* 農 村 契에 關한 硏 究. 農協과의 比 較를 中心으로 ,comp. Chang Tongsŏp 張 東 燮, [Kwangju 光 州 :] Chŏllam taehakkyo ch'ulp'anbu 全 南 大 學 校 出 版 部, 1973

97 *Richō kōnōsei no kenkyū* 李 朝 貢 納 制の 硏 究, comp. Tagawa Kōzō 田 川 孝 三, Tōyō bunko ronsō 東 洋 文 庫 論 叢, ed. Tōyō bunko, no. 47, Tōkyō: 1964

98 *Sae maŭl undong. Kŭ iron'gwa chŏn'gae* 새 마을 運 動. 그 理 論과 展 開, comp. Hongbo chosa yŏn'guso 弘 報 調 查 硏 究 所, publ. Munhwa kongbo pu (vid. no. 70), Seoul: 1972

99 *Tae Han min'guk chido* 大 韓 民 國 地 圖 *(The Standard Atlas of Korea)*, comp., ed. Im P'yo 林 豹, Seoul: Sasŏ ch'ulp'anbu 辭 書 出 版 部, 1960

100 *[Tae Han min'guk chido,* vid. no. 99], Kungnip kŏnsŏl yŏn'guso 國 立 建 設 硏 究 所, 353 leaves, scale 1:50.000, Seoul: Han kongjido kongŏpsa 韓 公 地 圖 工 業 社', 1963-1969

101 "T'arhae chŏnsŭng ko. Chŭgwiŭi chujirŭl chungsimŭro hayŏ" 脫 解 傳 承 考. 即 位의 主 旨를 中心으로 하여 ,comp. Kim Yŏlgyu (vid. no. 74), *Kim Chaewŏn paksa hoegap kinyŏm nonch'ong* (vid. no. 91), pp. 483-494

102 *Tongjok puragŭi saenghwal kujo yŏn'gu* 同 族 部 落의 生 活 構 造 硏 究 , comp. Kim T'aekkyu 金 宅 圭, ed. Silla Kaya munhwa yŏn-guwŏn 新 羅 伽 倻 文 化 硏 究 院, [Taegu 大 邱 :] Ch'ŏnggu taehak ch'ulp'anbu 青 丘 大 學 出 版 部, 1964

103 "Wan-do chibangŭi chimyŏng ko" 莞 島 地 方의 地 名 考, comp. Yi Tonju 李 敎 柱, *HMY*, vol. 4, 1966, pp. 213-252

104 "Wando-ŭp Changjwa-ri tangje" 莞 島 邑 長 佐 里 堂 祭,comp. Yi Tuhyŏn (vid. no. 71), *Yi Sungnyŏng paksa songsu kinyŏm nonch'ong* 李 崇 寧 博 士 頌 壽 紀 念 論 叢, Seoul: 1968, pp. 429-444

105 "Wan-dowa waegu. Yijo sidaerŭl chungsimŭro" 莞 島와 倭 寇. 李 朝 時 代를 中心으로 , comp. Song Chŏnghyŏn 宋 正 炫, *HMY*, vol. 4, 1966, pp. 203-211

106 *Yŏnggi* 令 旗 , comp. Ch'oe Kilsŏng 崔 吉 成 , Chungyo minsok charyo chosa pogosŏ 重 要 民 俗 資 料 調 查 報 告 書, no. 23, [Seoul: Munhwa kongbo pu], Munhwajae kwalliguk (vid. no. 70), 1970

Literature in Western Languages

107 Allott, Anthony N. "The Recording of Customary Law in British Africa and the Restatement of African Law Project", *La rédaction des coutumes dans le passé et dans le présent* (vid. no. 134), pp. 197-232

108 Bader, Karl Siegfried. *Das mittelalterliche Dorf als Friedens- und Rechts-bereich,* Studien zur Rechtsgeschichte des mittelalterlichen Dorfes, Erster Teil, Weimar: 1957, photolithogr. Nachdr. Graz/Wien/Köln: 1967

109 Bader, Karl Siegfried. *Dorfgenossenschaft und Dorfgemeinde,* Studien zur Rechtsgeschichte des mittelalterlichen Dorfes, Zweiter Teil, Köln/Graz: 1962, erg. Neuauflage, Wien/Köln/Graz: 1974²

110 Bader, Karl Siegfried. *Rechtsformen und Schichten der Liegenschaftsnutzung im mittelalterlichen Dorf,* Studien zur Rechtsgeschichte des mittelalterlichen Dorfes, Dritter Teil, mit Ergänzungen und Nachträgen zu den Teilen I und II der . . ., Wien/Köln/Graz: 1973

111 Biot, Edouard. *Le Tcheou-li ou Rites des Tcheou,* traduit pour la première fois du Chinois par . . ., 2 tomes, Paris: 1851, repr. 1939

112 Bishop, Isabella Bird. *Korea and Her Neighbours. A Narrative of Travel, With an Account of the Recent Vicissitudes and Present Position of the Country,* New York/Chicago/Toronto: 1898

113 Bodde, Derk. *Festivals in Classical China. New Year and Other Annual Observances During the Han Dynasty, 206 B.C.-A.D. 220,* Princeton/N.J.: 1975

114 Brandt, Vincent S. R. *A Korean Village. Between Farm and Sea,* Harvard East Asian Monograph Series, no. 65, Cambridge/Ms.: 1971

115 Bühler, Theodor. *Gewohnheitsrecht und Landesherrschaft im ehemaligen Fürstbistum Basel,* Rechtshistorische Arbeiten namens der Forschungsstelle für Rechtssprache, Rechtsarchäologie und Rechtliche Volkskunde beim Rechtswissenschaftlichen Seminar der Universität Zürich, hrsg. Karl Sieg-fried Bader, Bd. 8, Zürich: 1972

116 Burmeister, Karl Heinz. *Die Vorarlberger Landsbräuche und ihr Standort in der Weistumsforschung,* Rechtshistorische Arbeiten namens der For-schungsstelle für Rechtsgeschichte beim Rechtswissenschaftlichen Seminar der Universität Zürich, hrsg. Karl Siegfried Bader, Bd. 5, Zürich: 1970

117 Carles, W. R. *Life in Corea,* with illustrations and maps, London: 1888

118 Chai, Alice Y. *Community Development in Korea. A Bibliography of Works in the Korean Language,* comp., annotated . . ., Occasional Papers of Research Publications and Translations, Annotated Bibliography Series, ed. Institute of Advanced Projects, East-West Center, University of Hawaii, no. 5, Honolulu: 1968

119 Chavannes, Edouard. *Les mémoires historiques de Se-ma Ts'ien,* traduits et annotés par . . ., 5 tomes, Paris: 1895—1905, repr. Collection UNESCO d'oeuvres représentatives, série chinoise, Leiden: 1967 + tome VI: Traduc-tion des chapitres XLVIII—LII, compléments et index général, préparés par Timoteus Pokora, avertissement par Paul Demiéville, Paris: 1969

120 Chavannes, Edouard. *Le T'ai-chan. Essai de monographie d'un culte chinois.* Appendice: Le dieu du sol dans la Chine antique, Annales du Musée Guimet, Bibliothèque d'Etudes, tome 21, Paris: 1910

121 Couvreur, Séraphin. *Li Ki. Mémoires sur les bienséances et les cérémonies,* 2 tomes, Ho Kien Fou: 1913, repr. Paris: 1950

122 Couvreur, Séraphin. *Cérémonial,* [trad. par . . .], Les Humanités d'Extrême Orient, Paris: 1951

123 Davis, F. James/Foster, Henry H./Jeffery, C. Ray/Davis, E. Eugene. *Society and the Law. New Meanings for an Old Profession,* New York: 1962

124 Eikemeier, Dieter. *Elemente im politischen Denken des Yŏnam Pak Chiwŏn (1737—1805). Ein Beitrag zur Geschichte der kulturellen Beziehungen zwischen China und Korea,* Monographies du T'oung Pao, vol. VIII, Leiden: 1970

125 Eikemeier, Dieter. "Villages and Quarters as Instruments of Local Control in Yi Dynasty Korea", *T'oung Pao,* nouv. série, vol. LXII, Leiden: 1976, pp. 71-110

126 Eikemeier, Dieter. "Rechtswirkungen von heiligen Stangen, Pfeilergottheiten und Steinhaufengottheiten in Korea", *Oriens Extremus,* 21. Jg., Heft 2, Wiesbaden: 1974, pp. 159-190

127 Eliséeff, Vadime/Bobot, M. T. Catalogue de l'exposition *Trésor d'art chinois. Récentes découvertes archéologiques de la République Populaire de Chine,* rédigé par . . ., Paris: 1973

128 Fél, Edit/Hofer, Tamás. *Proper Peasants. Traditional Life in a Hungarian Village,* Viking Fund Publications in Anthropology, vol. XLVI, Chicago: 1969

129 Fél, Edit/Hofer, Tamás. *Bäuerliche Denkweise in Wirtschaft und Haushalt. Eine ethnographische Untersuchung über das ungarische Dorf Átány,* Veröffentlichungen des Instituts für mitteleuropäische Volksforschung an der Philipps-Universität Marburg/Lahn, A: Allgemeine Reihe, hrsg. Gerhard Heilfurth, Bd. 7, Göttingen: 1972

130 Foster, George M. "Peasant Society and the Image of the Limited Good", *American Anthropologist,* ed. American Anthropological Association, vol. 67, Menasha/Wn.: 1965, pp. 293-315

131 Gehring, Paul. "Um Weistümer", *Zeitschrift der Savigny-Stiftung für Rechtsgeschichte, Germanistische Abteilung,* Bd. 60, 1940

132 Gierke, Otto von. *Das deutsche Genossenschaftsrecht,* 4 Bd., Berlin: 1868—1913

133 Gifford, Daniel L. "Korean Guilds and Other Associations", *The Korean Repository,* vol. II, [Seoul:] 1895, pp. 41-48

134 Gilissen, John. *La rédaction des coutumes dans le passé et dans le présent. Colloque organisé les 16 et 17 mai 1960 par le Centre d'Histoire et d'Ethnologie Juridiques sous la direction de . . .,* Etudes d'histoire et d'ethnologie juridiques, no. 3, Bruxelles: 1962

135 Gilissen, John. "La rédaction des coutumes dans le passé et dans le présent. Essai de synthèse", *La rédaction . . .* (vid. no. 134), pp. 15-61

136 Gillet, P[hilip] L. "The Village Gilds of Old Korea", *TKB*, vol. IV, part II, 1913, pp. 13-44

137 Gluckman, Max. *Ideas and Procedures in African Customary Law. Studies Presented and Discussed at the Eighth International African Seminar at the Haile Sellasie I University, Addis Ababa, January 1966,* ed. . . . ., with an introduction by A. N. Allott/A. L. Epstein/M. Gluckman, publ. Oxford University Press for the International African Institute, London: 1969

138 Gompertz, G.St.G.M. "(The First Sections of a Revised and Annotated) Bibliography of Western Literature on Korea from the Earliest Times Until 1950. Based on Horace G. Underwood's *Partial Bibliography of Occidental Literature on Korea",* *TKB*, vol. XL, 1963

139 Grimm, Jakob/Grimm, Wilhelm. *Deutsches Wörterbuch,* bearb. Alfred Götze und der Arbeitsstelle des Deutschen Wörterbuches zu Berlin, Bd. 1, Leipzig: 1854

140 Gutt, Etienne. "Le *Restatement of American Law* au XXe siècle", *La rédaction . . .* (vid. no 134), pp. 185-196

141 Hahm, Pyong-Choon [Ham Pyŏngch'un 咸 秉 春]. *The Korean Political Tradition and Law. Essays in Korean Law and Legal History,* Royal Asiatic Society, Korea Branch, Monograph Series, no. 1, Seoul: 1967

142 Hegel, Karl von. *Städte und Gilden der germanischen Völker im Mittelalter,* 2 Bd., Leipzig: 1891, Nachdr. Aalen: 1962

143 Henderson, Dan Fenno. *Village "Contracts" in Tokugawa Japan. Fifty Specimens with English Translations and Comments,* Asian Law Series, [ed.] School of Law, Washington University, no. 2, Seattle/London: 1975

144 Henderson, Gregory. *Korea. The Politics of the Vortex,* Cambridge/Ms.: 1968

145 Henthorn, William E. *Korea. The Mongol Invasions,* Leiden: 1963

146 Hentze, Carl. "Schamanenkronen zur Han-Zeit in Korea", *Ostasiatische Zeitschrift,* Bd. 19, Berlin/Leipzig: 1933, pp. 156-163

147 Kang, Chang Kyu [Kang Ch'anggyu 姜 昌 圭]. *The Influence of "Ke" Societies Upon Ri-Dong Agricultural Cooperative Association,* [ed.] Economic Planning Board, Republic of Korea/United States Agency for International Development to Korea [Ch'ŏngju 清 州 :] Choong-Puk National College, 1969

148 Keim, Willard D. "A Survey of Two Korean Villages to Determine the Attitudinal Aspects of Progressiveness", *Journal of Korean Affairs/Han'guk munje,* ed. Young Hoon Kang, vol. V, no. 3, Silver Springs/Maryl.: 1975, pp. 1-13

149 Kim, Chewon/Kim, Won-Yong. *Korea. 2000 Jahre Kunstschaffen,* übers. aus dem Engl. I. Schaarschmidt-Richter, Fribourg/München: 1966

150 Kollnig, Karl. "Probleme der Weistumsforschung", *Heidelberger Jahrbücher,* hrsg. Universitäts-Gesellschaft Heidelberg, Göttingen/New York/

Berlin: 1957, pp. 13-30, Nachdr. *Deutsches Bauertum im Mittelalter,* hrsg. Günther Franz, Wege der Forschung, Bd. CCCCXVI, Darmstadt: 1976, pp. 394-423

151 Kumagai, Kaisaku. "On the Formation of a Customary Law on *Allmende* in Japan *(iriai)*", *The Osaka University Law Review,* no. 20, Ōsaka: 1973, pp. 1-9

152 Lee, Hyo-chai. Review of Roh Chang Shub *et al., A Study of Three Developing Rural Communities, Journal of Social Sciences and Humanities (Bulletin of the Korean Research Center),* no. 23, Seoul: 1965; pp. 45-48

153 Lee, Man-gap [Yi Man'gap 李 萬 甲]. "Korean Village Politics and Leadership", transl. Glenn D. Paige, *The Korean Affairs,* vol. 1, no. 4, 1962, pp. 398-412, repr. "The Village Political and Social Structure", *A Pattern of Political Development: Korea,* ed., introd. C. I. Eugene Kim, The Korea Research and Publication, Inc. Series, 1964, pp. 107-125

154 Lee, Man-gap [vid. no. 153]. "Rural People and their Modernization", *Aspects of Social Change in Korea,* ed. C. I. Eugene Kim/Ch'angboh Chee, Kalamazoo/Mich.: 1969, pp. 70-91

155 Legge, James. *The Chinese Classics. With a Translation, Critical and Exegetical Notes, Prolegomena, and Copious Indexes,* by . . ., 2nd rev. ed., 7 vols., preface from December 1892, repr. in 4 vols., Taipei: Wen-hsing shu-tien, 1966

156 McCune, Evelyn. *The Arts of Korea. An Illustrated History,* Rutland, Vt./ Tōkyō: 1962

157 Mills, J. E. *Ethno-Sociological Reports of Four Korean Villages,* Seoul: 1960

158 Osgood, Cornelius. *The Koreans and Their Culture,* New York: 1951, photomech. repr. Tōkyō: 1954[3]

159 Pak, Ki-Hyuk/Gamble, Sidney D. *The Changing Korean Village,* publ. for the Royal Asiatic Society, Korea Branch, by Shin-hung Press, Seoul: 1975

160 Pospíšil, Leopold. *Anthropology of Law. A Comparative Theory,* New York/ Evanston/San Francisco/London: 1971

161 Puchta, Georg Friedrich. *Das Gewohnheitsrecht,* Erster und Zweiter Teil, Erlangen: 1828/1837, photomech. Nachdr., 1 Bd., Darmstadt: 1965

162 Radcliffe-Brown, Alfred R. "Primitive Law", *Structure and Function in Primitive Society. Essays and Addresses,* with a foreword by E. E. Evans-Pritchard/Fred Eggan, London: 1956, pp. 212-219

163 Reischauer, Edwin O. *Ennin's Travels in T'ang China,* New York: 1955

164 Reischauer, Edwin O./Fairbank, John K. *East Asia: The Great Tradition,* A History of East Asian Civilization, vol. 1, London: 1960

165 Rickett, W. Allyn. *Kuan-tzu. A Repository of Early Chinese Thought,* a translation and study of twelve chapters by . . ., foreword by Derk Bodde, vol. 1, Hong Kong: 1965

166 Ross, John. *History of Corea, Ancient and Modern. With Description of Manners and Customs, Language and Geography,* Paisley: no date

167 Rutt, Richard. "The Chinese Learning and Pleasures of a Country Scholar. An Account of Traditional Chinese Studies in Rural Korea", *TKB*, vol. XXXVI, 1960, pp. 1-100

168 Rutt, Richard. *Korean Works and Days. Notes from the Diary of a Country Priest,* ed. Royal Asiatic Society, Korea Branch, Rutland, Vt./Tōkyō: 1964

169 Rutt, Richard. *James Scarth Gale and His History of the Korean People. A New Edition of the History Together with a Biography and Annotated Bibliographies,* by . . ., Seoul: 1972

170 Scalapino, Robert A./Lee, Chong-sik. *Communism in Korea,* part II: The Society, ed. under the auspices of the Center for Japanese and Korean Studies, University of California, Berkeley, Berkeley/Los Angeles/London: 1972

171 Scheiner, Irwin. "The Mindful Peasant. Sketches for a Study of Rebellion", *Journal of Asian Studies,* vol. XXXII, no. 4, 1973, pp. 579-591

172 Shin, Susan. "The *Kye.* A Study of Social Change in Korean Villages", *Papers on Japan,* vol. 4, from seminars at Harvard University, publ., distributed by the East Asia Research Center, Harvard University, Cambridge/Ms.: 1967, pp. 177-214

173 Shin, Susan. "The Social Structure of Kŭmhwa County in the Late Seventeenth Century", *Occasional Papers on Korea,* ed. James B. Palais, no. 1, March 1974, pp. 9-35

174 Shiratori, Kurakichi. "The Legend of the King Tung-ming 東 明 王 the Founder of Fu-yü-kuo 夫 餘 國 ", *Memoirs of the Research Department of the Toyo Bunko,* no. 10, Tōkyō: 1938, pp. 1-39

175 Vos, Frits. "De traditionele vormen van dramatische kunst in Korea", *forum der letteren,* Jg. 1972, nr. 4, Amsterdam: 1972, pp. 9-31

176 Vos, Frits. *Die Religionen Koreas,* Die Religionen der Menschheit, hrsg. Christel Matthias Schröder, Bd. 22.1, Stuttgart/Berlin/Köln/Mainz: 1977

177 Watson, Burton. *Ssu-ma Ch'ien. Grand Historian of China,* New York/London: 1963[2]

178 Wolf, Eric R[obert]. *Peasants,* Foundations of Modern Anthropology Series, ed. Marshall D. Sahlins, Englewood Cliffs/N.J.: 1969

179 Yang, Lien-sheng 楊 聯 陞. "The Concept of *Pao* as a Basis for Social Relations in China", *Chinese Thought and Institutions,* ed. John K. Fairbank, Chicago: 1957, pp. 291-309

180 Yi, Kyu-Bo [李 奎 報]. "A Lay of King Tongmyŏng", transl., annot. Richard Rutt, *Korea Journal,* ed. Korean National Commission for UNESCO, vol. 13, no. 7, Seoul: July 1973, pp. 48-54

Errata in the Bibliography
No. 14: For 卽 read 卽
No. 27: For 集馬 read 淨 則

INDEX

VERLAG OTTO HARRASSOWITZ · WIESBADEN